D0882494

CATKILLER 3-2

Map of Southeast Asia showing the four Corps Tactical Zones (CTZ). I Corps is bordered on the north by North Vietnam and on the west by Laos. Note location of the DMZ, Dong Ha, MMAF and Hue Phu Bai (220th company headquarters).

CATKILLER 3-2

An Army Pilot Flying for the Marines in the Vietnam War

RAYMOND G. CARYL

Naval Institute Press
Annapolis, Maryland

Naval Institute Press
291 Wood Road
Annapolis, MD 21402

Library of Congress Cataloging-in-Publication Data
Names: Caryl, Raymond G., author.
Title: Catkiller 3-2 : an Army pilot flying for the Marines in the Vietnam war / by Raymond Caryl.
Other titles: Memories of an Army birddog pilot flying for the Marines in Vietnam
Description: Annapolis, MD : Naval Institute Press, [2018] | Includes bibliographical references and index.
Identifiers: LCCN 2018020780 (print) | LCCN 2018025409 (ebook) | ISBN 9781682473535 (epub) | ISBN 9781682473535 (mobi) | ISBN 9781682473535 (ePDF) | ISBN 9781682473528 (alk. paper)
Subjects: LCSH: Caryl, Raymond G. | Vietnam War, 1961–1975—Aerial operations, American. | Air pilots, Military—United States—Biography. | United States. Army. Aviation Company, 220th. | Vietnam War, 1961–1975—Reconnaissance operations, American. | Vietnam War, 1961–1975—Regimental histories, American. | Vietnam War, 1961–1975—Personal narratives, American. | Port Angeles (Wash.)—Biography.
Classification: LCC DS558.8 (ebook) | LCC DS558.8 .C379 2018 (print) | DDC 959.704/348092 [B] —dc23
LC record available at https://lccn.loc.gov/2018020780

♾ Print editions meet the requirements of ANSI/NISO z39.48-1992 (Permanence of Paper).
Printed in the United States of America.

26 25 24 23 22 21 20 19 18   9 8 7 6 5 4 3 2 1
First printing

This book is dedicated to every man who served as a Catkiller, whether on the ground or in the sky. To the Army, Navy, and Marine Aerial Observers who flew with us in those cramped, unprotected back seats, trusting us to bring them back safely from each mission, and to all of those awesome Marine Corps grunts for whom the Catkillers were "the Eyes of I Corps."

CONTENTS

ACKNOWLEDGMENTS

I would like to thank the many individuals who helped make this project possible. Special thanks go to Thomas Wildenberg, for without his guidance, encouragement, and editing this material would have remained an accumulation of short stories. I would also like to thank Maj. Gen. Jerry Curry, USA (Ret.), Maj. Gen. Frank Libutti, USMC (Ret.), and Brig. Gen. Michael Seely, USA (Ret.), for reviewing a draft of this manuscript and giving generous words of encouragement. Thanks to Col. Eugene Wilson, USA (Ret.), for his tireless effort in researching and compiling the history of the Catkillers, which proved to be of immense help. Last, I would like to thank the following individuals who helped fill in many of the missing pieces of my story: Rob Whitlow, David O'Hare, Richard Johnson, Kenneth Trent, Charles "Larry" Deibert, Don Pepe, Don Ricks, John Pfeiffer, Dick Messer, Bob Ford, Jack Mayhew, and Ms. Laurel McDaniel.

TERMS AND ABBREVIATIONS

AHC	Assault Helicopter Company
ANGLICO	Air Naval Gunfire Liaison Company
AO	aerial observer
ARVN	Army of the Republic of Vietnam
BDA	bomb damage assessment
Button Orange	pre-set UHF frequency radio
CAB	Combat Aviation Battalion
CAR	combat assault rifle
CAS	close air support
CIDG	Civilian Irregular Defense Groups
CO	commanding officer
CQ	charge of quarters
DASC	Direct Air Support Center
Deuce and a Half	two-and-one-half-ton-load capacity truck
DMZ	Demilitarized Zone
FAC	forward air controller
FAST	flight aptitude selection test
FO	forward observer
FM	frequency modulated
GCA	ground controlled approach
GP	general purpose
HE	high explosive
Helos	helicopters
IFR	instrument flight rules
IP	instructor pilot

IR	infrared
Klick	one kilometer or one thousand meters
Lima Charlie	loud and clear
LRRP	long range reconnaissance patrol
LZ	landing zone
MAC	Military Assistance Command
MAP	missed approach point
Medevac	medical evacuation
MIBARS	Military Intelligence Battalion Air Reconnaissance Support
MMAF	Marble Mountain Air Facility
NCO	non-commissioned officer
NVA	North Vietnamese Army
OCS	Officer Candidate School
OIC	officer in charge
OPCON	operational control
Op Order	operation order
P	Piaster (South Vietnamese currency, exchange rate of 385:1 to the U.S. dollar)
PA	public address system
PFM	pure freaking magic
PSP	perforated steel planking
RAC	Reconnaissance Airplane Company
RIO	radar intercept officer
ROTC	Reserve Officers' Training Corps
RPG	rocket-propelled grenade
R&R	rest and recuperation
RTB	returning to base
SAM	surface-to-air missile
SLAR	side-looking airborne radar
STOL	short takeoff and landing

TACA	tactical air controllers, airborne
TAOR	tactical area of responsibility
TOC	Tactical Operations Center
UHF	ultra high frequency
VC	Viet Cong
VFR	visual flight rules
VHF	very high frequency
VNAF	Vietnamese Air Force
VOR	VHF omni directional radio range
VR	visual reconnaissance
WP	white phosphorous

Introduction

The Vietnam War has faded into history. It has been described from many viewpoints, ranging from "we lost the whole thing" to "we lost the interest and support of the folks back home" to "we never lost a major battle so we won, but at a terrible price." Somewhere in there lies the truth, but one thing remains without question: for those who were there, the bonds forged in the crucible of combat knew no limits and left no room for reservation or doubt. We served our country and we served each other in the common cause of mission accomplishment and survival.

Being a Birddog pilot gave me a unique perspective of the war. I could see things others could not: Grunts could rarely see more than a few hundred feet in any given direction, close air support jets were going too fast to clearly see details, and helicopters tended to fly in gaggles in which separation from other helicopters was more important than looking at the ground. My mission was primarily visual reconnaissance, then bringing artillery, naval gunfire, and close air support jets to bear when the enemy was located. Birddog pilots spent hours flying low and slow over the same general areas, getting to know what normally went on there, and becoming as familiar with those areas as with their own backyard at home.

Birddog pilots flew single-pilot airplanes. We never flew in gaggles. Sometimes we flew in pairs, but most often we flew single ship with an observer in the back seat. We had a lot of discretion in how we flew and where we flew, but we always flew with the specific intent of supporting the troops on the ground. Ours was a solitary kind of war; yet, by virtue of the slow speed and low altitudes we operated at, we had a perspective few others had. In addition, we controlled a tremendous amount of firepower, which was only a radio call away. Because of our mission we were set apart from most Army pilots in Vietnam. The unit I flew for—the 220th Reconnaissance Airplane Company, named the Catkillers—was even more unusual: we flew most of our missions in direct support of the Marines with a Marine aerial observer (AO) in the back seat. The bond formed between Catkiller pilots and their Marine AOs was extremely close. They were our friends, brothers, and—most of all—mentors who set the bar very high. They helped us develop a skill set that went well beyond any training the Army had given us in flight school.

Not until several years after my tour of duty in Vietnam did I begin to realize how unique the 220th was and how special the relationship was between our Army pilots and the Marine Corps aerial observers. I began to feel that maybe we really were just a bit different. Yes, we flew the same aircraft other Army pilots in Birddog companies flew; and yes, a lot of what we did, like visual reconnaissance and artillery adjustment, they did as well. But there was something deep inside that made us different: It was the mission of supporting the Marines on the ground, realizing their warrior ethos, listening to our Marine AOs as they proudly told us about their Marine Corps and its illustrious history. For a brief period of time, we Catkillers were allowed to become a part of that long, unwavering tradition of warriors and join the brotherhood of The Corps. And we were all the better for it.

My original intent, rather than to write a book, was to provide a written account of my tour so that my grandchildren might find out what "Gramps" did in Vietnam. Over the years memories of the events I had seen and experienced in Vietnam continued to percolate; I became convinced the unit I had served in was unique and the stories I had been telling my buddies needed to be told to a wider audience.

What intrigued me was not human conflict per se, but the very human humor, pride, compassion, fear, grief, and—yes—love that swirl around us no matter what the circumstances. What I remember is how combat seemed to evoke these emotions in quite surprising ways. Everything I experienced from July 1967 to July 1968, I experienced through the lens of the emotions that bind us as human beings.

This is my story and the story of the men I flew with, the Marines we supported, and the things I experienced. I loved what I did, and every day was another opportunity to directly influence the safety of Marines on the ground. Nothing else mattered.

Everything I have written is true and accurate to the best of my recollection, with the exception of a few names and call signs that I could not recall. The dialogue I have quoted is accurate in general but not exactly as stated nearly fifty years ago. Some readers may find what I write about difficult to believe or understand. After a few months in country, I couldn't believe some of it either. At one point I attempted to read Joseph Heller's novel *Catch-22*. I got about eighty pages into it then put it down thinking, *Why in the world am I reading this? Hell, I'm living it.*

1 | A Fear of Flying

grew up in the small town of Port Angeles, Washington, located on the Olympic Peninsula about sixty miles west of Seattle. My parents divorced when I was six, and my mother remarried when I was twelve. My stepfather had been a B-24 flight engineer in World War II. He was shot down over Germany and spent nearly two years as a prisoner of war (POW). I had trouble accepting him as a substitute for my real father, and we did not get along very well.

My stepfather was interested in aviation and owned several light aircraft over the years. He tried to share his love of flying with me, but I was too immature and stubborn to accept it. Had I listened to him I could have had my private pilot license at seventeen years old, most likely been the envy of all my pals, and caught the attention of some of the girls in high school.

He tried his best to get me interested in flying. He even had one of his World War II fighter pilot buddies take me up in his Aeronca Champ for my first flight. Instead of taking it easy, so I could become accustomed to the wonders of flight, he took it upon himself to "impress" me with steep turns, stalls, and a couple of spins. All that did was scare the hell out of me, and he seemed to think it was funny. I was convinced he had done it to me on purpose. After that my stepfather couldn't get me near one of his airplanes. Feelings of not "measuring up" spilled over into other aspects of my growing up. I shunned playing sports in school because I was afraid I wouldn't be good enough. I discovered I could get by academically without really applying myself. Avoiding challenges and barely getting by became my credo.

I was what some would call an underachiever. I wasn't lazy; if something didn't come easily, I tended to avoid risk and direct my attention elsewhere. This lack of motivation didn't really catch up with me until college. I wound up at Seattle University in Seattle, Washington, unprepared to study. The good Jesuits actually gave me two opportunities over the next three years to perform, but the only thing I managed decent passing grades in was the two-year mandatory Army Reserve Officers' Training Corps (ROTC) program.

At jobs between my two failing years at Seattle University, I had set chokers for a logging operation near my hometown of Port Angeles and done shift work at a local paper mill. Neither of these appealed to me, so when I received my notice from the local draft board to report for a physical, I complied. Those were the days of "the draft," and as a lower-middle-class, blue-collar, perfectly healthy kid, the thought of not serving my country never entered my head. I had just wanted to put it off as long as possible.

Out of excuses, lacking any prospect of a good job, and uncertain when I would be drafted, I elected to salvage what small modicum of self-determination I still had and went to the Army recruiter and enlisted. I figured that getting to do something I wanted by enlisting for three years was better than waiting to be drafted and having zero choice in what I would be doing for two years. The Army recruiting sergeant was more than happy to see me and, after I signed the required papers, told me where to report for an enlistment physical and battery of written tests.

Less than a month later I found myself in Army basic training at Fort Ord, California, on the Monterey Peninsula. During basic training I began to find my way. The two years of ROTC at Seattle University had given me a leg up on what to expect. Apprehension gave way to excelling. I suddenly discovered the magic of achieving short-term goals. The military is very good at telling you exactly what it expects of you and exactly how it wants you to do it. If you need training to do what is required, it will give you that as well. I was offered a leadership position and then an opportunity to attend Infantry Officer Candidate School (OCS) at Fort Benning, Georgia. I jumped at the chance. Funny how quickly the military can change the path of a young man from becoming the flotsam and jetsam in society to someone looking forward to challenges and opportunity.

Following OCS came an opportunity to become Airborne qualified at the Army's Airborne School at Fort Benning. Success begets success. I applied and was accepted to Army fixed-wing flight training at Fort Stewart, Georgia, and Fort Rucker, Alabama. Graduating in June 1967 as a newly minted Army aviator, I knew my next assignment would be Vietnam; but now that I was armed with the skills and a sense of purpose I had never possessed as a civilian, I looked forward to it. This would be my chance to prove my worth, and I was ready: I no longer had a fear of flying.

2 | Silver Wings

Matthew Perry delivered this line to Salma Hayek in the movie *Fools Rush In*: "You are everything I never knew I always wanted." That's a pretty fair description of the beginning of my lifelong love affair with flying. My story actually began August 1965, at Fort Benning, Georgia, during the Tactics Phase of Infantry Officer Candidate School (OCS). I was a Senior Candidate and less than a month from being commissioned a second lieutenant in the Army. The final phase of our tactics training was an introduction to the Army's latest concept in warfare: an air assault on an enemy force.

The concept of an air assault on an enemy, known as air mobility, emerged out of the Howze Board findings, an entity established in 1962 under the chairmanship of Gen. Hamilton H. Howze. In its final report the board recommended the creation of air assault divisions equipped with organic aircraft supported by heavy-lift helicopters and de Havilland Caribou transport aircraft. In 1963 the 11th Air Assault Division (test) put this concept into practice. On July 3, 1965, at Fort Benning, the 11th Air Assault Division colors were cased and retired, and the colors of the 1st Cavalry Division (Airmobile) were raised. Soon after, on July 28, 1965, President Lyndon Johnson ordered the 1st Cavalry to Vietnam. Deployment of the division to Vietnam, by both air and sea, took two months. Suddenly the skies above Fort Benning seemed devoid of any aircraft save the commanding general's highly polished green and white

Huey. Fortunately, there were a few de Havilland DHC-4 Caribous left for our Tactics Phase of training.

To the Air Force generals, the Howze Board findings that allowed the Army to field fixed-wing transport aircraft sounded suspiciously like the Army was trying to create a tactical air force of its own. The Army's focus had always been on supporting the troops on the ground with everything needed, when needed; that required keeping all aviation assets under the senior ground commanders' direct control. The Air Force didn't see it that way. It wanted a more centralized control of aviation assets, which required extra levels of command approval for mission scheduling. This put the Army and Air Force at odds, resulting in the 1966 Johnson-McConnell agreement between Army Chief of Staff Gen. Harold K. Johnson and Air Force Chief of Staff Gen. John P. McConnell. As part of this agreement the Army was allowed to have helicopter gunships in direct support of ground troops as well as transport and heavy-lift helicopters. In return, the Army gave up its fixed-wing Caribou transport aircraft, and the Air Force limited its use of helicopters, primarily for the search and rescue of downed aviators. The bottom line was that the Air Force was that not about to allow the Army to have its own fixed-wing air force. If an aircraft had fixed wings, the Air Force generals wanted it.

When I entered the final phase of OCS training, air assault had become the Army's way of taking the fight to the enemy. Our tactics training had begun at the platoon level and worked through company-level operations, followed by combined arms, which involved mechanized infantry and armor and culminated in an air assault attack of an imaginary enemy force. Normally this attack would have been conducted using helicopters, but the 1st Cavalry Division had taken all of the helicopters at Fort Benning with them. As a result, the Caribou was our air assault aircraft, not the helicopter; thus began my desire to fly instead of walk.

The Caribou, an off-the-shelf short takeoff and landing (STOL) twin-engine cargo aircraft, was capable of carrying thirty-two combat troops or up to four tons of cargo. The Army had purchased a total of 159 Caribous from the de Havilland Aircraft Company. The Caribous were the largest fixed-wing aircraft in the Army inventory. The Army would eventually lose them to the Air Force, but for a while they filled a vital role for the Army's field commanders in troop transport and limited resupply.

On the morning of our air assault training we climbed on board several Caribous at Lawson Army Airfield, all decked out in our infantry combat gear. After takeoff we flew around the outer reaches of Fort Benning for a while and then rapidly began circling in a descent. I was looking out of the round window behind my web seat and noticed a very small opening in the thick Fort Benning woods with a dirt road running through it. I remember thinking to myself that there was no way we were going to land in that little clearing in the woods, but we did! We slammed onto the ground, then there was a tremendous roar as the pilot reversed the propellers and applied heavy braking, bringing us to a stop in a cloud of dust. The flight engineer quickly lowered the rear ramp and yelled at us, "Get off!" We did as ordered and ran toward the nearby tree line to take up firing positions, securing the landing area.

Special attachments on the barrels of our rifles allowed us to fire blank ammunition, creating the sounds of combat without the possibility of injury that real bullets would have inflicted. All around were the sounds of most of my classmates firing into the trees to "suppress any nearby enemy forces." I, on the other hand, took position at the base of a Georgia pine and turned to marvel at that magnificent machine that had safely delivered us. I figured the pilot was going to turn around and taxi back to the end of the clearing, which wasn't much larger than a football field, so he could take off. He didn't. He had landed and stopped at less than midpoint of the field. Now the pilot stood on the brakes, applied full power to the engines, released the brakes, and to my total amazement took off. Granted, he was thirty-two bodies lighter, but I knew that there was no way he could clear the fifty-foot pine trees at the departure end of the field. To my complete amazement, he did! In that instant I knew I wanted to become an Army aviator and fly Caribous.

On September 6, 1965, I was commissioned a second lieutenant. At the last minute, twenty-eight of us had our assignments changed to remain at Fort Benning. We had all been assigned to the new Basic Training Brigade that was being created at Sand Hill, located on the sprawling Fort Benning complex. The war in Vietnam was heating up and there was an increased demand to train more soldiers for Vietnam. I soon found myself the officer in charge (OIC) of a rifle range, responsible for teaching young soldiers the proper actions of the individual soldier in the defense of a position. It was not a particularly difficult job. Before long, I was able to convince my commander that, as an infantry second lieutenant stationed at Fort Benning—the home of the Army's Airborne School—it would be an excellent opportunity for me to become Airborne qualified if he could just see his way clear to let me go for three weeks.

While I was in Airborne training I encountered another lieutenant, who told me he was waiting for orders to go to flight school. I immediately asked him how he had gone about applying and found out that all I had to do was go to the Fort Benning personnel office and ask to take the Flight Aptitude Selection Test (FAST).

As soon as I completed Airborne training and pinned on my jump wings, I headed for the personnel office and requested to take the FAST. I was determined to have another set of wings as well—those of an Army aviator. Admittedly I was pretty naive about the inner workings of the military and how the system operated, particularly when it came to something like being selected for flight school. I was Infantry Branch, so any long-term training had to be approved at branch level. I took the written exam for entry to flight training and scored quite high. The first lieutenant who administered the test told me he could guarantee I was qualified (provided I pass the Class One flight physical) and would be accepted for training.

The most difficult part of the flight physical was the eye exam. Back then, the interocular tension of the eye was determined by placing a small metal device directly on the eyeball, a very uncomfortable sensation that caused a natural reaction to either close the eyelid or turn away, neither of which action was appropriate. Passing the eye test was critical, and a military flight school candidate had to have at least 20/20 vision. This was the one requirement for initial entry into military flight training that could not be waived. Many otherwise highly qualified applicants for military flight training have been turned away because of that one, set-in-stone requirement. Once in flight training or after becoming a rated military aviator, it was acceptable if vision degraded to as much as 20/200, if correctable to 20/20 with glasses. My problem was I just could not avoid turning my head when the medic tried to place the metal device on my corneas, so he had two of his fellow medics hold my head in place. After that ordeal I drove home squinting through dark sunglasses as tears ran from my dilated eyes, the discomfort mitigated by the knowledge I had passed the flight physical.

Next came the waiting. Days passed and became weeks. I had just about given up hope of being accepted to flight training when a letter from Infantry Branch at the Pentagon arrived telling me I had been approved; however, I had not been assigned a class date.

The last sentence of the letter said that if I had any questions, I could call a certain Autovon number (Autovon was the military telephone system that allowed free official long-distance telephone calls). I had questions. So I called, without knowing who I would be talking to or exactly what I would say. I was simply seeking reassurance that the acceptance letter was for real. The woman who answered was quite friendly, and I admitted to her that I was concerned that someone might change his mind. She laughed and told me, "No, you are going to flight school, I just don't have a class date for you yet." Still unsure that I could trust the system, I asked if I could call her from time to time to get updates. She said that I could call her every week if I wanted to, so I did. I was always polite. This went on for another five weeks until I received a telephone call from her one morning: "Lieutenant Caryl, I'm making up the class list for next month. I can put you in the helicopter class if you want it, or if you are willing to wait a couple of months, I can put you in a fixed-wing class." I hesitated and told her that I really wanted to go to fixed-wing training and asked again if someone would change his mind about sending me to flight school if I declined helicopters. Her next statement left me with a momentary terrible sinking feeling, followed by complete relief.

She said in a serious tone, "Lieutenant Caryl, I don't think you realize who you are talking to."

Instantly, I'm thinking, *Oh no, I've screwed up.*

Then I heard her say, laughing, "I'm the one who makes the flight school class assignments for Infantry Branch."

Holy Cow! Here I thought that I had been talking to just a civilian secretary at the Pentagon. And all along I had been talking to the Aviation Assignment Officer for the United States Army Infantry Branch, who just happened to be a woman and a civilian. I never met her or knew anything about her, but she must have been a mom and realized that this poor dumb lieutenant really needed a mother's help, and so she gave it. I have yet to meet another Army aviator who actually got to choose whether he went to rotary-wing or fixed-wing flight training.

I can only contribute my good fortune to having been polite on the telephone to that woman. All those years as a kid, being reminded by my mom to "be polite to others," had borne fruit.

At the time, the Army's primary need was for helicopter pilots in Vietnam; most of those assigned to flight school were sent to rotary-wing training. When I graduated from flight school in June 1967, there were 382 in the rotary-wing class and only 51 of us in the fixed-wing class: a ratio of over seven to one. I will always feel that woman saved my life, because of the 4,347 Army flight crew members killed in Vietnam, nearly all were in helicopters. Their names are inscribed on the walls of the Vietnam Memorial room in the Army Aviation Museum at Fort Rucker, Alabama. A solemn reminder of the hazards of flying in combat.

In August 1966 I left Fort Benning and headed to Fort Stewart, Georgia, for the Officer Fixed-Wing Aviator Course, Class 67–5 (OFWAC 67–5). I was beginning a career as a pilot that would span thirty-eight years and encompass both military and civilian flying—fixed-wing and rotary-wing aircraft. Just before I began flight school the Army had been required to give its Caribous to the Air Force, per the Johnson-McConnell Agreement. Sadly I was not to realize my dream of flying a Caribou.

Almost immediately after the agreement was signed, the Air Force set up a transition program at Fort Benning for its pilots who had been selected to fly the Caribou. Army Caribou pilots, primarily warrant officers, had been selected as instructor pilots (IPs) to teach the Air Force pilots, largely lieutenant colonels, majors, and lieutenants, the art of flying this relatively small cargo aircraft.

At the Lawson Army Airfield Officers Club at Fort Benning late one afternoon during the transition period, I noticed a bunch of Army and Air Force pilots in their flight suits sitting at the bar complaining about the transition. Flight suits were really nothing more than gray cotton coveralls with the appropriate aviator wings, rank insignia, and unit patches sewn on them. Typically, pilots were not allowed in the main bar area of an Officers Club, but were permitted in the casual bar that every club had. The Army pilots were grousing that they were being forced to give up their beloved Caribous, and the Air Force pilots were grumbling they were being forced to fly those slow, baby cargo airplanes. Their main complaint seemed to be that once in Vietnam, they would be relegated to landing on small, unimproved runways at remote Army Special Forces outposts, often placing them at great distance from their home airfield; and when compared to larger Air Force cargo aircraft, the slow Caribous would put them in jeopardy of being late for Happy Hour at their Air Force O-Club. None of the Army warrant officers seemed very sympathetic toward this whining. I was siding with the Army pilots. Somewhere there were some happy Air Force generals, but at the operational level—where it really mattered—neither Army nor Air Force pilots were pleased.

Prior to the fall of 1966 fixed-wing flight training was conducted exclusively at Fort Rucker, Alabama. Because of the increased need for aviators, the entire Army flight-training program was expanded to such an extent that skies over Fort Rucker were crowded with aircraft. Thus the first two phases of fixed-wing training were moved to Fort Stewart.

Primary flight training at Fort Stewart consisted of one hundred hours in the air learning the basics of flying. The Cessna O-1 Birddog was the Army's primary flight trainer at the time. It was the first airplane that I ever flew. It was also the airplane most of us in OFWAC 67–5 would fly in Vietnam. My class—known as the Red Hats because we wore red baseball caps throughout our flight training—was the last class to fly the Birddog in the first two phases of the Army's flight training program.

The course at Fort Stewart was divided into two phases: A and B. A-Phase included day and night takeoffs and landings, airport traffic patterns, emergency procedures, and cross-country navigation. Most of us qualified to fly solo after about ten or twelve hours of dual instruction. We were also taught basic air maneuvers such as steep turns, spins, and stall recovery. B-Phase consisted of dual and solo work that involved landing in, and taking off from, short grass strips with a variety of obstacles, including fifty-foot pine trees and other assorted barriers located around the perimeter of the grass strip. The landing strips were scattered over a large area and had to be located by using navigation charts. We were learning how to use maps as a navigation tool while flying in unfamiliar areas without becoming lost, something we just might be able to use in Vietnam. It was challenging, but fun too; and my confidence grew with each flight.

The Birddog was easy to fly. It was a "tail dragger" though and could quickly get away from the inexperienced pilot who got sloppy with his landings, especially in a crosswind where it was highly susceptible to a ground loop—the tendency of the tail of the aircraft to rotate forward after landing. This phenomenon causes the aircraft to go sideways, often resulting in a wing tip striking the ground, damaging the aircraft. Also, the main landing gear could collapse or other damage could render the aircraft unrepairable. Ground loops were rarely fatal but never failed to damage the pilot's ego.

The students in the class behind us were flying the brand-new T-41 Mescalero, the Army's 230-horsepower version of the Cessna 172 Skyhawk with a variable-pitch propeller and beefed-up landing gear. The T-41s were purchased without any of the frills normally found in the civilian version. The seats were canvas and designed so the occupants of the two front seats could wear parachutes, which was required when performing aerobatic maneuvers. The T-41s were faster than our Birddogs and had new radios and tricycle landing gear with a nose wheel instead of a tail wheel. Eliminating the tail wheel made them much easier to land. Those students who followed us would rib us about flying "old" airplanes that theirs could easily outpace. We just smiled knowing that most of them, like us, would be flying the Birddog in Vietnam and that we would have one hundred more hours in it than they would when they got to Vietnam. "Just wait until you get to Fort Rucker and have to land a tail dragger," was our common response to their ribbing.

Shortly after we began B-Phase, the movie *Blue Max* came out. I think the entire class attended the Friday night showing, and we all hooted and hollered as George Peppard flew his World War I airplane under bridges and between trees. Our instructors must have seen the movie the same weekend, because Monday morning our briefing from the flight commander, Maj. Bill Everett, included the stern caution not to try anything stupid like flying under bridges. To my knowledge, none of us did.

Upon completing primary flight training at Fort Stewart, I was transferred to Fort Rucker, Alabama, the home of Army Aviation. There I began C-Phase, which was my introduction to instrument flying. C-Phase also included multi-engine qualification. More than four hundred aircraft were in the sky above and around Fort Rucker's numerous training fields on any given day. Most of them were helicopters.

For the fixed-wing students, instrument flight training at Fort Rucker was conducted in the spiffy new T-42 Beechcraft Baron. The T-42 had retractable landing gear and a nose wheel. It was a low-wing, four-place aircraft with two engines instead of one, and it was twice as fast as what we had been flying. On this aircraft we would learn to fly by referring only to the flight instruments. We wore a hood that restricted our vision to the instrument panel; no more looking outside the airplane to stay right side up. I really struggled in C-Phase. I had become pretty confident with my flying skills in the Birddog, but the T-42 was a handful and I found myself falling behind.

All of our instrument instructors were civilian pilots under contract to the Army. Most were former military aviators. My first instrument instructor was a retired Air Force colonel who chain-smoked and had zero empathy for anyone like me who had trouble grasping the concept of flying without a visual horizon outside the aircraft. Eventually he handed me off to another instructor because I "just wasn't getting it." My second instrument instructor wasn't much better at helping me "get it."

Finally I was handed off to a retired Navy fighter jock who told me I had been awarded five additional flight hours to master instrument flying or I was out, and he was the last instructor I was going to get. So this was make-or-break time for me. There weren't going to be any second chances. I was hanging on the verge of being set back or tossed out of flight school and naturally nervous as hell. He seemed pretty sincere when he said that he was determined to help me meet the standards for instrument flying, but when he told me to file a flight plan for Columbus, Georgia, I knew that I was doomed.

The airport at Columbus had four different runway directions with a different instrument approach (e.g., VHF Omni-Directional Radio Range [VOR], Instrument Landing System [ILS]) to each one. Because of this, the instructors could have a student "shoot" one approach after the other, each to a different runway, requiring a different approach plate (chart), with different minimum descent altitudes and different missed approach criteria. These approaches occurred in such rapid succession that the student could eventually fail to perform correctly, earning an unsatisfactory grade for the flight. Unsatisfactory grades were written up on a pink grade slip; thus, Columbus became known as Pink Slip Alley among the students.

SILVER WINGS **17**

After giving me a preflight briefing, McClary, my IP, accompanied me to flight operations where I got my weather briefing and filed my instrument flight rules (IFR) flight plan. The weather at Columbus was forecast to be "severe clear," but even as fledgling pilot I was learning to distrust the weather guessers. We then went out to our aircraft, and I performed a walk-around preflight, carefully following the checklist. Convinced that I was under additional scrutiny, I was hoping to make a good first impression with my new IP. We then climbed into the cockpit and again following the checklist, I started the engines; received, copied, read back my IFR clearance to Cairns Clearance Delivery; and taxied out to the runway for takeoff. We departed runway 06 and climbed to our assigned altitude as I pointed the T-42 toward Columbus and what I was certain would be the end of my career as an Army aviator.

Nearing Columbus, we were handed off to approach control. McClary then shut off my radio receiver that was set to the Columbus Approach Control frequency so I could not hear him talking to the controller. He would now be my approach controller, and I was to talk to him on intercom. This was common practice for the instrument IPs and often used in visual flight rules (VFR) conditions where they could see out of the aircraft. This technique gave them more latitude in what they had us do, making it easier for them to load us up to the point of failure.

All instrument approaches to airports are designed to get the pilot and his airplane safely on the runway when he cannot see the ground because of low clouds, fog, heavy rain, or any obstructions to visibility. Different approaches have different degrees of precision and therefore allow the pilot to descend to different altitudes above the runway before requiring him to abort the approach and "go around," that is, fly a missed approach. The approaches take into account vertical obstacles such as terrain, tall buildings, and towers that lie within a certain distance of a particular runway.

The Federal Aviation Administration regularly flies each instrument approach at an airport, certifying the level of precision and obstacle clearance. Each approach is printed on an "approach plate" or chart that is contained in booklet form and updated and replaced on a recurring cycle. This process takes into account changes in the height of obstacles, for example, a radio tower near the airport that is about to have an additional fifty feet added to it. If the changes impinge on the published approach path, then the approach needs to be changed and the changes updated on the approach plate. The approach plate will depict the proper way to enter the approach, the course to be flown, and the different minimum altitudes at which the pilot can be at certain specific points along the approach path to the runway. It will also depict the minimum altitude to which the pilot can descend without seeing the runway and the procedures to follow to execute a missed approach if he does not see the runway. We were learning to execute these approaches precisely, using the proper communications terminology while flying the airplane solely by instruments with no outside visible horizon. This procedure had to be done while referring to the approach plate without violating any minimum descent altitudes or course restrictions. It does get easier the more you do it, but getting to that point can be a struggle.

McClary cleared me for three approaches and their published missed approaches in rapid succession. The last one, with instructions to enter holding at a specific point in the sky, shown on the approach plate known as GEMMY Intersection. Without a break, I was hand flying the aircraft the entire time plus tuning radios, finding the correct approach plates, and quickly studying them for a dozen different bits of necessary information. Because the T-42 had no autopilot, I never had a moment to sit back and gather my thoughts. Somewhere in the process of flying the last missed approach and cross tuning radios to enter holding, I lost it.

Man, I was a mess and embarrassed beyond belief. McClary who had now become my tormentor calmly said, "I've got the controls. Let's just fly around here a bit until you settle down. I purposely pushed you to your limit today so I could see where you stand. You know, you are your own worst enemy. You are worrying about things way beyond what you need to be thinking about. Let's start over and I'll show you how to prioritize what you should be doing. I'll show you how to get everything set up in advance that needs to be set up and then you can relax and fly this thing. You know how to fly the aircraft, tune the radios, read the approach plates, and fly the approaches. All you need to do is relax."

And I did. Under his calm tutelage, everything seemed to fall into place and suddenly I was flying on instruments and enjoying it. As they say in Georgia, "Every now and then, even a blind hog finds an acorn." I had just found mine.

With instrument flying under my belt, I moved on to the next training syllabus: D-Phase. For those of us in the Red Hat class, D-Phase was a walk in the park because we had flown Birddogs in primary flight training. D-Phase was designed to be a transition into an airplane with a tail wheel. For those who have never flown one, an airplane with a tail wheel can quickly become a real handful during takeoff and landing. A ground loop is only a heartbeat away for those who, as old aviators like to say, fail to "fly a tail-dragger until its brakes are set, the wheels are chocked, and it is tied down." I think that, for the instructors who would be teaching it to the classes that followed us, our class became a training ground for them to work out any bugs in the program.

For the Red Hats, D-Phase was a retake of our B-Phase at Fort Stewart. We did all of the same things: flying into and out of grass strips near Fort Rucker, navigating between them, performing power-on and power-off landings, and landing over barriers with 60 degrees of flaps. The big difference was that at D-Phase I was much better at it and my confidence level soared. After twenty-eight hours of really fun flying, I moved on to Tactics, the last phase of flight training.

By then we were all very proficient at flying the Birddog, and the Tactics syllabus simply seemed like something that someone, somewhere had tacked on at the end of flight school just to keep us at Fort Rucker for another month. It became more of a test of patience than actual flight instruction. Someone way up the chain of command must have pulled the World War II manual of Liaison Aircraft Operations off the shelf, dusted it off, and sent it to Fort Rucker. This phase was supposed to teach us fledgling aviators how to use the Birddog in combat, but it had apparently been written by those who had not considered how quickly Army aviation was evolving in Vietnam and how Birddogs would be used there.

During the Tactics Phase, I had to land and take off from a curved dirt road with tall pine trees lining each side—something I never did later in Vietnam. I practiced flying with large bundles attached under each wing, which created an enormous amount of drag and severely degraded the Birddog's already limited performance. Allegedly this exercise was to train us to "resupply" troops on the ground—something the Army may have done in World War II and Korea; but that was before Vietnam and Huey helicopters. We did practice adjusting artillery. I may have called one artillery fire mission and adjusted two or three artillery rounds under the tutelage of an instructor in the back seat. These were not enough rounds to really get the hang of it, but they were short of artillery rounds at Fort Rucker that week and that's all I got. We also fired 2.75-inch rockets at an imaginary target on the ground. The rockets had a 10-pound warhead containing 2.3 pounds of high explosives (HE). These HE warheads could be lethal to unprotected personnel, and although I fired rockets from my Birddog in Vietnam, none of them were HE.

The process instructors at Fort Rucker taught for firing rockets was overly complicated. First we had to climb up to three thousand feet above ground level from our normal visual reconnaissance (VR) altitude of eight hundred to one thousand feet. This took nearly five minutes. After gaining altitude, we were to arm a rocket using the overhead switches, pull on the carburetor heat, retard the throttle, lower 45 degrees of flaps, pull the safety pin from the trigger located on the handgrip of the control stick between our legs, neutralize the controls, remain lined up on the target, and squeeze the trigger.

This process may have looked good on paper, but it didn't work well for me in training and it sure as hell didn't work in Vietnam. By the time I had lowered the flaps to 45 degrees and lined up on the target, I was in a screaming-ass dive and had to hold forward pressure on the control stick to keep the nose pointed at the target. The airplane then wanted to pitch nose up, but I was preventing it with the forward pressure. However, when I fired the rocket, it shot out of the tube and started to "climb" relative to the direction the nose of the airplane was pointed in. Since the controls were definitely not neutralized when I squeezed the trigger, the rocket wound up missing the target by a distance of at least two football fields. All I could think was there had to be a better way to fire rockets. If I was trying to hit anyone, they would be long gone by the time I had spent the last five minutes climbing. Also, I was just a bit concerned about being right over whatever I was shooting at (and missing): they might be shooting up at me.

Pilots who flew Birddogs in Vietnam fulfilled the role of eyes in the sky for commanders on the ground. Their primary mission was visual reconnaissance, but in many ways the Birddog was the ground commander's secret weapon. Even though the aircraft was virtually unarmed, it was a lethal asset. It did have two 2.75-inch diameter rocket tubes under each wing—some Birddog units carried more, but that load tended to degrade aircraft performance—and either high explosive or white phosphorous (WP) rockets could be carried and fired from them. The WP rockets left a lingering plume of white smoke at their point of impact, whereas the HE rockets simply exploded in a flash of flying shrapnel and a brief puff of black smoke. Most Army Birddog companies may have carried the HE rockets, but the pilots of the unit I would fly for in Vietnam used the WP rockets exclusively to mark their targets for jet attack aircraft. Any additional armament on the Birddogs consisted of whatever weaponry the pilot and observer chose to carry on board. We all carried a pistol and a rifle, but these were intended to be used in the event we went down someplace hostile and needed to protect ourselves until help arrived. Occasionally someone would fire their rifle out an open side window, but accuracy became a problem due to aircraft movement and leading the target issues. Every now and then some enterprising Birddog pilot would attach an M-60 machine gun under a wing and fire it using a long piece of wire to pull the trigger.

This may have worked, but it didn't really fit the mission profile of the unit I would fly for in Vietnam. We were there to locate the enemy and then accurately adjust artillery and naval gunfire or mark the target for jet attack aircraft. Attempting to play the role of attack fighter-bomber in a Birddog would likely get a pilot shot down.

In addition to visual reconnaissance, artillery adjustment quickly became one of the primary tasks of Army Birddog pilots in Vietnam. Even the Army's 1st Cavalry Division, composed almost exclusively of helicopters, had its own Birddog detachment whose sole job was to accurately adjust the division's artillery batteries. Their call sign was Woodpecker, something they seemed delighted in shortening to just "Pecker" when they made radio calls. The Birddog's ability to stay aloft over twice as long as a helicopter before having to refuel made it an ideal platform for artillery adjustment. Cessna's little two-seat airplane was aptly named. Just like a hunter's bird dog, its job was to find the quarry, then bring about its demise.

3 | Becoming a Catkiller

On June 6, 1967, I was one of fifty new Army aviators of Fixed-Wing Aviator Course 67–5 who walked across the stage at the Fort Rucker post theater and received silver wings. Nearly all of us received orders to Vietnam and nearly all of us would be flying Birddogs after we got there. I didn't know what Birddog unit I would be assigned to; that would happen after I got to Vietnam. I just knew that "Above the Best" is the motto of Army Aviation, and I was determined to live up to it in my next duty assignment, Vietnam.

After a brief bit of leave and goodbyes at home, I flew military standby to San Francisco and then processed through the Overseas Replacement Station in Oakland where I received what seemed like an endless number of shots. They were administered by enlisted medical personnel who really seemed to enjoy jamming very large needles into both arms of young men standing in long lines in their skivvies. It was obvious that the military didn't want me to die in Vietnam from some strange disease. The irony wasn't lost on me either, since I was going to Vietnam where people that I didn't know were going to try to kill me with bullets. Then it was travel by bus to Travis Air Force Base near San Francisco where I boarded a Braniff Airlines charter jet. A two-day odyssey began on July 21, 1967, when the charter jet landed at Tan Son Nhut Air Base near Saigon.

The heat and humidity were the first thing to hit me when I stepped off the aircraft; Georgia in July barely comes close to Saigon. The next thing to assail my body was the smell—pungent and foreign to my nostrils. The third thing was the line of GIs waiting to board the aircraft I had just arrived in. This was their "Freedom Bird" that would take them back to the "land of the big PX." They were in faded fatigues, obviously on their way home, taunting us new arrivals with shouts of derision.

"Look at the new meat!"

"You're going home in a body bag!"

"I'll be seeing your girl tomorrow!"

I just tried to ignore it. We were herded on board some Air Force blue buses and driven to the 90th Replacement Battalion at Long Binh. Chicken wire covered the open windows to prevent hand grenades from being tossed inside. Long Binh was sarcastically referred to by those who had been in country a while as Long Binh Junction, or LBJ—a less than complimentary nod to our current president. It was where everyone was checked in after arriving in Vietnam and then routed to their unit of assignment. The place was a madhouse. Newly arrived first-tour people had no idea where they were. If they did just happen to know where they were going, they had no idea how to get there. The noise of vehicles and aircraft was constant. Added to that cacophony was a blaring public address (PA) system that called off names of those who were moving on to their units.

There was a mess hall, but the food was lousy; there were barracks with cots and bedding, but no place to secure anything of value. Going to take a shower or even relieve yourself might mean leaving your belongings under the watchful eye of a complete stranger that you might or might not be able to trust. Total chaos best describes time spent at the 90th Replacement Battalion.

The next two days were a blur. The only things I paid any attention to were my suitcase and the PA system, which was so loud and garbled I wasn't sure I'd recognize my name when it was called. As luck would have it, I was in the latrine when I thought I heard my name being announced. I scrambled to finish, gather my gear, and find out where I was heading. The orders I had been issued when I first arrived merely read "assigned to the 90th Replacement Depot for further assignment," and by then I was willing to go anyplace just to get out of there. Fortunately, they actually had been calling my name, and I was issued a new set of orders assigning me to the 223rd Aviation Battalion of the 17th Aviation Group. I was finally on my way.

After a two-hour ride in the back of a noisy Air Force C-123 and several landings at places with names like Pleiku and Vung Tau, I found myself in Nha Trang.

Two of my flight school classmates, Capt. Royal Peterson and 1st Lt. Lloyd Raduege, and I were seated in the office of Maj. Ronald Wilson, the executive officer of the 223rd Aviation Battalion.

"Well gentlemen, welcome to the 223rd. I'll quickly go over some admin notes and then we'll get to your unit assignments."

I missed most of the admin stuff because I was semi-dozing off, but I perked up when he started talking about unit assignments.

"I've got three Birddog pilot slots that need to be filled. Two of them are with the 219th and one is with the 220th. The 219th is here in Two Corps [II Corps]. You may have heard of them. Every aviation unit here in Vietnam has given itself a name. They are known as the Headhunters. The 220th is called the Catkillers. They're up north in Eye Corps [I Corps]. A couple of months back, one of the 220th pilots was shot down and captured. The VC [Viet Cong] dragged him through the local villages for about five nights and then they broke every bone in his body and tried to make a lampshade out of him. His body was finally located in a shallow grave a few weeks later. The VC don't like Birddog pilots and there's a ten-thousand-dollar reward for you guys, dead or alive."

Hearing that, I immediately thought, *Yikes! They broke every bone in his body and then tried to make a lampshade out of him? Maybe the 90th Replacement Depot wasn't such a bad place after all.*

"You gentlemen have any preferences as to which Birddog company you'd like to be assigned?"

Peterson immediately piped up with, "I've already written to the CO [commanding officer] of the 219th and he said that he was saving a slot for me, sir."

"Okay, captain, I'll put you down for the 219th," replied the major, making a note on a paper on his desk.

That made sense. Peterson had already done a tour in Vietnam as a ground-pounder artillery forward observer in II Corps and was a captain. Rank has its privileges. The major then looked at Raduege and me and said, "Either of you lieutenants have a preference?"

I think that we both definitely had a preference; I know that I did. Neither of us wanted to be the odd man out, especially when the odd man would have to go up north where they shot you out of the sky, dragged you through villages at night, broke all the bones in your body, and tried to make a lampshade out of what was left.

Neither one of us said a word. It just wouldn't have been good form to say that we'd rather go to the 219th, so we just sat there staring at the major.

"Okay then. It's about lunch time," announced Major Wilson, looking at his watch and sliding his chair back. "Let's go eat while you two are making up your minds."

So off we went to the mess hall. Along the way we passed a corner of the aircraft parking ramp, and a de Havilland Beaver that was sitting there. The venerable Army U-6A, fondly referred to as the Ugly Six Alpha by those who flew it, had been manufactured in Canada as a bush aircraft, specifically for hauling people and cargo into and out of small, unimproved backcountry landing areas, and was a natural for the U.S. Army and its needs.

"Either of you two fly the Beaver?" asked the major, looking at Raduege and me.

"I do," I said.

Now that wasn't totally a lie. I had flown in a Beaver back at Fort Stewart, in one of the back seats, not the front. It was a tail-dragger though, just like the Birddog, and I did know how to fly those. How much harder could it be to fly a Beaver? It was just a larger version of the Birddog, albeit with a radial engine. I figured that I could find a warrant officer who was checked out in it to give me a few pointers, then I'd be good to go. Nha Trang had a beach, and it was the location of a major headquarters, so it had a post exchange and other amenities. And there was a hospital, which meant nurses. Yes, I definitely wanted to stay here and fly that Beaver.

"You two go on, we'll be along in a minute," the major said to Peterson and Raduege. To me he said, "Go ahead and jump up in there and start it for me, lieutenant."

I bravely climbed up into the left seat of the Beaver and began frantically looking around. If you have never actually started a Beaver, you are not going to figure it out just sitting there and looking at all of the switches and levers. There is a process. There is a primer that you pump (slowly) three times located on the floor to your lower left, a mixture lever on the throttle quadrant in front of you that you push forward, a throttle lever that you push forward just a bit and then don't touch again until the engine is running (or you can blow a cylinder off of it), a wobble pump that you "wobble" holding the fuel pressure at 5 psi (no more), and three guarded toggle switches on the lower left of the instrument panel that you move up in a specific sequence, and—the one thing I did recognize—a red magneto switch.

I'm screwed, I thought as I just sat there, knowing that any hope of remaining at Nha Trang had disappeared.

"Nice try, lieutenant," Major Wilson said smiling, without a trace of anger in his voice. "I can't blame you for wanting to stay here, but I really do need you in one of the Birddog companies." And off we went to lunch.

Later, back in Major Wilson's office and in our original seats, the major asked, "Well, did you two make up your minds which unit you want to go to?"

Raduege and I just sat there, neither one of us saying a word. I knew that I was a lousy poker player; and a poker face was not something that I possessed, so I began staring intently at one of the plaques on Major Wilson's wall, silently hoping that Raduege would say that he wanted to go to the 220th. Seconds dragged by in total silence, and finally I blinked.

"Major, do you have a list of pilots in the 220th?" I asked.

"Sure," he said, sliding a piece of paper across his desk in my direction.

I quickly scanned the list of names, thinking that if I couldn't go to a company with someone I knew, maybe someone I knew would already be in the company I ended up in. Then I saw a name I recognized . . . 1st Lt. Richard Johnson.

Rick and I had been roommates at Fort Stewart, Georgia, during our first four months of flight school. He was a graduate of Virginia Military Institute and had taken a commission in the Marine Corps upon graduation. He had wanted to become a Marine fighter pilot and was accepted to Navy flight training at Pensacola, Florida. Several months into his training he was told that because his eyesight was something less than 20/20 (but still within limits), he was not going to be in the front seat piloting a Marine Corps jet fighter but in the back seat as a Radar Intercept Officer (RIO). That news did not sit well with Rick, so he managed to pull some strings, transfer his commission to the Army, and attend Army flight training. He figured that he would rather fly in the front seat of a Birddog than the back seat of an F-4 Phantom. Less than a month into our training, the Army realized Rick already knew how to fly, so he was moved up two classes and graduated two months before I did. Rick owed me forty dollars for his share of our phone bill and had forgotten to pay me. I was determined to get it back. Losing forty dollars on a bet was one thing; getting stiffed for it is another.

"I'll go to the 220th," I said. "Johnson owes me forty dollars on a phone bill."

Raduege looked at me like I was nuts. He was no doubt thinking, *You would go up there where pilots that get shot down get turned into lampshades for forty bucks?* Peterson shook his head and chuckled, and the major just smiled and leaned back in his chair. His job was done; he had successfully assigned three new aviators to their respective units.

That very afternoon Peterson and Raduege went to the 219th Reconnaissance Airplane Company, and later I boarded an Air Force C-130 transport aircraft headed north to I Corps and the 220th Reconnaissance Airplane Company.

If it wasn't for a young Marine sitting next to me on the C-130 when it landed at Hue Phu Bai, I would have wound up at the wrong airfield. After glancing at my orders, he was nice enough to tell me, "There are two Hues, sir, and I don't think this C-130 can land at the other one because the runway is too short, so you had better get off here." How was I to know there were two Hues: Hue Citadel (pronounced Way Citadel), the ancient imperial city of Vietnam, and Hue Phu Bai (pronounced Way Foo By), where I was dropped off.

So here I am in the late evening of July 23, 1967, alone on the tarmac standing next to my suitcase in Vietnam, in a war zone, at night, in the dark, without a weapon. *Well,* I thought to myself, *You're off to a great start. Here you are in a combat zone, unarmed, not exactly sure where you are, and without the foggiest idea where to go next or how to get there.* Just then an aircraft-towing vehicle, known as a tug, rumbled up out of the darkness and stopped.

"Can I help you find something, sir?" said the voice from the driver's seat.

"Uh, yes, I'm looking for the 220th aviation company," I replied.

"Toss your gear up on the hood and I'll give you a ride, it's right across the ramp. I'm Specialist Parker. Are you assigned to the 220th?"

"Yep, I was just sent up here from battalion today. Been riding on that C-130 for what seems like hours. Sure feels like I've arrived at the end of the world."

"Well, sir, you could say that's just about where you are. We're only fifty miles or so south of North Vietnam."

With that, my young specialist-savior crunched the tug into gear, and we headed off across the ramp to my new home for the next year: the 220th Reconnaissance Airplane Company, headquartered at Hue Phu Bai, Thua Thien Province, Vietnam.

My orders upon graduating from flight school had merely instructed me to report to the Oakland, California, Army terminal for transport to Vietnam and further assignment to the 90th Replacement Battalion. That didn't tell me which unit I was to be assigned to when I got to Vietnam, so my journey to this very spot had been rather interesting.

My benefactor stopped his tug at the edge of the ramp and announced, "There it is, sir. Just go across the road and under the archway. The CQ is in that first building on the left. He'll get you settled for the night. Welcome to the 220th."

I slid off the seat of his tug, thanked him, grabbed my suitcase, and walked across the dirt road to the dimly lit building that held the Charge of Quarters (CQ). Every military unit, from a company on up to world level with a command structure, has someone who is awake and ready to respond all night long. Notification of the person in charge is but a phone call or waking nudge away. That's one of the strengths of the military services: they are always ready.

I dropped my bag outside the door on the sidewalk and entered the building. A sergeant was sitting at a small desk, probably the one the company clerk sat at during the day. One light bulb hanging from the ceiling illuminated the room.

"Yes sir, what can I do for you?" the young sergeant asked.

"I'm just checking in sergeant," I said. "I sure hope this is the 220th because it's been a long day and I'm still not sure exactly where I'm at."

"You've come to the right place, lieutenant. This is the 220th. It's pretty late, how about I get you a place to bunk up tonight and you can formally check in tomorrow?"

"I'd really appreciate it sergeant. Just point me to where you want me to go."

"Follow me, sir, and I'll lead you to a hooch with an empty bunk. This is the orderly room and the CO's office is here. You'll want to see him in the morning."

We went outside, and as he led me to my hooch, he pointed out the important stuff.

"That's the mess hall over there. Breakfast is from 0600 to 0730. The coffee and eggs are pretty good and every now and then we get pancakes. That's the latrine over there," he said, pointing to a building two hooches away. "No hot water for the showers, so I'd recommend taking one at night. It's not too bad this time of year, but it's pretty cold in the winter."

Right about then I was thinking, *As hot as I am right now this late at night, a cold shower sounds pretty good.*

"Here's your hooch. There should be some clean sheets on the first bunk to your left. Here's a flashlight you can use to get settled. You can just bring it back to the orderly room in the morning. If you need anything else, I'll be up all night, so just let me know."

"Okay, thanks, sergeant. I think I can take it from here," I said as I took the flashlight and opened the screen door to my new home. Less than fifteen minutes later, I collapsed on the promised clean sheets and fell into a deep sleep.

The next morning, July 24, I awakened to the sound of people talking and airplanes running up on the ramp just across the dirt road. Mother Nature wasn't just calling, she was screaming, so my first order of business was to head to the latrine. I grabbed my shaving kit and towel, tossed on some shorts, slipped into a pair of sandals, and headed out the door. The shower was cold, but not really that bad as the temperature outside seemed to already be in the nineties. Then back to the hooch and into a clean set of fatigues and boots.

Stepping out the door of the hooch, I saw the friendly face of Lt. Gary O'Shields, one of my flight school classmates. As soon as I saw him I thought, *Finally, someone that I know.* Things were starting to look up.

"Gary! Man, it's good to see you. How are you doing?" I asked.

"Good, Ray," Gary responded, shaking my proffered hand, "You just get here?"

"Yeah, I got in late last night. How long you been here? Let's go grab a cup of coffee and you can bring me up to speed."

"I got here a week ago. I'd really like to have coffee, but I've got a mission and have to get going. Catch you later, okay?"

"Okay. Good to see you."

Watching him hurry off with purpose, I couldn't help but think, *Wow, he's been here just a week and he's off flying a mission. They sure didn't waste any time getting you into the saddle around here. I'd better grab some breakfast and check in with the CO.*

I wandered over to the mess hall and was settling into a chair at one of the tables with my tray of breakfast when the captain sitting at the next table nodded in my direction.

"Lieutenant, grab a seat here at this table," he said with a grin. "I'm Ken Trent. Are you just checking into the unit?"

"Yes sir," I said, shaking his hand. "Just got in last night and already found someone that I know from flight school."

"Good. I'm the supply officer. After you finish signing in, come over to the supply hooch and I'll fix you up with all of your gear and weapons."

We chatted a bit as Captain Trent finished his breakfast, and then he was gone. Next on my agenda was a visit to the orderly room and check-in with my new commanding officer.

"The major will see you now," announced the first sergeant as I stood in his orderly room, just a bit nervous. Everyone that I'd encountered so far in the 220th had been more than friendly, but this was a combat aviation unit in Vietnam and we were at war, so I didn't want to screw up my first encounter with my CO.

"Thanks, first sergeant," I said as I passed him and stepped through the doorway to the CO's office. I strode up to the required three feet in front of his desk, came to attention, and snapped an Infantry OCS salute.

"Sir, Lieutenant Caryl reports," I said in a loud, clear voice.

"At ease, lieutenant," Maj. Courtney Smith said, returning my salute. "Grab a seat in that chair and tell me a little bit about yourself."

We talked for a few minutes, and Major Smith made me feel at ease as he welcomed me to the 220th RAC. He gave me an overview of our mission, told me where each platoon was located, and in general made me feel right at home.

Army helicopter companies tended to fly in large gaggles and therefore returned to one location at the end of every flying day. Army Birddogs normally worked alone, so their companies typically operated as separate platoons that were located throughout their area of responsibility.

The first platoon, I was told, was located on the coast at Quang Ngai near the southern edge of I Corps and was the farthest distance away.

The second platoon flew out of a small dirt runway inside the ancient walled city of Hue Citadel, about five miles to the northeast of our company headquarters, at Hue Phu Bai (or Phu Bai). The pilots ate and slept in the Military Assistance Command, Vietnam (MACV) compound just across the Perfume River to the south of the Citadel. The enlisted members of the platoon resided in a villa inside the walled city. The third platoon was located at Marble Mountain Air Facility near Da Nang, and the fourth platoon was located at Dong Ha, the northernmost airfield in South Vietnam just ten miles south of North Vietnam.

———

"Lieutenant, I'm going to assign you to the third platoon down at Marble Mountain. Go ahead and sign in with the company clerk and then go over to supply to draw your gear. When you are finished with that, come back here and I'll have my operations officer, Captain Sutherland, give you your in-country checkout. Welcome to the Catkillers."

"Yes sir," I said, then stood up, saluted, turned, and walked out of his office. It was official, and I was not only in my new home, I was a Catkiller.

After signing in, I asked the company clerk which way to supply and was given directions. As I walked in the front door of supply, my breakfast buddy, Captain Trent, greeted me.

"Hey, Ray, I started to get your basic issue of gear out for you. There's a flak jacket, a pistol belt, your survival radio, a poncho, a couple of blankets, and a steel pot. You brought your flight helmet and gloves with you, right?"

"Yes, I've got all my flight gear."

"Great. What size fatigues do you wear? I'll issue you three sets of jungle fatigues for now. If they wear out, don't throw them away. Just bring 'em back to me and I'll exchange them for new ones on a one-to-one basis."

"I probably wear large. Where can I get my patches and stuff sewn on?"

"What platoon are you assigned to?" he asked.

"The 3rd Platoon at Marble Mountain," I replied.

"There will be someplace down at Marble where you can get it done on the local economy. The guys down there will help you take care of that. Now here's the important stuff."

Captain Trent reached under the counter and brought up a leather holster with a flap and "U.S." stamped on it. He popped open the flap, pulled out a Colt .45, Model 1911, cleared it, and gently placed it on the counter.

"Here's your pistol and a couple of magazines and a box of bullets. You've shot one of these before haven't you?"

"Yep, I was a range OIC for a year back at Fort Benning and I must have put 500 rounds through one."

"Great, here's another little treat for you. How would you like a CAR-15 for your issue rifle?"

"Yeah, you have one?" I asked, barely able to contain the excitement in my voice.

"Yep, just got one in a couple of days ago and you're the first one who has been in that needs a rifle, so it's yours if you want it. The CAR-15 fits a lot better in the cockpit than a regular M-16."

I'm sure that from the grin on my face, Captain Trent could read the thoughts running through my mind: *My lucky day! The CAR-15 has a collapsible stock, a shorter barrel than the regular M-16, and a neat flash suppressor on it. Really a slick-looking little thing, and I think he's right about it fitting better in the cockpit too.*

Capt. Kenny Trent had become my new very best friend. He was a senior pilot in the 220th and would rotate home in December, so his tour was half over and probably at least some of the reason for his magnanimous nature. Kenny could also sing and play the guitar. His rendition of the song "Catkiller 801," to the tune of "Wabash Cannonball," was legend among the Catkiller clan.

After dragging my newly issued gear to the orderly room, I was introduced to the company operations officer, Capt. John Sutherland. Captain Sutherland explained that we were just going to do some touch-and-go landings here at Phu Bai to make sure I was up to speed on flying the

Birddog. He said this ride was important because the aircraft here were heavier than the ones I had been flying in flight school and did handle a bit differently. I realized that this was to be a check ride of sorts but never once doubted my ability to pass. Heck, I had 150 hours flying the Birddog in flight school, and it was almost second nature to me by then.

Captain Sutherland and I flew together for an hour making touch-and-go landings, a simulated forced landing (due to engine failure), and then finished with a full-stop landing. It was pretty much uneventful, and I was proud that I'd done well. First impressions are important.

He then told me to go ahead and fly solo traffic patterns for an hour and that he would fly me down to the 3rd Platoon right after lunch in the company Beaver. I was beginning to feel like I was making progress and would soon be flying actual missions, just as O'Shields had done.

After lunch we loaded my gear and suitcase on the Beaver, and I settled into the copilot's seat. It was going to be just a thirty-minute flight, and I would be landing at my new home, Marble Mountain Air Facility (MMAF), or simply Marble Mountain.

4

Catkiller 3-2

The flight to my new home at Marble Mountain was comfortably cool at our 2,500-foot cruising altitude, a most welcome change from the oppressive July heat on the ground at Phu Bai. I could really appreciate the beauty of the countryside from this altitude. I Corps from the air was breathtaking! To our left was the sparkling blue South China Sea. Beneath us was an expanse of relatively flat terrain dotted with what appeared to be rice paddies that extended inland from the beach a few miles and then rose rapidly on our right to peaks a thousand feet high, covered with lush green vegetation. This wasn't at all like the swamps and marshlands of the Mekong Delta near Saigon that I had seen on the evening news.

As we crossed Hai Van Pass just north of Da Nang, I could make out the city of Da Nang and the 12,000-foot runway of the Air Force base at Da Nang Main. Captain Sutherland pointed to our left front—a much shorter runway was right next to the beach, just a few miles to the east of Da Nang. "That's Marble Mountain, lieutenant, home of the 3rd Platoon. We call it the Country Club. It's not a bad place to be as long as you have to be in Vietnam." With that, he got busy calling the tower for landing instructions, and I tried to take in as much as I could as we made our approach and landing.

MMAF was loaded with helicopters. It was used primarily by the Marines as a helicopter facility but had an Army component there as well. It was constructed in August 1965 after President Lyndon B. Johnson's decision to increase the number of forces in Vietnam led to the rapid saturation of the airfield and facilities at Da Nang, the northernmost major air base in South Vietnam. The apron and parking area were already crowded with Air Force F-4s, Marine Corps A-6s, and a multitude of large transports, all of which benefited from its long runway, leaving little room for helicopters. The air base at Da Nang also served as an emergency recovery airfield for B-52s flying over North Vietnam out of Guam.

The lack of space at Da Nang forced the 1st Marine Air Wing to seek an alternate site for its helicopter operations. The Marines chose a stretch of sandy beach on the South China Sea about five miles southeast of Da Nang, just north of a series of red marble mountains. American military construction units were overtasked at the time, so the initial construction of the airfield was done by Raymond, Morrison-Knudson/Brown, Root & Jones, a consortium of civilian construction companies. By the end of August 1965, they had completed a two-thousand-foot runway, and on August 26 Marine Air Group 16 (MAG 16) officially moved in.

The 3rd Platoon of the 220th RAC had been operating out of Da Nang along with the Marine Birddogs and helicopters. When the Marines moved their helicopters and Birddogs to Marble Mountain, the 3rd Platoon moved with them. By the time I arrived in summer of 1967, the perforated steel planking (PSP) runway had been extended to 4,500 feet and was sufficient for both MAG 16 as well as a smaller Army contingent. The Marines were located on the east side of the runway. Their aircraft consisted of H-34, H-46, H-53, and UH-1 helicopters, plus their small Birddog detachment. Most of the west side of the runway seemed to belong to the Army. The 3rd Platoon of the 220th RAC shared this space with the 282nd Assault Helicopter Company and a detachment of the 18th Aviation Company flying a U-1A Otter. The Otter guys appeared to operate on a schedule like a small airline. Their plane carried everything from Special Forces personnel to Vietnamese civilians, whose carry-on baggage often included chickens and pigs in little bamboo cages.

The de Havilland Otter was manufactured in Canada. Like its smaller cousin the (U-6A) Beaver, also manufactured by de Havilland, the Otter was a "bush" airplane designed to operate in and out of short, unimproved landing strips and therefore a natural for the Army. It had one large radial engine like the Beaver, but it was just a bigger airplane. It could carry up to twelve passengers or two thousand pounds of cargo. Some used to say that the Otter was the box that the Beaver came in and the Beaver was the box that the Birddog came in. They all had one engine, high wings, and a tail wheel. As airplanes go, neither the Beaver nor the Otter was particularly attractive. The planes' beauty lay in the fact that they could carry heavy loads and land and take off almost anywhere.

The largest Army presence at MMAF was in the form of the 282nd Assault Helicopter Company (AHC), nicknamed the Black Cats. The 282nd AHC directly supported a battalion of Army of the Republic of Vietnam (ARVN) Rangers. They had three lift platoons (slicks) and one gun platoon (gunships). The slicks were D and H model Bell UH-1 "Hueys," and the gunships were Bell UH-1 B and C model Hueys. The slicks were the troop carriers and had a free-swinging, stanchion-mounted 7.62-mm machine gun manned on each side of the helicopter for self-protection. The gunships carried 7.62-mm machine guns and 2.75-inch-high explosive rockets mounted on each side of the helicopter that were controlled by one of two pilots seated in the front. Some of the gunships also had a 40-mm grenade launcher mounted under the nose of the aircraft. They also had a free-swinging 7.62-mm machine gun, suspended from a bungee, manned on each side for additional firepower and protection. The job of the gunships was to protect the slicks as they inserted and extracted their soldiers. The slicks all had a large yellow ball painted on the nose with a black cat standing in the middle on just three legs with one of its front legs raised. This particular posture supposedly brought good luck. The gunships all had the same yellow ball, but on some of the gunships the cat was sort of a pale green, had patches of fur missing, a chunk out of one ear, and an Ace bandage wrapped around a crooked tail. It had wild-looking eyes and a hideous grin and was firing a machine gun tucked under its raised paw. A normal request from the tower for departure by one of the slicks would go something like this:

"Marble Tower, Black Cat 1-3, flight of four to lift from the ramp for a south departure."

The gunship guys, who referred to themselves as Alley Cats because they were always looking for a fight, had their own special way of doing things and often could be heard to say something like "Marble Tower, Alley 2-2, flight of two, lift from the litter box for a south departure." Army gunship pilots, few of them over the age of twenty-one, always had their own special brand of cool.

Marble Mountain's 4,500-foot runway lay north–south and was parallel to a beautiful, pristine, 100-foot-wide beach with a gentle surf breaking on it. MMAF was also the location of the Marines' in-country rest and recuperation (R&R) facility. And this was where I was going to have to spend the war? Not bad for a combat zone.

After we had landed, taxied to our ramp, and shut down, I removed all of my belongings from the aircraft and took a look around. The ramp area was perforated steel planking, just like the runway. There were several Birddogs parked nearby, and in the near distance I could see revetments filled with Hueys belonging to the 282nd AHC.

We walked into the 3rd Platoon line shack where I was introduced to my new platoon leader, Capt. Nate Stackhouse, and platoon sergeant, SSgt. Lee Berry. Nate was a graduate of USC with a degree in enology—the study of wine and wine making. His dream was to eventually own and operate a vineyard. In the meantime he could often be found wandering around the platoon area after a day of flying, holding a wineglass and sipping away at something from his private stock. We never knew where he got the stuff from, but he never seemed to be without.

I was shown to my room in one of the hooches, and one of the guys helped me drag all of my belongings there so I could settle in. After that I wandered up to the small Quonset hut that was our line shack. One of the warrant officer pilots had just landed and shut down his aircraft.

He walked into the line shack, and someone introduced me to him as his replacement. He grinned, shook my hand, and said, "Glad to see you. Now that you're here, I can go home. I'm already packed, and anything you find in the hooch that belongs to me, you can have. I'm outta here!" And he was gone. Funny, I didn't get his name and I never saw him again. That's when it began to sink in that being in Vietnam for a whole year meant I would be a long way from home in both distance and time.

Outside the line shack was our Birddog ramp where the platoon's aircraft were parked. Several of the guys were busy shoveling sand from the back of a two-and-a-half-ton truck into fifty-five-gallon drums. Figuring the best way to fit in was to pitch in, and with nothing else to do, I went outside and offered to help.

"Sure, we're glad to have you," grinned Capt. John Mulvany, sticking out a hand for me to shake.

John was from Boston and had a Boston accent that sort of rolled his vowels as he spoke.

"What are you guys doing with the sand and barrels?" I asked.

"We're building revetments to park the aircraft in. We had a mortar attack a week ago and a couple of the birds were damaged, so this is our solution."

"Sounds like a good idea to me," I said. Stripping down to my T-shirt like John, I grabbed a shovel and began filling one of the barrels. After a bit, John said, "Ray, you might want to pace yourself a little, this heat and humidity will nail you if you don't."

The voice of experience had just spoken, and like the inexperienced newbie that I was, I chose to ignore it. "I feel fine John," was my response as I kept shoveling at a rapid pace, wanting to show that I was not only a team player, but a tough one as well . . . very dumb! It wasn't long before I suddenly experienced a massive headache and felt woozy. John had been keeping an eye on me, knowing that my over-exuberance could lead to heat exhaustion. He saw the first signs before I did and asked, "Ray, how are you feeling?"

"Man, I've suddenly got a real bad headache," was my reply.

"Better go drink some water and lie down. You stay out here much longer and you're going to pass out."

"Yeah, you're right. Guess I did push it a little hard," I replied.

John laughed, "You've got a whole year ahead of you so you'll have plenty of time to adjust to the heat." As I headed off to my room in the hooch, I was thinking, *So much for showing my new friends what a stud I am.*

Acclimation to the summer heat and humidity of Vietnam generally took a week or two, especially if you were exerting yourself physically. Increasing your water intake was mandatory, and I hadn't bothered to do that either.

The next day I was on schedule to get my area checkout from Captain Stackhouse. I was asked what call sign I would like and noticed that the number 3-2 was available. The 3 would stand for the 3rd Platoon, and since I considered 2 a lucky number, I asked for it.

"It's yours," said Captain Stackhouse. "Use it instead of your aircraft tail number in all of your radio calls. From now on, when you are flying, you are Catkiller 3-2." He gave a short mission brief and showed me on a large map on the line shack wall where we would be flying.

"We'll head down to the Que Son Valley and I'll show you our Tactical Area of Responsibility (TAOR). You won't be flying that right away because I want you to get some experience under your belt first. After your area checkout, you will be assigned to fly high ship in the two ship missions back into Indian Country and the milk runs on the north and south coast missions. When we get back, someone will help you put your maps together. Learn how to use them because you will need them every flight. Right now I just want you to get a feel for the general area and show you what we do."

After going over the radio frequencies I would need to know and after a thorough preflight, we climbed into one of the available Birddogs, Stack in the back seat. He talked me through the rocket-arming procedure, and our crew chief armed the rockets. I called ground control for taxi clearance, taxied out to the end of the runway, performed the engine run-up checks, called tower for takeoff clearance, advanced the throttle, and after a bit longer takeoff run than I had expected, we rose into the clear blue I Corps sky.

"Took a little longer to get off the ground than it did back at Fort Rucker, didn't it, lieutenant?" Captain Stackhouse asked over the intercom after we had departed the traffic pattern.

"Yes sir, it sure did. The rate of climb is a lot less too," I replied.

"That's because we are four hundred pounds heavier than you are used to. Keep that in mind when you are in situations where you might need both altitude and airspeed at the same time."

The rest of the flight went quite well. Captain Stackhouse made a point of trying to cram into my skull as much knowledge as possible about flying techniques, minimum altitudes, what to avoid, and what to look for. It wasn't overwhelming, but I realized a pretty steep learning curve lay ahead for me.

"Don't think you are going to start seeing the enemy right away, lieutenant. It will take you a couple of weeks to get familiar with the area and with what sort of activity at any given place at any given time is normal. Once you've figured that out, anything that isn't normal will suddenly jump right out at you. Just be patient and don't be afraid to ask questions. The job we do is serious business, but that doesn't mean we can't have fun doing it."

Two and a half hours later we returned to Marble Mountain, and I shot a couple of touch-and-go landings and then a final landing to a full stop.

"You did real well out there today, lieutenant, and your landings were all good, even in this crosswind. We'll get you up on the mission board tomorrow, probably for either a north or south coast mission with one of the Navy observers. Let's taxi back to the ramp and shut it down. You can get your maps squared away for tomorrow and be at the line shack ready to go at oh-seven hundred."

"Yes sir," I responded, barely able to keep the pride and excitement out of my voice.

I'm checked out and ready to go and my boss said that I did a good job! All of the confusion of the 90th Replacement Depot, the hours spent in the back of Air Force C-123s and C-130s, and the embarrassment of not knowing how to actually start a Beaver were now but distant memories. I was where I had spent nearly a year of my life training to be: flying an airplane that I loved to fly, doing a job that I really wanted to do, directly supporting troops on the ground in combat!

5 220th RAC

A s I settled into the flying routine of the 3rd Platoon at Marble Mountain, I came to realize how very fortunate I was to receive a Catkiller call sign and become a pilot in the 220th, the most unusual Army Birddog company in all of Vietnam. We were unique because we were under the operational control of the Marines, not the Army. Operation experience early on convinced the Marine leadership they did not have enough aircraft to perform forward air control—Tactical Air Controller, Airborne (TACA) in Marine Corps terminology. So they requested that an Army Birddog unit be assigned to them to fill the breach. Fortunately, the Army agreed and thus was born at the operation level a unique interservice relationship between the 220th RAC and the Marine Corps. Being under the operational control of the Marines and not the Army provided Catkiller pilots opportunities that pilots of other Army Birddog companies were never granted.

Unlike the other Army Birddog companies, which would often disperse their aircraft individually to outlying units, each platoon of the 220th had its assigned aircraft return to their home airfield at night and then sent them out singularly or in pairs each day to accomplish their missions. This practice meant each platoon could centrally perform maintenance on its aircraft on a daily basis and that there could be variances in aircraft and pilot assignments. The result was an exceptionally high rate of aircraft availability and mission readiness.

220th pilots were authorized to control Air Force, Navy, and Marine jet attack aircraft in the close air support (CAS) role and flew in arguably the most dangerous area of Vietnam—I Corps. The adversaries they faced daily were not so much Viet Cong, the antigovernment South Vietnamese rebels; rather, every day the Marines in I Corps and the pilots of the 220th RAC battled the professional soldiers of the North Vietnamese Army (NVA). For several months in 1967 and again in 1968, Catkiller pilots flew over North Vietnam as well, being shot at by the same anti-aircraft guns attempting to down Navy and Air Force jets, which were much faster than the piston-engined Birddogs. The Catkillers did all that, every day, and sometimes at night, in small single-engine, two-place airplanes. They were the "Eyes of I Corps," and very few of them would trade that year of their lives as a Catkiller for anything else.

Pilots of the 220th flew the Cessna O-1, formerly known as the L-19. This aircraft came from a lineage of small single-engine, two-seats-in-tandem, high-wing, fabric-covered, tail-wheeled aircraft that had been used in World War II for artillery adjustment and light liaison work. The World War II versions had four-cylinder engines and were manufactured by several different American aircraft companies.

In the summer of 1949 the Army and Air Force issued a joint specification for the construction of a new all-metal, light observation aircraft. The Cessna Aircraft Company in Wichita, Kansas, presented the winning design and held a contest within the company to name its new little airplane. Ten names were selected by a board of military officers and forwarded to Gen. Mark W. Clark, chief of Army Field Forces. General Clark had agreed to select the winning entry and sent a letter to Derby Frye, then sales manager, listing his five choices in order of priority. General Clark's first choice, "Skyhawk," could not be used because it was copyrighted and being used by another company. So his second choice, "Birddog," was declared the winner. This name seemed to fit perfectly because the primary mission of the airplane was to seek out targets, just like a hunter's bird dog.

The Birddog was larger and, at 1,400 pounds, somewhat heavier than its predecessors with an all-metal fuselage and a 36-foot wingspan. It also had a Continental 6-cylinder engine that produced 213 horsepower and spun an all-metal propeller. It was not fast; cruise speed was around 100 miles per hour. But the Birddog proved reliable and well suited for operating in the field. It had conventional landing gear with extremely durable spring steel main landing gear struts and a tail wheel. The pilot could lower up to 60 degrees of flaps, giving it a very slow landing approach speed that allowed landing in surprisingly small, unimproved landing areas. The Army loved it and changed its designation from L-19 (Liaison) to O-1 (Observation).

U.S. Army aviation had been involved in Vietnam since 1962, with two aviation companies primarily serving the needs of the MACV, which included U.S. Special Forces and advisers to the ARVN. One company, the 18th Otter Company, flew the de Havilland Otter, a large, single-engine cargo/passenger aircraft designed to operate in remote environments. The other was the 73rd Airplane Company, Surveillance Airplane Light that flew Cessna O-1 Birddogs. Both companies had air-craft stationed all over South Vietnam, and they were moved around as need and requirements changed. It was quickly realized that the Bird-dog performed perfectly in the role of visual reconnaissance and artil-lery adjustment. By 1965, with the impending buildup of U.S. forces in South Vietnam, more Birddog companies were needed to augment the increase in ground units, so the 73rd was disbanded (later re-formed as an OV-1 surveillance airplane company); in its place, three new Birddog companies were formed and dispatched to Vietnam. The 74th assumed the assets of the 73rd and was headquartered at Phu Loi in III Corps; the 219th was formed at Fort Hood, Texas, and shipped to Vietnam in June 1965 to be headquartered at Pleiku in II Corps.

The 220th, which had been organized at Fort Lewis, Washington, on April 16, 1965, spent just two months gathering equipment, signing in personnel, training, and receiving new Cessna O-1 aircraft from the Cessna factory. It then shipped to Vietnam in June 1965, and the advance party arrived in Saigon on June 26. The remainder of the company was transported on C-130 aircraft, departing McChord Air Force Base on July 1 and arriving at Phu Bai on July 4, 1965. Further buildup of U.S. troops included two battalions of the 3rd Marine Division's 9th Marine Expeditionary Brigade that waded ashore at Da Nang on March 8, 1965, recorded by news reporters and photographers strategically positioned on the beach. On May 7, 1965, the 9th Marine Expeditionary Brigade and its assets were absorbed into the III Marine Amphibious Force (MAF). In August 1965 the Army's 1st Cavalry Division established itself near Pleiku in II Corps. The United States was changing its advisory role to one of aggressive pursuit of the enemy.

South Vietnam had been divided into four military regions or corps tactical zones—I Corps through IV Corps—progressing from north to south. Instead of staying near Saigon in III Corps, as its orders initially read, the 220th was to move immediately to I Corps. The company headquarters were to be located at Hue Phu Bai, north of Da Nang and only fifty miles south of the Demilitarized Zone (DMZ) and North Vietnam. This single act set the course for the 220th to become unique in all the Army Birddog companies in Vietnam.

When the Marines had moved into I Corps in 1965, their command saw their mission as pacification, clear, and hold; the requirement for aerial control of CAS was minimal under those conditions. Visual reconnaissance, convoy cover, and general liaison work could be accomplished with the number of Birddogs the Marines had on hand. This changed when General Westmoreland mandated "search and destroy" as the only acceptable way to prosecute the war. This change in tactics required the extensive use of jet aircraft in the CAS role and more tactical air controllers to control them.

The Marines found themselves critically short of Birddogs to accomplish the visual reconnaissance/airborne artillery adjustment/airborne naval gunfire adjustment/airborne tactical air controller mission, with only a dozen or so Birddogs throughout I Corps. They had tried to fill the breach using their organic Bell UH-1 gunships, but found their 1.5-hour flight time wasn't long enough to provide the support that ground troops needed. So the Marine Corps requested an Army Birddog company be placed in I Corps to directly support the Marines. The timing of this request apparently coincided perfectly with the 220th's arrival in Vietnam. When its commander, Maj. Jerry Curry, and his advance party arrived in Saigon, thinking the 220th would be assigned to III Corps, they found their area of assignment had been changed to I Corps and that the 220th would be under the operational control of the Marine Corps. Curry, who later retired as a major general, was a no-nonsense, extremely well-organized, and knowledgeable officer who saw to it that the 220th excelled.

Every aviation unit serving in Vietnam had a name in addition to the military numerical designation. This name usually was intended to imply something special about the unit, the unit aircraft, its mission, or attitude. The Catkiller story had its own special twist.

When the 220th arrived in Vietnam, it had not selected a unit name. It had simply been too busy getting ready to go to war. Ironically, the name Catkiller came about by accident. When the first flight of Birddogs from the 220th was flying north in I Corps from Saigon to Phu Bai and requesting permission to transit the airspace at Da Nang, Capt. Richard "Dick" Quigley, who was leading the flight of four aircraft, suddenly found himself in a quandary. He had called Da Nang Approach and requested permission to transit their airspace. He told Da Nang Approach Control they were a flight of four Army aircraft requesting transit from south to north. Da Nang Approach responded wanting to know their call sign. Dick told them they didn't have a call sign. Da Nang Approach told him every aircraft unit in Vietnam had a call sign and wanted to know, "What's yours?" Stumped, but thinking quickly, Dick decided that since they were flying Birddogs and since dogs kill cats, why not call themselves "Catkillers"? He then transmitted, "This is Catkiller [using the tail number of his aircraft], flight of four requesting transition through your airspace from south to north." This seemed to satisfy Da Nang Approach Control, and the Catkiller name was born.

The 220th remained in the Army chain of command but fell under the operational control of the 1st and 3rd Marine Divisions. From June 1965 the 220th was under the command of MACV. At the time, MACV was the overarching command for all Army aviation. In 1966, due to the rising number of aviation units in Vietnam, the 17th Aviation Group was created as the top level of command for Army aviation and formed several aviation battalions to oversee subordinate units. The 220th Airplane Surveillance Company, Light came under the administrative control of the 223rd Combat Aviation Battalion (CAB) located at Nha Trang. In August 1967, as Army aviation presence in I Corps grew, a new battalion, the 212th CAB, was formed and headquartered at Marble Mountain. The 220th was redesignated the 220th RAC and became a subordinate unit of the 212th CAB. In 1969 the 220th was again redesignated as the 220th Utility Airplane Company. Regardless of the name changes imposed by the Army, the 220th Catkillers remained loyal to their one true mission, that of directly supporting and protecting Marines on the ground.

One benefit of the 220th pilots being under the operational control of the Marines was approval to control jet fighter aircraft in the CAS of troops on the ground. The Air Force jealously guarded this task, and in II, III, and IV Corps areas, when an Army Birddog pilot in support of U.S. ground troops encountered a situation requiring Air Force jet attack aircraft, he was required to call for an Air Force forward air controller (FAC) to do the job. This often caused a delay in repelling the enemy. Fortunately the Marine Corps controlled I Corps and didn't agree with the Air Force's attitude when it came to rapidly supporting Marines on the ground. Under pressure, the Air Force reluctantly agreed to allow certain Marine aerial observers (AOs) to train 220th pilots in the art of controlling jets in the CAS mission. After several training missions under the watchful eyes of our AOs, 220th pilots were issued Marine Corps orders designating them Tactical Air Controllers, Airborne (TACA). It was a proud moment for me when I received my orders, knowing it set me apart from Army Birddog pilots in other units; I also felt a sobering sense of responsibility because of the lethality the jets could bring as well as their being another tool to use in supporting the Marines.

In 1970, as the Marine 1st and 3rd Divisions were leaving Vietnam and the Army gradually took operational control of I Corps, the same rules of operation that existed in II, III, and IV Corps began to change some of the mission profiles of the 220th pilots. They were quickly eliminated from the role of TACA to primarily that of just visual reconnaissance and artillery adjustment. They no longer flew with a Marine AO in the back seat; an Army artillery Forward Observer (FO) now filled that seat. The Air Force insisted that its pilots were the only ones qualified to control jet attack aircraft; apparently the mere thought that an Army Birddog pilot might be as capable of doing the job ruffled its blue feathers.

Never mind that Army pilots of the 220th had been successfully controlling Marine, Navy, and Air Force jet attack aircraft since 1965—Catkiller pilots were again deemed unfit and unqualified to control Air Force CAS aircraft. Sometimes the turf wars that are conducted at world level really tend to piss off the professionals operating at the tip of the spear.

I find it interesting that the only jet attack aircraft I sent home with a zero-over-zero Bomb Damage Assessment (BDA) was a flight of Air Force F-4s who couldn't seem to follow instructions or hit my well-marked target. Part of our job as TACAs was to provide a BDA after the jets were finished dropping their ordnance. A BDA consisted of two numbers: the first number was the percent of bombs on target, the second was percentage of target destroyed. A zero-over-zero BDA meant none of the bombs had impacted the target and none of the target was destroyed. In other words, they had done a crappy job.

The jets simply didn't have the ability to quickly, and accurately, identify their intended targets, especially when the enemy was in close proximity to friendly troops; such identification became the Birddog pilots' job. The slow-moving Birddog was able to remain airborne for several hours at a time and when flown close to the ground became a lethal instrument with the ability to identify the exact location of the bad guys, mark the target with a white phosphorous rocket, and control the jets in their attack. Naturally this became an item in the turf wars between the Army and the Air Force. The Air Force claimed exclusive rights to controlling the jets, based on the argument that only Air Force pilots flying as FACs had the knowledge and skills required to safely and accurately control CAS—an argument that is probably the reason why Army pilots were never trained as FACs in flight school.

Ironically, nearly all the Air Force FACs, during the years of heaviest fighting, were majors or colonels who had been transport or Strategic Air Command pilots, not fighter pilots. Fighter pilots, the ones who understood fighters and their tactical use, were in short supply and needed in the cockpits of fighter aircraft, not little Birddogs. So the Air Force trained transport pilots, who never got close to the ground except to take off and land, the art of finding the enemy and controlling attack jet fighters. Of course, Army Birddog pilots who were ground oriented by virtue of their branch of service were unqualified to do the job in the eyes of the Air Force high command.

The role of TACA in Vietnam meant that the pilot was responsible for the safety not only of the Marines on the ground but also of the pilots of the attack aircraft. We had to know what ordnance the jets carried and how close to the friendlies on the ground they could safely drop it. The target briefing for the jets included location of friendlies, location of the enemy, whether or not the drop was to be "danger close," the run-in heading, direction to turn after dropping ordnance, terrain elevation, type of enemy ground fire, direction it was coming from, and sequence of dropping their ordnance.

The TACA adjusted each drop relative to the previous drop in order to cover the target and was responsible for accurately placing a white phosphorous rocket to mark the target. Each drop had to be closely observed to ensure proper alignment of the jet in relation to the target and the location of friendlies. A "cleared hot" from the TACA was required for each drop, and every FAC/TACA took that responsibility very seriously. We talked to the jets on the UHF radio and to friendlies on the ground on the FM radio. We might also be adjusting friendly artillery on the target, which needed to be shut down when the jets attacked to avoid hitting them. This situation was always fluid when the ground troops were in direct contact with the enemy and required a cool head and full attention, especially when we were taking fire ourselves. Close coordination between the Catkiller pilot and the Marine AO in the back seat was critical. We quickly became a very close-knit team and knew what the other was going to do at all times.

My less than satisfactory encounter with firing rockets in flight school accidentally resolved itself early in my tour. I was deep in the Que Son Valley one afternoon, when I spotted two young Vietnamese men walking along a paddy dike. Four things gave cause to take a closer look:

1. As soon as they realized I was heading toward them, they began walking faster.
2. They were wearing black short-sleeved shirts and shorts but no conical hats like Vietnamese peasants normally wore.
3. They were swinging only one of their arms; the other was being held close to their sides, as though they were carrying something they did not want me to see, like a weapon.
4. As I drew closer, they kept looking up at me. Normally Vietnamese peasants would seem to go out of their way not to look up, as though doing so would draw unwanted scrutiny.

I circled them once, verifying that they were each carrying an AK-47 rifle, then flew off some distance to see if I could bring up some artillery. None was available. The closest battery was already engaged in a fire mission, and rather than scramble a flight of bomb-laden jets out of Chu Lai just to whack two men, I decided to shoot a couple of rockets at them. Because I had not continued to circle and had actually flown on a tangent away from them, they must have thought they had fooled me and were safe. What they didn't realize was that even flying slightly away from them, I was still keeping a close eye on them over my shoulder.

In earlier VR missions I had figured out that once my wing tip was past enemy soldiers from their perspective, even those who were perfectly camouflaged would turn their heads to look up at me and I could actually see their faces in the bushes. This resulted in my spending quite a bit of time looking back over my left and right shoulders when I was performing visual reconnaissance. This technique was never mentioned in flight school. As a matter of fact, we were taught to look forward and down in roughly a 45-degree arc. This technique completely ignored that the enemy could hear us coming with enough time to hide. Recurring little details like this had me convinced Tactics Phase at Fort Rucker needed some serious upgrading.

Under the standard procedures taught during the Tactics Phase of flight school, I should have climbed to three thousand feet above the ground. This would have taken four or five minutes and by then they would probably have been gone. More out of exasperation than anything else, I simply turned back toward the two rifle-toting characters, armed a rocket, pulled on the carburetor heat, retarded the throttle, and as the nose dropped, felt my sweet little Birddog line up on them perfectly. I pulled the safety pin and squeezed the trigger. A loud *BANG— WHOOSH!* and the white phosphorous rocket left its tube and flew straight toward the now suddenly running Viet Cong. The rocket impacted on the paddy dike just below where they had been a moment before. I kicked a little right rudder then neutralized the controls as I armed another rocket and, using a bit of Kentucky windage, led the two Viet Cong who were now in full stride trying to get to a tree line a hundred yards or so away. They didn't make it. This time the rocket impacted on the paddy dike right between them, knocking them off the dike. I flew over them and circled, neither of them moving, their two AK-47s clearly visible in the dirt beside them. There weren't any friendlies nearby to confiscate the AKs and confirm them as dead, but white phosphorous is nasty stuff when it comes in contact with flesh. It just keeps burning through until it burns itself out. Scratch two bad guys and a new rocket-firing technique was born—an enormous departure from the cumbersome technique being taught at Fort Rucker, but one that actually worked in combat and one that I used with great success throughout the rest of my tour.

The 220th RAC might have been located in the farthest north tactical zone and its pilots might have faced the most prolonged intense resistance from the NVA, but the tools we had at our disposal were many. As young officers we had at our beck and call everything from artillery and naval gunfire to jet attack aircraft and the authority to use them all at our discretion. We had an enormous amount of death and destruction at our fingertips for officers of our rank and age. During my entire year in Vietnam involving over nine hundred hours of combat flight time, my decision to use these tools was never questioned or challenged. Yes, I had truly been fortunate in finding my way to the 220th RAC, the Catkillers.

6

Just a Little Bit Different

Flying for the Marines was different from flying for the Army. While the 220th was under the operational control of the 1st and 3rd Marine Divisions in the I Corps Tactical Zone, Army Birddog pilots in the II, III, and IV Corps Tactical Zones all flew under the control of the major Army command in their tactical zones. They all flew VR, adjusted artillery, and performed convoy cover just as we did; some even flew with a Vietnamese observer in the back seat who controlled Vietnamese Air Force (VNAF) attack aircraft in the close air support role for Vietnamese ground troops. However, none of them were authorized to control U.S. Air Force close air support aircraft for U.S. ground troops.

Looking back, I would say a few other things separated us from our Army Birddog brothers farther south. I Corps bordered both North Vietnam and Laos, which meant we flew the DMZ between North and South Vietnam. Our pilots encountered flak (yes, just like in World War II movies) when we flew the DMZ, and we did lose two pilots and their observers to North Vietnamese anti-aircraft fire over North Vietnam. I Corps comprised the five northernmost provinces of South Vietnam; all but one bordered on Laos and its deeply imbedded Ho Chi Minh trail, which was actually a network of trails and roads constantly travelled by North Vietnamese soldiers infiltrating weapons, supplies, and themselves into South Vietnam. This activity never stopped; attempts to stop it cost American lives and massive amounts of resources.

When the 220th first arrived in I Corps, the 4th Platoon had been detached from the 220th and attached to the 219th RAC that was operating in II Corps Tactical Zone. Since II Corps encompassed a larger land mass area than I Corps, senior Army commanders decided the 219th could use a little assistance. The 220th was then left with just three operational platoons (twenty-four aircraft) to cover all tasked missions in I Corps during its first twenty months in Vietnam. In April 1967 the 4th Platoon was brought back home and assigned to fly the DMZ out of Dong Ha, some ten miles south of North Vietnam. Their primary mission was adjusting friendly artillery located at Camp Carroll, just west of Dong Ha, on North Vietnamese troop encroachment into the DMZ.

During the spring and summer of 1967, pilots of the 4th Platoon were tasked with flying missions north of the Ben Hai River into North Vietnam. One day an Army colonel showed up and told them they were going to be flying up to twenty-five miles into North Vietnam (this information came from then Capt. Charles "Larry" Deibert, 1st Lt. Rick Johnson, who experienced being fired on by the SAM, and 1st Lt. David O'Hare). These missions were to be referred to as "Banjo" and were to log flights as such in their aircraft logbooks. Supposedly, for every five missions flown over North Vietnam, they would receive a one-day drop in their tour. They were to adjust U.S. artillery firing out of Camp Carroll on any NVA artillery sites they found in North Vietnam. To discourage any attempts at visual reconnaissance, the NVA quickly responded by moving 12.7-mm, 37-mm, 57-mm, and surface-to-air missile (SAM) sites into southernmost North Vietnam.

Heavy NVA artillery bombardment of the Dong Ha Marine base and airfield eventually necessitated evacuating 4th Platoon aircraft from Dong Ha beginning on August 17, 1967. The 4th Platoon permanently relocated to the company headquarters at Phu Bai in October 1967. Missions were then flown from Phu Bai to Dong Ha where the aircraft were refueled and then performed VR and direct combat support of Marines on the ground throughout the DMZ. Just two aircraft and pilots and one crew chief remained overnight at Dong Ha on a rotating basis, to preclude massive aircraft loss during NVA artillery strikes but still provide immediate response if needed. The Banjo missions were discontinued and flights over North Vietnam were not authorized again until Operation Thor, which ran from July 3, 1968, to November 1, 1968. Those missions were referred to as "Tally Ho."

Our adversary at the DMZ consisted of NVA soldiers, who were generally better trained and better equipped than their comrades to the south and more inclined to stay and fight than cut and run when they encountered Marines. Engagements with the NVA could become very intense and prolonged.

Since flying with the 220th RAC and the Catkillers was new to me, at first I just assumed we were like every other Army Birddog company in Vietnam; and we were, in terms of visual reconnaissance, artillery adjustment, and convoy cover, but I soon learned that in several ways we weren't. I kept my eyes and ears open and tried my level best to learn as quickly as I could the myriad techniques and lifesaving tidbits of information the old hands had to share. Anything and everything seemed important. Back in flight school, controlling the Birddog after landing and preventing a dreaded ground loop were the major concerns. Now, landing was something I barely thought about. It was just something I did. The act of controlling the aircraft quickly became second nature because it was secondary to what I was actually doing: either looking for targets or, once found, trying to destroy them. The one thing I did not do was fly straight and level.

I flew between 800 and one 1,000 feet above the ground when performing visual reconnaissance. This not only permitted me to see and accurately analyze what I was looking at but also kept me just at the outer limits of accurate ground fire from enemy rifles, although well within range of enemy heavy machine guns. The cruising airspeed of the Birddog varied from 100 to 110 miles per hour, depending on which model I was flying. This slow airspeed made me an easy target for a determined enemy on the ground with a rifle or a machine gun. Because of these factors, I was constantly turning left or right to avoid a predictable flight path. The enemy could hear me coming and, given an opportunity, would have been delighted to shoot me down. Flying a predictable flight path would have made it easier for him at those altitudes and airspeeds. Generally speaking, the VC and NVA soldiers did not want a Birddog pilot to see them because that would most likely bring down the wrath of Zeus upon them; however, it was combat and there was rumored to be a $10,000 reward riding on a Birddog pilot's head. So I preferred to place the odds in my favor: no straight and level flying for me while I was working. I wanted, as General Patton was quoted as having once said, "the other poor, dumb bastard to die for his country."

Catkillers and their AOs were the eyes in the sky for the Marines on the ground. We sorted out friendly and enemy positions so our troops would have the advantage. We located reconnaissance teams so they could continue their missions or be extracted, sometimes under intense enemy fire. We were the map readers and accurate coordinate-givers for the friendly artillery batteries whose job it was to bring first round destructive fire upon the enemy without hitting our own troops. We were the low-flying, slow-moving controllers of the fast-moving jet attack aircraft that needed our WP rockets to accurately mark the enemy positions so they could drop their ordnance on the enemy without hitting our guys. We did these things every day, and the days were busy, especially when we were working with Marines in contact with the enemy. All of these tasks required our full attention focused outside the aircraft. Flying was just the means by which we did our job of protecting the grunts on the ground. The six or seven hours we spent in the air each day passed very quickly.

Our primary mission was VR. VR is an art learned backward, almost like the negative of a photograph. My platoon leader, Captain Stackhouse, had told me to become familiar with what normal activity looked like in a given area during certain periods of the day. That was the negative of a photo. Then, when something unusual popped up it would jump out at me, just like the actual print of the photo.

A good example would be the foot traffic moving toward a village market in the early morning on the trails. The women carried their goods to sell or barter in buckets or baskets suspended from each end of a split bamboo pole balanced on their shoulders. They all wore black pajama-like shirts and pants with conical white straw hats. They walked with a peculiar rolling gate that I surmised prevented the bamboo poles from flexing up and down. A normal gait would have caused the contents of the baskets or buckets to spill out. On most days they would be hurrying *toward* the village, not away from it, because that was where everyone was gathering to do business. My suspicions would be raised if a group of black-clad, conical white hat–topped people with no bamboo poles with something suspended from the ends were moving *away* from the village at that same time of day. If these people were moving with the longer strides of young males and holding one arm to their side as though pressing something close to their body while swinging the other arm as in a normal walking gate, my suspicions would really spike. Eventually I could tell the difference between a walking male and a walking female as I flew one thousand feet above the ground, even though they dressed in the same black "pajamas" and conical white hats. The women walked with the same rolling gait even when they weren't carrying a bamboo pole on their shoulders. Oddly, these simple observation techniques were never mentioned during flight training, but they were certainly passed on and quickly learned in Vietnam.

Accurate artillery adjustment had been a major staple of Army Birddog pilots back in World War II right along with VR. Army aviation had initially survived in the Signal and Artillery Branches of the Army after the Army Air Corps had split off and become the Air Force in 1947. Until the advent of helicopters and their acceptance as the new way of movement in combat, Army aviation had existed almost exclusively as an artillery asset. In all four of the Vietnam Corps tactical zones, Army Birddogs continued this long-standing tradition of artillery adjustment.

A variety of observers flew with the Catkillers in the back seat of their aircraft. The pilots of the 1st, 2nd, and 3rd platoons of the 220th RAC flew Vietnamese observers from time to time, depending on requirements assigned by the G-2 Air section of III MAF headquarters at Da Nang. The Catkillers of the 3rd Platoon sometimes flew coastal missions with a U.S. Navy observer in the back seat. The Navy observers were officially known as ANGLICOS, an acronym for Air Naval Gunfire Liaison Company. They basically did the same job as the Marine AOs but focused more on what the enemy was doing on or near the water. Occasionally the 2nd or 3rd Platoon pilots would be tasked to fly a cameraman from the Army's Military Intelligence Battalion (Air Reconnaissance Support) MIBARS detachment, headquartered in Da Nang. Although the task of photographing enemy positions and activities was normally assigned to Air Force photo recon jets or the Army's OV-1 Mohawks, every now and then someone from MIBARS would show up with a 35-mm camera and want us to fly them over a specific set of coordinates so they could take black-and-white photos for further detailed interpretation at their facility. The results of these photos and the debriefing reports we filled out after each VR flight were fed into the intelligence gristmill, analyzed, and then presented to the senior decision makers for action. Once a week a lieutenant from the G-2 Air would come over to give us an update on the location of enemy anti-aircraft fire and radio transmissions reported and plotted in our area of operations. He would also tell us how any information that we had submitted had been acted upon. It was always nice to know how we fit into the puzzle.

I felt the mission with our Marine AOs in the TAOR really had some meaning: here the rubber met the road for me as a Catkiller. For those of us in the 3rd Platoon, that meant the area immediately south of Da Nang and in the Que Son Valley where it seemed the Marines were never able to completely eradicate the NVA soldiers who lurked there. A TAOR mission meant my AO and I would be working directly with a Marine unit on the ground. A typical mission involved a company on a sweep through the countryside—slow, tough going for a grunt who was always wondering if the tree line ahead was going to explode in a hail of enemy bullets directed at him and his buddies. I'm certain that the sound of the 6-cylinder Continental engine of my little two-seat Birddog growling around above brought them some comfort, because they knew if they did run into trouble we were there to control the destruction of whoever was shooting at them. All we ever got was a simple thanks, but in combat that's all you really need from a brother. The bond between men at risk is strong, even when you are eight hundred feet above the grunt in the dirt below.

What really set the 220th apart from any other Army Birddog company was our being under the operational control of the Marines. This meant the Marines could pressure the Air Force into allowing Army pilots of the 220th to become qualified to control jet attack aircraft. With the brief and limited exception of a handful of pilots from the 21st RAC being awarded TACA orders, Catkiller pilots were the only Army Birddog pilots awarded long-term approval and orders designating them qualified to control U.S. Air Force, Navy, and Marine high-performance, close air support aircraft.

Because our Birddogs were small, were painted a dull Army green, and flew over basically green vegetated terrain, jets coming to us at 20,000 feet had difficulty seeing us. So that we could be seen more easily from above, maintenance had painted the tops of the flaps, ailerons, and elevators white. Unfortunately, this didn't always work well if there were scattered clouds or other obstructions to visibility. Never let it be said that Catkillers weren't creative when they needed to be—Capt. Rick Johnson, a Catkiller pilot, came up with a solution that worked amazingly well. He had maintenance rivet a metal plate to the outside of his aircraft just below the right rear passenger window. Metal straps attached to the plate secured up to three smoke grenade canisters of varying colors (yellow quickly became the choice de jour of all the Catkillers). That solution worked and very soon most of the 220th Birddogs acquired the modification. When a jet seemed to be having a problem finding one of us over a target, our AO could simply reach out and pull the pin of a smoke grenade, and within a few seconds the pilot would go into a tight 360-degree turn, trailing the brightly colored smoke. I'm pretty sure the 220th RAC was the only Army Birddog company in Vietnam to have a smoke grenade attachment on the side of its aircraft.

When I called in jets they had to check in with me before dropping their ordnance. The lead jet (they always showed up in pairs) would give me his lineup, or what ordnance they were carrying. If it was a flight of Marine A-4s, they would normally be armed with Delta One-Alphas (250-pound high-drag Snake Eye bombs) and Delta Sevens (napalm canisters, "Nape"). The Snake Eyes were preferred for close air support of ground troops; they had fins that opened when dropped, retarding the rate of fall long enough for the aircraft to be clear of the blast zone upon impact. This delay allowed the jets to drop from a very low altitude, thus improving accuracy. If they were carrying Snake and Nape, they always got rid of the napalm first. Getting hit by accurate ground fire and igniting a napalm canister hanging on their wing was not jet jocks' favorite thing. If they told me they had Pistols, that meant they were also carrying 20-mm cannon rounds—not a lot, but enough to mess up a determined enemy's day, should the Snake and Nape not have already done so.

After checking in with the jets and giving them a thorough target description and situation, I marked the target with a WP marking rocket. I then watched the jets as they made their attack to ensure they were on the proper run-in heading and then transmitted a "cleared hot" for each run. This was critical, particularly if the grunts were in close contact with the enemy (which was usually the reason we were there). If the run-in heading didn't look right for any reason, it was my job to not clear him hot and to sort out the problem before making another try. This was something every AO and Catkiller took very seriously.

Adjusting naval gunfire was the other role that set us apart from our Army Birddog flying brothers in the other Corps tactical zones: not just any naval gunfire, but gunfire that the U.S. Navy's battleship *New Jersey* directed on targets in North Vietnam.

7

Birddogs, AOs, and the Bonds Forged in Combat

The Marine AOs that we Catkillers were privileged to fly with were our mentors, our benefactors, and our brothers. The Army pilots of the 220th were mostly in their early twenties, newly minted, and eager to learn. The single biggest difference between the Marine Birddog pilots and us was that we were more "ground oriented." The Marine pilots were all fighter jocks who for one reason or another had become tactical air controllers. I've been told that some of them volunteered for the job and some of them were "assigned" because of prior recalcitrant behavior.

The Marine AOs all flew with us as well as with their own Birddog pilots. The Marine Birddogs were C-models; square tailed, with enlarged engine cowlings and supercharged engines. The Cessna Aircraft Company made only a few of them, and only the Marines had them. According to the Marine AOs they were maintenance nightmares. The Marines had pressed the C-model Birddogs into service because the anticipated North American Rockwell OV-10 counterinsurgency aircraft didn't arrive in Vietnam until midsummer of 1968. The supercharged C-models did have an increased maximum gross weight over our O-1 D and G model aircraft, but if you can't keep them flying, the more powerful engine doesn't do you any good.

Both the Marine and Army Birddogs did suffer from one common malady. Because of the type of aviation fuel available in Vietnam, they went through spark plugs at a horrendous rate: the only avgas available was 115/145 octane. This was great for all of the piston-engined aircraft operating in Vietnam, except for the O-1 Birddogs. Their six-cylinder opposed engine was designed to run on 80/87-octane aviation fuel. If we ran 115/145-octane fuel in them, they ate spark plugs like a four-year-old going through a package of M&Ms. The higher-octane aviation fuel fouled our spark plugs in very short order, resulting in an engine running on less than its six cylinders. This would scare the bejabbers out of the average civilian pilot flying his Cessna 172 over Nebraska on a clear blue day; experiencing a "rough-runner" over triple canopy jungle near Laos or over a bunch of NVA soldiers trying to shoot a pilot out of the sky would definitely elevate his heart rate. Our mechanics were constantly replacing fouled spark plugs in our aircraft. Whoever was manufacturing them for the Army, Marine Corps, and Air Force Birddogs was making a fortune!

In the military today, unmanned aerial vehicles (UAVs) have replaced the Birddog pilots and their AOs who flew in Vietnam. UAVs are "flown" by young officers safely sitting in comfortable chairs in an air-conditioned room, sometimes thousands of miles away from hostile fire, in front of a computer screen, with a joystick, and probably sipping on a Coke and eating a pizza. Granted, these modern "eyes in the sky" are not placing themselves in harm's way as we did flying around in our little unarmed Cessna O-1s. On the one hand that is a good thing, as fewer Americans are exposed to the threat of death; on the other hand, there is something they are missing: they are not directly involved in what the grunts on the ground experienced. The controllers of the UAVs can see only what their sophisticated optics are pointed at. They have no peripheral vision as we did. Yes, they can go to a wider field of view, but just like a camera, that puts them visually farther away from what they are looking at. They are just a voice on the radio to the grunts on the ground, while we were living, breathing brothers flying directly overhead, exposed to the same dangers as the grunts were. There is a bond of understanding and trust we had with the grunts on the ground that has to be extremely difficult to duplicate with UAVs. There were times that we could see a threat developing and neutralize it before contact was made with friendly troops. In combat, it is the little things that are often "tells" to what the enemy is planning to do. I'm convinced that even though UAVs can see in the dark and detect the body heat of humans hiding in the bushes, the personal touch of another human overhead who understands and is directly involved in the experiences of the grunts on the ground is an invaluable asset in combat.

The pilots in the 220th RAC were assigned to one of four platoons, each located some distance from company headquarters at Phu Bai. We were all a long way from our higher headquarters, or any Army flagpole for that matter, and we liked it that way. The upper command structure of the 1st and 3rd Marine Divisions assigned general mission tasks to their AO sections but allowed quite a bit of latitude in how tasks were actually accomplished, so together, we simply did our own thing. The wonderful result was the freedom we had to fly and directly support the grunts on the ground as much as we cared to. And we cared to every chance we got. We had an operational view of the war that virtually no one else had and the freedom to assist ground commanders with visual reconnaissance, artillery adjustment, naval gunfire, and close air support. Few officers below field grade (majors and above) had the authority to control the level of death and destruction that we did. Virtually everything we did in support of the Marines on the ground was completely up to us.

The Marine AO section, under the command of a major, comprised an interesting mix of captains and lieutenants. All of them attended the Marine Corps Aerial Observer Course before they went to Vietnam, and most were commissioned through normal channels via ROTC at a university such as Virginia Military Institute or the Naval Academy at Annapolis. A precious few were Mustangs. These men came from the enlisted ranks and had served as warrant officers or non-commissioned officers (NCOs) before they accepted commissions as 2nd lieutenants. Their level of experience and institutional memory was incredible; many had already served as infantry leaders on the ground before they got in the back seat of a Birddog and flew as an AO. They knew what the Marines on the ground needed and had a vested interest in giving it to them. Such was the level of their professionalism that many continued to serve in the Marine Corps after Vietnam, eventually retiring as captains and majors.

To say the 1st and 3rd Marine Division AO sections were staffed with the cream of the crop would be a tragic understatement. They included men like Bill "The Mox" Moxley, who had fought in Korea, endured the hardship of the "Frozen Chosin," and been a highly decorated drill instructor; Jim Sanders, an NCO promoted first to warrant officer and then commissioned officer, with a background in cryptology and related secret squirrel stuff who could recite passages from Conrad and Kipling with equal ease; and Denny Kendig, who had been a drill instructor at Parris Island for years and could keep us laughing hysterically for hours as he regaled us with stories of his adventures in a voice much like that of a very large truck driving across gravel.

Entry into the inner circle of trust with these men was not simply a matter of achieving a successful landing for every takeoff, nor was it entirely dependent on how quickly we mastered the art of accurately adjusting artillery or displayed competence in becoming a proficient TACA. Because we were Army and they were Marines, there was a natural rite of passage for us young, impressionable Army pilots. There were no free passes.

Every now and then some of the 3rd Platoon pilots and a few of the Marine AOs would gather in one of our hooches to toss back a few cold ones and share tales of the day's events. Sometimes the conversation would drift to talk about loved ones back home or food. Big old cheeseburgers and cold milkshakes seemed to be missed the most, with mom's home cooking a close second. Then there were the bitch sessions regarding how our politicians were making us fight with one hand tied behind our backs and, in our view, imposing rules of engagement that favored the enemy and prevented us from unleashing the full might of the U.S. military.

To young Army pilots like us, the more seasoned Marine AOs, especially the Mustangs, always brought an interesting perspective to the conversation. "Know what we ought do?" one of the AOs asked rhetorically. "We should load all of the friendly Vietnamese on ships and sail them out into the South China Sea. Then we should nuke this entire country. Then we should sink all of the ships."

Naturally, we all laughed at this piece of dark humor, which only men engaged in mortal combat can relate to. We were there risking our lives trying to "win the hearts and minds" of the Vietnamese, but sometimes events just didn't seem to jibe with that concept and lives were lost because we weren't allowed to do our job of eliminating the enemy.

Amid the frank talk, search for answers, and ribbing were initiation rituals for new Catkiller pilots that best be left unsaid. No permanent injuries were ever the result, but we did tend to press the envelope of common sense and propriety. For those who have experienced it, the bond formed between men in combat may be beyond comprehension by those who have not. Rest assured that these initiations cemented the bonds between pilots and AOs and resulted in making us a formidable foe for our enemy.

These Marine AOs were the men the young pilots of the 220th RAC flew with and learned from. Our learning curve was nearly vertical—we knew how to fly the airplane, but the art of accurate artillery and naval gunfire adjustment and controlling jet attack aircraft was learned from our Marine AOs. Flying with these warriors wasn't the only thing we did. We listened to their wild tales of decadent behavior in some of the world's exotic locations they had visited. The stories cannot be repeated here, but find yourself a former United States Marine Corps gunny, buy him a couple of drinks (good booze only), and be prepared to enjoy some really good stories! We commiserated with the Marines regarding the war and the politicians. We also gained tremendous respect for the United States Marine Corps and its warrior ethos. Every year I quietly celebrate November 10, the birthday of The Corps.

8

Wild Night in the Valley

Flying visual reconnaissance was primarily a daytime operation. Flying at night wasn't very practical. Pilots couldn't see anything on the ground, unless there was a full moon and even then it was marginal. We did fly night mortar and rocket watch over the airfield when intelligence reports warned of a possible attack, but if the bad guys just dropped a few mortar rounds and disappeared we couldn't really do much. Nevertheless, maybe our higher-ups felt that the sound of us flying around overhead on a dark night would deter any hostile behavior. I hated night flying—droning around in the dark all night, trying to stay awake while everyone else was at the O-Club or sleeping. A few of the guys seemed to like it. They probably thought their chances of getting shot at were reduced. Night missions were always scheduled missions, and the guys who flew them knew well in advance when they would be flying. That's why the loud banging on my door at 9:30 at night on September 6, 1967, startled me out of a sound sleep.

"Lieutenant, are you awake?" asked my platoon leader.

"Yes," I mumbled, looking at my clock and wondering, *What does Stack want me for at this time of night?*

"You had anything to drink tonight?" he demanded.

"No sir, I've got an early flight tomorrow so I decided to turn in early."

"Well, get your butt up. You've got a mission in the Que Son. Your AO is on his way over right now. He'll brief you when he gets here. You've got five minutes."

With a groggy "Yes sir," I rolled out of bed, got dressed, grabbed my flashlight, flight gear, and weapons, and headed for the line shack.

As I walked over to the line shack I was thinking, *This can't be good. I wonder what the hell is going on. I have only a few hours of night time back in the States and none over here. What if I get lost? Man, it sure is dark out here. How do they expect me to see anything on the ground?* I walked out to one of our Birddogs being readied for flight by one of our crew chiefs, Sp4 Jerry Warren.

"She's good to go, sir," Warren said as he handed me the logbook. "You've got four Willie Petes and the tanks are full of gas."

"Thanks Warren," I said, taking the logbook, quickly scanning the write-ups on the Dash 13, and tossing it on the pilot's seat as I turned on my flashlight and began my walk-around inspection.

About then a Mighty Mite, the Marines' excuse for a jeep, screeched to a stop next to the line shack with my AO, Lt. Jim Sanders, behind the wheel. The Mighty Mite, manufactured by American Motors for the Marines, was smaller than the Army's M-151 jeep and lighter. And, according to our AOs, it was far less reliable than our M-151 jeeps. It did seem as though Marines were cussing at theirs an awful lot of the time. Sanders, one of our more experienced AOs, got out and strode over to me. He didn't waste any time on preliminary greetings.

"They've got a real shit sandwich going in the Que Son. They want us to fly down there and see if we can give them a hand. A couple of companies are heavily engaged with the NVA, and the gomers aren't backing off."

Oh boy, this is sounding better all the time, slithered through my mind.

"Okay, I'll be ready to go in just a second," I said as I finished checking the oil in the engine and secured the latches on the cowling. "You go ahead and jump in the back."

We climbed into the small cockpit, secured our seat belts and shoulder harnesses, and I shouted "Clear!" and started the engine. Once it was running and I had the instrument lights on and checked my engine gauges and switches, I turned on the radios, got a quick communications check with Jim, and then put both of my hands up on the crossbars just above the instrument panel. This signified to Warren that I had checked the rocket arming switches "off" and was ready for him to arm the four rockets suspended under the wings. This also showed him my hands were not near any of the switches required to fire the rockets. This was important because the crew chief had to stand to the rear and off one side of the rocket tubes and flip a metal arm over the back of the rocket, completing an electrical contact. If the circuit was "hot" the rocket would fire, severely burning him. The switch circuitry was a military "add-on" and wasn't completely reliable, as I was to learn a few weeks later.

Warren gave me a thumbs-up, indicating that arming was complete. It was time to get the show on the road.

"Marble Ground, Catkiller 3-2, Catkiller ramp, ready for taxi," I transmitted as I rolled forward a bit and checked the brakes.

"Catkiller 3-2, Marble Ground, cleared to taxi runway 1-7, winds calm, altimeter two nine eight seven."

I taxied to and stopped short of the runway, performed a magneto check, saw that we were good to go, and called the tower.

"Marble Tower, Catkiller 3-2 ready for takeoff runway 1-7."

"Catkiller 3-2, Marble Tower, cleared for takeoff runway 1-7." After takeoff and climbing to one thousand feet and heading southwest toward the Que Son Valley, Jim and I tried to formulate a plan of action. We both knew that because of the darkness it would be next to impossible to discern the enemy's exact position in relation to the Marines. We were certain the NVA soldiers would use their tactic of "grabbing the enemy by the belt." This meant simply that they would position themselves as close as possible to the friendlies to try to prevent us from using close air support and artillery. They had done this before, and they would surely use it again.

"Got any ideas how we're gonna do this?" I asked over the intercom, wondering how in the hell we were going to be able to help the troops on the ground.

"We should be able to see muzzle flashes," Jim replied. "Hopefully there will be a flare ship overhead. We're just gonna have to wait until we get there and see what develops. As soon as we get a bit closer, I'll see if I can raise anybody on the ground and see what they need. Tune your FM to 41.5 and I'll tune mine to 35.7. That will give us both the artillery frequency and one of the ground frequencies to start with."

Our aircraft had two FM radios, so we could tune in two different frequencies. We could monitor both frequencies at the same time but could only transmit on one. This process required switching back and forth between the two transmitters. One transmitter was located overhead near the front seat (my seat) and the other was on a small panel to the side of the back seat.

"Okay. I'm going to check in with the DASC [Direct Air Support Center] and let it know we're up, so at least somebody will know we are out here and where we are headed."

"Sounds good."

The DASC was in a bunker at division headquarters in Da Nang. It was responsible for coordinating all air assets used in support of ground troops. These were the folks we talked to when we needed air support and would be the ones who had handed off the jet attack aircraft to us. Their call sign was Land Shark.

I contacted Land Shark on my UHF radio to see if there were any other friendlies in the area. "We have a Basketball flare ship and a Spooky working there at this time," the DASC controller responded. "They should be talking directly to the ground. No altitude information on either one. No other reported aircraft at this time, over."

"Roger Land Shark, Catkiller 3-2 copies."

The universal call sign of all Air Force AC-47 gunships was Spooky; the civilian version was the venerable Douglas DC-3 nicknamed the Gooney Bird. It was a large, all-metal cargo aircraft that had been around since the 1940s. It could seat twenty to thirty people and had two radial engines and a tail wheel. It had served the U.S. military well in World War II during the invasion at Normandy and earned great notoriety flying supplies over the Hump in Burma. It had been resurrected as a very lethal gunship in Vietnam with M-60 machine guns. Three General Electric, Mark 134 mini-guns were soon added, replacing the M-60s, all of which were mounted to fire through the window openings on the left side of the aircraft. Each six-barrel Mark 134 "Gatling Gun" could fire up to six thousand rounds per minute, an awesome amount of firepower. Once over the target at three thousand feet, the pilot placed the gunship in a pylon turn. In this flight maneuver an aircraft banks into a circular turn in such a way that an imaginary line, projecting straight out the side of the aircraft along the wing, points to a fixed point on the ground. The pilot took aim by using both a concentric-circle sight mounted by his left window and angle of bank and rudder inputs. The tremendous firepower of a Spooky wrought death and destruction on enemy forces on the ground. The ground troops loved Spooky because it had lots of bullets and fuel and could thus stay overhead protecting them for long periods of time.

Besides Spooky, the DASC controller had advised there was also a flare ship in the area with the call sign Basketball—probably a Fairchild C-123, a cargo aircraft, bigger than the AC-47, with two big radial engines augmented by a gasoline-burning jet engine under each wing. The jets, which consumed massive amounts of fuel, were normally used only for takeoff, providing additional thrust to get the aircraft off the ground on short runways. They were shut down once the aircraft was in the air and had attained normal cruising speed. The C-123's job was to illuminate the area under attack using large magnesium flares suspended under small parachutes.

After talking with the DASC controller, I thumbed my intercom button, asking Jim if he had gotten all of that. "Yeah, I got it. Sounds like they don't have any fixed wing dropping on the gomers yet," he replied. "That's probably what we are being called down there to do. They'll want us to see if we can sort out who is where too, but I don't know how successful we'll be because it's so dark. We'll just have to wait until we can talk to somebody on the ground."

To someone flying his first night mission in Vietnam, lack of a better plan of action was rather disconcerting. But I had learned to trust the Marine AOs that I flew with and always felt that we were a team up there and could work together no matter what the circumstances.

Jim tuned in his FM radio to one of the ground frequencies he had been given, and I was almost sorry he had. All we could hear was near total chaos. Everybody seemed to be talking at once, and nobody was getting in a complete sentence before being "stepped on" by someone else on the same frequency. The end result was that nobody seemed to be getting what they needed. As we flew closer, we began to pick up a light show that was nearly as beautiful as it was lethal.

There was no moon, but stars were visible and there was just enough residual light to expose the dark outlines of the mountains that ran along the north and south sides of the valley and the distant outline of the hills and mountains that lay to the west. The valley floor was devoid of any lights except hundreds of muzzle flashes emanating from the pitched battle going on there. It looked like sparklers on the Fourth of July and gave us no clue as to who was shooting at whom, or which direction they were shooting. A lot of bullets were flying around.

"Are you seeing what I'm seeing down there?" I asked Jim on intercom.

"Yep. A real shit sandwich, just like I said. Can't tell our guys from the gomers 'cause all the flashes look the same," he responded. "Everybody is talking at the same time, and I can't get a word in edgewise either."

By this time I was thinking, *There is no way that we are ever going to be able to sort this out*, when I spotted Spooky doing his thing over the middle of the valley. To say it was impressive would be an understatement. I couldn't actually see Spooky because the aircraft was blacked out. What I could see were the red tracers spewing death toward the ground from its three mini-guns. Only one out of every five rounds was a tracer, but it still looked like red water pouring from a fire hose.

I could also see the green tracers from NVA 12.7-mm machine guns going back up searching for Spooky. A lot of lead was changing places in that dark sky.

Somewhere above Spooky, completely invisible and talking to no one, Basketball was kicking out flares every minute or so. The magnesium flares burned with an intense bright light, illuminating large areas that grew smaller the closer they got to the ground. There was no way of controlling them as they swayed back and forth under their small parachutes, carried by the wind and casting strange shadows that constantly changed as they descended. It seemed surreal from our vantage point a few miles away.

I decided the best thing to do was circle east of all the action until Jim could sort out where the Marines were on the ground and exactly what they needed from us. But it was beginning to sound pretty hopeless based on all the overlapping chatter coming from the radios.

A sense of frustration had replaced my initial feelings of apprehension. Gone now were my concerns about flying around Vietnam after dark. I was almost overwhelmed by the near visual overload and the simultaneous knowledge that Marines were dying and we couldn't do a damn thing to help. We were witnesses to a raging battle that seemed even more pronounced than it would have been during the day because all the tracers were putting on a light show unlike anything I would ever see back in the U.S.A. We were there to help, but because of the darkness and total confusion on the ground, we were reduced to mere onlookers. This went on for nearly thirty minutes, and then someone slapped the proverbial icing on the cake: we were almost knocked out of the sky by another aircraft!

I had just turned back west toward the raging battle when I suddenly saw a red rotating beacon rapidly descending over the top of us, heading in the same direction, and, a moment later, the flash of bombs exploding on the ground. Someone was controlling a flight of jet attack aircraft, and it wasn't us. I had had enough experience controlling flights of fixed-wing attack aircraft to realize I had been directly in his flight path as he was descending to drop bombs. By pure luck he missed me. I had turned off my wing tip and tail position lights as well as my red rotating beacon when we entered the valley because I didn't want the bad guys shooting at me—I had seen all the tracers going up toward Spooky and didn't want to become their target too. Turning my lights off had worked against me because the jets couldn't see me either.

Marine infantry companies often had attached TACs on the ground. Like us, they were trained to control jet attack aircraft providing close air support, but unlike us, didn't fly . . . they walked. We were known as

TACAs, with the same job but a different perspective and mode of travel. I didn't know if the TAC on the ground had used Land Shark in ordering up their jets or possibly used a different line of communication. What I did know was that Land Shark had not told us of the impending arrival of a flight of fast movers, and they probably hadn't told the fast movers we were also out there. Chalk up another one to the "fog of war." I also knew they never sent out a ground attack jet alone; there were always two of them, and that meant the other one was out there somewhere, maybe heading straight toward me. Getting knocked out of the sky by a friendly jet was not on my wish list. As soon as I realized what was going on, I turned my lights back on so they could see me, keyed my intercom button, and, almost shouting into the mic, asked Jim if he had seen the rotating beacon.

"We almost got mid-aired by that jet, somebody on the ground must be controlling it."

For a moment the intercom was silent. I couldn't tell if my AO, like me, was angry, was speechless from fear, or had experienced a heart attack. Then I heard Jim's calm, steady voice coming through my ear-phones: "Ray, let's go home. We aren't doing anybody any good out here and if this keeps up, we'll probably wind up getting mid-aired."

Man, if I could have, I think I would have crawled into the back seat and hugged Jim Sanders that night. We had come as close to buying the farm as I ever wanted, and the sad truth was we weren't doing anybody any good, no matter how badly we wished we were.

I turned back toward Marble Mountain, checked out with Land Shark, and thanked Jim for making the decision. I was still pretty new at the job, but I learned something very important that night from a solid Marine AO and friend: You can't always do what you so desperately want to do to help the guys on the ground, but it's always better to live to fight another day.

The pitched battle we had witnessed occurred on the third night of Operation Swift. The battle continued until September 15 but diminished in intensity until the Marines drove off the enemy. Both sides needed to lick their wounds for the time being. But the NVA and Viet Cong would never be completely driven from the Que Son Valley.

9 | Convoy Cover

onvoy cover was one of the least interesting missions that I flew. Simply being overhead probably provided the troops in the convoy more of a psychological benefit than a tactical one. The major threat to a ground con is a command-detonated mine, unless the bad guys actually assault a convoy en masse. When a mine exploded, we would lose one or two vehicles without ever seeing who detonated it. This happened to a convoy going over Hai Van Pass just north of Da Nang. The road was extremely crooked and not very wide, with a serious drop-off on the ocean side. There was literally no place to go if attacked and virtually no room to go around the vehicle if it were damaged or rendered inoperative. Everything would grind to a halt until a wrecker could drag the damaged vehicle out of the way.

On a clear blue autumn day I was to provide cover for a Marine convoy of some twenty or so vehicles that was forming up on Highway 1 just on the north edge of Da Nang. I had been given an FM radio frequency and their call sign, Dandy Dancer, prior to takeoff so I dialed it up as I approached them. I instantly knew I was on the right frequency because of the constant stream of chatter that assaulted my ears.

"Dandy Dancer 2-6 X-Ray, this is Dandy Dancer 2-2. You copy, over?"

"Dandy Dancer 2-2, this is Dandy Dancer 2-6 X-Ray, I read you Lima Charlie, over."

Dandy Dancer was the call sign of all the elements of the convoy. Each element had a separate number, and these guys were using absolutely correct tactical radio procedures every time they made a radio transmission. The problem for me was that the many elements in the convoy seemed to be talking to each other constantly. Each element's call sign began with Dandy Dancer and ended with a particular number identifying that element; I had "Dandy Dancer" literally dancing around inside my helmet without letup.

Maybe this was how the elements needed to get organized, but their order of movement, departure time, route of travel, destination, and actions to take upon enemy contact should have all been covered in the pre-mission Op Order and briefing. I thought they talked to each other constantly out of apprehension and the need for psychological support. I couldn't really blame them because the odds of losing at least one vehicle to a mine were very real. However, when two or more radios were transmitting on the same frequency at the same time it was almost impossible to understand what was being said; also, radios are line-of-sight devices, so ground units separated by terrain such as a curve in the road could not always receive each other's transmissions. To someone like me in an aircraft overhead (with "line of sight" to all of the transmissions), their stepping on each other generally meant that instead of words, all I heard was a loud electronic squeal in my flight helmet. Not a good thing, especially when it continued for the duration of the convoy's journey.

To help pass the time while flying convoy cover, I usually tried to dial up armed forces radio on my automatic direction finder (ADF) navigation radio and put a little music in the background. The best part was I could sing along at the top of my lungs (I could not carry a tune in a five-gallon bucket) and nobody could hear me unless I keyed the mic button. Heck, I couldn't even hear myself above the sound of that mighty Continental engine roaring away about five feet in front of me.

In the meantime the convoy was still getting organized, and the Dandy Dancer crowd was broadcasting their every move to anyone who happened to be listening on their FM frequency. Then two civilian gasoline tanker trucks pulled out of the tank farm on the north side of Da Nang. One was a bright yellow and white Shell Oil tanker and the other a bright red and white Esso tanker. Both trucks passed Dandy Dancer's convoy stopped by the side of the road getting organized and began the climb up the hill over Hai Van Pass. Neither truck had any sort of armed escort, and their drivers appeared to be conducting business as usual while a war raged around them. At that point some uneasy thoughts began to gnaw at me and raised some serious questions regarding possible payoffs and who was getting rich and being protected while the young Marines I was watching below me were heading into harm's way.

Twenty minutes after the Shell and Esso tankers passed it, the Marine convoy finally started moving north over Hai Van Pass and on to Phu Bai. I was making lazy circles overhead, listening to the music on my ADF that was constantly being interrupted by FM radio transmissions from the convoy below, while I watched the road ahead for any signs of ambush. It was impossible for me to tell if a mine had been buried in the asphalt roadway because of the nearly constant patchwork of previous repairs.

Command-detonated mines were usually made from unexploded U.S. artillery rounds. The VC or NVA would dig them up and lug them to the nearest road that U.S. or ARVN convoys would use. The mines would then be wired to a detonating device and buried. The bad guys would conceal the wires, and the person doing the detonating would hide in a vantage point somewhere within visual range. When one of our vehicles was in range he'd detonate the buried explosive, blowing up the vehicle along with anyone on board, then melt away into the jungle or blend in with any civilians in the immediate area. Even if the explosion failed to do serious bodily harm, the psychological damage was instant and often lingered for quite some time. It was hard to find an Army or Marine truck driver who wasn't just a bit nervous. Either kind of harm was a check mark in the enemy's win column. In defense, the Marines running convoys began placing layers of sandbags on the floor of their vehicles in an attempt to mitigate the extent of injury should an explosion occur. I'm not sure just how effective that was, but not doing anything would have been worse.

When the convoy was three-quarters of the way up the narrow Hai Van Pass road, one of the 2.5-ton trucks suddenly bucked several feet into the air in a cloud of dirt and black smoke. The convoy commander, whose vehicle was near the front of the convoy, was immediately on his radio asking me what had happened.

"I saw the explosion. It's a Deuce and a Half about two-thirds of the way back in your convoy," I responded.

The convoy commander wanted to know if I could see who set off the explosion and the extent of the damage. I told him I did not see any movement on either side of the road; it looked like the right front tire and wheel of the truck were gone and he was going to need to move up the wrecker from near the rear of the convoy to tow it. I also told him it looked like he had some injured people in the truck.

Sadly, this was about all I could do when performing a convoy cover mission unless an NVA or VC force attacked the convoy directly, in which case I could bring artillery or air support to bear on the enemy. Otherwise it was always a hit-and-run event. I suppose the NVA/VC's true intent was to inflict some physical damage and maximize any psychological damage. I sometimes felt like a cop called to the scene of an assault after it had already happened. About all I could do was search the immediate area for bad guys, ask if anyone saw anything significant, and remain vigilant for further hostile action. Beyond that, there wasn't much I could do.

That's when I began thinking again about those Shell and Esso tankers. They had driven up and over the top of Hai Van Pass without even the slightest interruption, let alone an attack. How was it that these guys could drive around with apparent impunity while I lost a Marine vehicle to a command-detonated mine? Was somebody working for Shell or Esso paying off the bad guys to escape damage to their trucks?

This question remains unresolved in my mind to this very day. Fortunately, there were only a couple of minor injuries to the Marines in the Deuce and a Half, and after a corpsman attended to them, the convoy again got under way with the wrecker towing the damaged truck.

The day wasn't over, however. Just to the north of Hai Van Pass and several kilometers south of Phu Bai was a narrow causeway/highway spanning the inlet to a large bay. As luck would have it, an ARVN convoy was heading south toward Da Nang at the same time my Marine convoy was heading north. The first vehicle in each convoy met at the north end of a bridge on the causeway.

In the United States, bridge etiquette requires that whoever arrives later must yield to the first to arrive. Not so in Vietnam it seemed. Although the U.S. Marine convoy arrived first, the commander of the ARVN convoy would not move his vehicles to the side of the narrow road and in fact appeared to be demanding that the Marine convoy back up off the bridge and let his convoy through. From my overhead perspective, unable to hear the conversation but watching a lot of arm waving and pointing, it was quickly evident the Marines weren't about to comply with the ARVN commander's demands.

U.S. Marines are trained to be polite to everyone but always have a plan to annihilate. The Marine commander—and his convoy—had already been through one nearly tragic event without being able to get his hands around the throat of the perpetrator, so facing down the ARVN convoy commander was the natural course of events. He wasn't going to budge! This, of course, presented an unwanted problem for all of us. Now there was not just one juicy convoy target for the bad guys, but two. The secret to a successful convoy movement is movement, continuous movement, and we weren't getting any.

As I circled the traffic jam, watching the two convoy commanders standing in the middle of the road engaged in what appeared to be less than convivial conversation, what should suddenly appear on the scene but a VNAF Birddog. Aha! Just what I needed to erase the boredom of circling over the two arguing convoy commanders. Things were looking up. Somebody for me to play with. Now we were both circling the mess eight hundred feet below and neither of us talking to the other, although I imagined he could talk with his convoy commander just as I could with mine.

This went on for several minutes, and then temptation reared its ugly head and I began thinking, *Hell, I'll just jump the VNAF Birddog and maybe he will tell his convoy commander to back off and let the U.S. Marine convoy through.* He wasn't the slightest bit interested in me other than trying to ensure we didn't collide. But he did seem to be hogging the airspace directly above the bridge; and I, being "ten feet tall and bullet proof," took that as a challenge to my superior flying skills (pilots, even Birddog pilots, rarely suffer from lack of inflated ego). We continued to circle as I slowly began to close the gap between us, working to position myself directly behind him. To a pilot this would be a clear "I gotcha" and to a military pilot, an ego-smasher. At some point the VNAF pilot realized what I was doing and quickly began to perform all sorts of evasive maneuvers, including very tight steep turns. I managed to remain right on his tail using flaps to turn inside his turns. What fun!

Suddenly he went straight and level and began to fly off to the south. Yes! He was yielding to my superior flying skills. I was busy mentally putting a trophy on my shelf when from out of nowhere two VNAF A-1E Douglas Skyraider attack aircraft came roaring at me head on, wing tip to wing tip. I think I nearly had a heart attack as they pulled up right in front of me less than two hundred feet away, their wing tips trailing vapor.

The VNAF Birddog pilot had gotten his revenge! He had called in a couple of his Big Brothers to crush the upstart Yankee Air Pirate and show him who really ruled the sky over I Corps. It did take a few minutes for my heart rate to subside, and by then the traffic jam below had been resolved and my convoy was allowed to pass.

Final score: USMC convoy: 1, ARVN convoy: 0, VNAF: 1, Army Bird-dog: 0. Some might consider that a tie; I considered it a clear message to NOT mess with VNAF Birddogs.

10 | Helicopters
The Other Way to Fly

A s a fixed-wing Army aviator I was not particularly fond of helicopters, especially after I witnessed more than one fall out of the sky and knew how hazardous flying them could be. The job of Birddog pilots was to fly over the action and control the direct support elements like artillery and close air support, whereas helicopter pilots had to fly the troops into the action, land to let them out, go get another load, and do it again. After that, they had to bring in supplies and take out the casualties, often under intense enemy fire. Theirs was not a job for the timid. Eventually the Army did get me into helicopters, although it was long after my tour in Vietnam. I suspect there are still two heel marks from when I was dragged across the ramp at Cairns Army Airfield, Fort Rucker, for my first training flight in a Bell UH-1 helicopter. The reasons I disliked helicopters are simple to understand:

- They are inherently unstable, and if you let go of the controls they will attempt to fall from the sky.
- They fly very dangerous missions, frequently placing their crews in harm's way.
- They are a mass of moving parts, most of which are moving counter to each other, thus creating a situation where, if given a chance, they will separate and depart the aircraft.
- They get shot at—a lot.

According to Shelby L. Stanton's numbers in his book *Vietnam Order of Battle*, I calculate the ratio of Army rotary-wing pilots and crew members killed to Army fixed-wing pilots and crew members killed in the Vietnam War was 23:1. When compared to the previously noted 7:1 ratio of rotary-wing graduates to fixed-wing flight school graduates, the elevated danger of flying helicopters in combat is very clear.

During my tour of duty in Vietnam I saw lots of different helicopters. The Marines fielded four different types of their own: the monster Sikorsky CH-53, a heavy-lift helicopter; the tandem-rotor Boeing CH-46, a slightly scaled down version of the Army's CH-47 Chinook; the Korean War–vintage Sikorsky H-34 with its massive, gasoline-powered radial engine; and the iconic Bell UH-1 "Huey." I observed the operations of all four of them from a distance, but the only one I experienced on a personal level was the CH-53 I bummed a ride in, from Phu Bai to Marble Mountain on the day I signed out of the 220th and headed home. Although I had no operational experience with helicopters in Vietnam, my encounters with these rotary aircraft left me with a series of images indelibly printed in my memory.

The venerable H-34 seemed called upon to do everything. On any given day I would see at least one or two of those distinctive silhouettes off in the distance, lifting out of or going into some remote location. They hauled everything from beans to bullets, and they were the prime mover for medically evacuating wounded, or medevac. My first memorable encounter with an H-34 was out near the western edge of Que Son Valley. A Marine company had engaged some NVA soldiers, had one seriously wounded, and requested medical evacuation. My AO and I were performing visual reconnaissance in the area, so we flew over to the scene.

As I circled above the Marines the FM radio crackled with, "Catkiller, Catkiller, this is Cottage Kilo 2-1, do you read?"

From the back seat, my AO, Marine Lt. Bill Amberson, transmitted "Cottage Kilo 2-1 this is Blackcoat 4, with Catkiller 3-2, read you loud and clear."

"Blackcoat 4, this is Cottage Kilo 2-1, we have a medevac in progress. Would you check out the surrounding tree lines for any enemy activity? We think there is at least one sniper in there somewhere. He's wounded one and may still be a threat."

"Roger, Kilo. We'll check out the area. Right now we're not seeing any movement, but we'll keep a close watch."

"Roger, Blackcoat, we appreciate it. Cottage Kilo 2-1 out."

About then I saw the stretcher with the wounded Marine on it being loaded into the H-34. I could not tell if he was conscious, but if he was, I was certain he was glad to see that medevac bird, his ride out of the bush. I watched as the H-34 pilot rolled his throttle up, and the helicopter lifted up and out of the small landing zone (LZ). He rolled into a hard right bank one hundred feet above the ground. I then watched in horror as the stretcher with the strapped-in Marine slid out the open door and fell to the ground, almost certainly killing the wounded Leatherneck. All I could do was look away. The stretcher must not have been secured inside the helicopter before the pilot lifted off.

"Ah, Cottage Kilo 2-1, Blackcoat 4. Looks like you won't be needing us anymore, copy?"

"Roger Blackcoat," came the obviously grief-stricken response.

"Well, that sure turned into a shit sandwich," grumbled Amberson over the intercom.

"Yeah, let's go find something else to do for a while," I replied.

It was just another sad day in the Que Son Valley.

The medevac flights had several issues. First, there was a helicopter shortage. The Marines simply did not have enough helicopters to carry troops, fly resupply missions, and pick up the wounded. Medevac was one of the primary missions of the H-34s, and the H-34 resources were frequently stretched to the limit. Second, the operational procedure followed during medevacs often required a Huey gunship escort, which of course revealed the medevac mission and added to the danger. Anyone seeing the two ships circling together with their unmistakable silhouettes—the bulbous-nosed high cockpit profile of the H-34 and the squat profile of the Huey gunship with its skids hanging underneath—knew the larger one would eventually descend to land and therefore become vulnerable to hostile ground fire.

This situation was made worse by forcing the medevac birds to circle the area while the pilots—as dictated by the standing orders issued from headquarters—asked a series of questions of the ground commander before descending to extract the wounded. Thus, the medevac pilot was forced to circle until he received satisfactory replies to questions including the following:

When was the last time you received fire?
What was it?
What direction was it from?
How heavy [intense] was it?
What caliber was it?

Why was this? I wondered. A Marine H-34 pilot said higher headquarters had informed their medevac pilots that if they were shot down while trying to extract a wounded Marine, "they would buy the aircraft with their wings," meaning they would be removed from flight status. So the Marine medevac pilots circled and circled asking their damn questions while the bad guys sat there hidden, knowing that eventually that bulbous helicopter was going to come down and land, then take off—an overripe target that they had been given more than enough time to prepare to shoot down.

This sad state of affairs resulted in Marines on the ground being as evasive as possible (without outright lying) when answering the questions. After all, it was one of their buddies lying there bleeding, waiting for extraction. War isn't pretty.

We Catkillers of the 3rd Platoon had come up with a backup plan. The Army's 282nd AHC, the Black Cats, was co-located with us at Marble Mountain airfield. They flew Hueys—both guns and slicks—and supported an ARVN Ranger Battalion. The Black Cat pilots had a common company frequency of 271.0 that they monitored among themselves to keep track of each other. They had given the frequency to us in case we ever needed to talk to them in flight. Sometimes, just cruising around, we would see them going someplace nearby and check in to see what they were up to. We knew a lot of their pilots, most of them young warrant officers. They were good guys—brave, aggressive— damn good pilots who, at nineteen and twenty years of age, were operating a $250,000 aircraft, were responsible for the lives of their crew and passengers, and would fly straight into the jaws of hell to save a life. Unlike some of their stateside peers, who needed drugs to get high, the only thing helicopter pilots needed for an adrenaline rush was to quickly pull up on the collective and fly. I had decided that if I was ever involved in a slowly developing medevac situation or ever needed to get a wounded Marine out quickly and no Marine medevac helicopters were available, I would put out a blanket call on the Black Cat common frequency. If any Black Cats were nearby, they would buzz over, pick up the wounded, and fly them to the hospital at Da Nang.

Just such a situation developed one day at the eastern end of the Que Son Valley near the coastal city of Hoi An. My AO and I were cruising in the vicinity and heard some chatter on the Fox Mike about a medevac request. I decided to fly over to see if we could assist.

When we arrived on scene, the Marine medevac H-34 and his Huey gunship entourage were just showing up and began their litany of questions as they circled. The Marines on the ground were having trouble convincing the medevac bird to come down because they were still receiving fire from a well-hidden enemy. This was beginning to look like a very long day for the wounded Marines.

About that time, I spotted a Black Cat helicopter heading south out of Marble Mountain and straight toward us, so I dialed up 271.0 on my UHF radio and gave him a call, "Black Cat just north of Hoi An heading south, this is Catkiller 3-2."

"Catkiller 3-2, this is Black Cat 2-7."

"Black Cat 2-7, I'm at your twelve o'clock. We have a medevac problem underneath us and maybe you can help."

"Sure, whaddaya need?"

Helicopter pilots were nearly always eager to help a fixed-wing guy in need, thus later garnering bragging rights and free drinks at the bar that evening.

"We've got a couple of wounded Marines down there, and it's a hot LZ so the medevac bird won't come down."

"We've got you and the helicopters in sight. Is the LZ right below you?"

"Yes, right below me, and the guys on the ground are begging for help."

"Okay, here's what I'm going to do. You tell the guys on the ground that I'm coming in low level from the north in about one minute. Tell them to pop smoke now."

"Roger. I'll tell 'em you're coming and not to keep trying to get the medevac to come down."

This exchange happened so quickly that I don't think the Marine pilots realized what was going on. They didn't say a word, they just kept circling. Black Cat 2-7 swooped in at treetop level, flared, and ever so gently (those kids were good) set the Huey down in the middle of the LZ right next to the yellow smoke billowing from a smoke grenade. Seconds later the wounded Marines were on board. As 2-7 lifted out, he transmitted, "3-2, 2-7's coming out; got the wounded and we're heading for the hospital at Da Nang."

"Roger 2-7. Thanks for your help. I know the guys on board appreciate it."

"No sweat 3-2, glad to help. Call anytime."

And there it was. A couple of young Army warrant officers grabbed the bull by the horns, and while the bad guys were watching and waiting for the H-34 to come down so they could shoot it out of the sky, the wounded Marines were snatched from the jaws of fate. Victory goes to the bold. Truthfully, I did feel a bit of remorse for the hapless Marine medevac pilots who I'm certain didn't appreciate being "snaked" by an Army helicopter, but they were probably at least somewhat relieved they didn't have to "buy" their ancient helicopter with their wings.

Just a week or so later in the same area near Hoi An, another medevac mission evolved beneath me. Even though he did not have a Huey gunship escort, the H-34 pilot was comfortable enough with the situation to have landed in the LZ and taken the wounded Marines on board. I was droning around overhead, keeping a close lookout for enemy troops. None were visible, but we knew they were there. What we didn't know was just how well armed they were. The H-34 lifted out of the LZ and was probably fifty feet or so in the air when a tremendous explosion erupted in the nose of the helicopter. I could hardly believe my eyes as I watched the H-34 wobble, then stabilize, and . . . continue flying! It looked to me like a B-40 rocket-propelled grenade (RPG) had struck the helicopter. *That's an anti-tank weapon! It blows up tanks!* That's when the H-34 pilot came up on his radio.

"We just took what looks like a B-40 round as we were coming out. We're still flying so I'm going to try to make it to Hill 55 before I put it down." I couldn't believe how calm his voice was as he went clattering the eight or so kilometers toward Hill 55 where the Marines had a fairly large artillery base.

"Catkiller 3-2 will follow you there," I transmitted as we fell in behind and above the now smoking helicopter as it made a beeline for Hill 55.

We watched as he made a successful landing and people began to get out of the aircraft. Two days later I found out the H-34 had indeed taken a B-40 round in the snout, but the enormous cast-iron reciprocating engine in that Korean War–vintage Sikorsky helicopter had completely absorbed the explosive force of the rocket-propelled grenade, leaving everyone on board without a scratch. Had it been a Huey CH-46 or CH-53, it would have been blown out of the sky. The explosion did blow a cylinder off the engine, but the engine continued to run, spewing oil and fuel as it staggered through the sky. When the pilot rolled the throttle off after landing, the engine seized; but when he needed that outdated machine to perform, it had. They just don't build 'em like that anymore.

During late 1967 the Marines began losing a lot of CH-46A helicopters in Vietnam. They were falling out of the sky for no apparent reason. Most of the accidents could not be properly investigated because many occurred over hostile territory. The cause or causes remained a mystery. I had the chilling experience of observing one such incident on a sunny afternoon late in August 1967. I was flying from Marble Mountain to Phu Bai on some administrative task, cruising along at about 2,500 feet where the air was cool. I noticed a lone CH-46 flying off to my 2 o'clock about a mile away. As I watched, the rear of the helicopter suddenly dropped; it began to flutter earthward with what looked like troops falling out the back. The CH-46 had a rear ramp and large overhead door and normally flew with the ramp up and the door retracted upward to allow airflow through the back of the aircraft to keep things cool. I was certain what I was witnessing was the death of a lot of Marines as they fell from the sky. Nobody was going to survive that. I called the DASC and gave an approximate location of the crash site as the helicopter exploded on impact. There was nothing else I could do. I continued on to Phu Bai. *Damn*, I thought.

The next day, September 1, 1967, I was returning to Marble Mountain from a North Coast mission just as a flight of two CH-46s was approaching the airfield from the north. Contacting Marble Tower, I was instructed to enter a right downwind landing to the north. The two helicopters were cleared for a straight-in approach, landing to the south. As I entered the downwind leg of the traffic pattern, the tower instructed me to do a 380 degree turn on the downwind to allow spacing from the helicopters. I rogered and went into a lazy circle, watching the two helicopters landing in trail on the runway below. What occurred next could not have been planned any better in a Hollywood script.

The two helicopters flared in unison, and just as their wheels were no more than five feet above the runway, a small explosion erupted at the top of the second helicopter's rear pylon, right where the rotor head was located. The rotor head and its attached three blades proceeded to depart the helicopter, still spinning until they deposited themselves in the sand between the runway and the parallel taxiway.

As I watched, the helicopter dropped five feet to the ground, and the four crew members exited their machine in something less than two heartbeats. I didn't know that a person could exit a helicopter that quickly. As luck would have it, the crash truck was parked right there, facing 90 degrees to the runway. All Crash had to do was start the engine of the truck, activate the pump, and shoot foam all over the aft pylon of the now totally empty helicopter.

For possibly the very first time the Marines now had one of their wounded CH-46 helicopters in captivity, with all of its parts and in a secure area where the origin of the mechanical failure could be properly investigated. In the years since, an official release of information about cause noted something about a faulty rear transmission or transmission mounts.

The real reason for these failures, according to one CH-46 pilot I spoke to back then, was somewhat different. According to his explanation, the CH-46 had a "hover aft" switch pilots could activate when hovering at a slow airspeed. This switch caused the aft rotor to tilt rearward independent of the aircraft, allowing the nose of the aircraft to be lower than it would be otherwise. The tilt gave the pilots better forward visibility when hovering. This switch was automatically disabled above a certain minimum airspeed and not designed to be used in cruise flight.

Somewhere along the way, Marine CH-46 pilots discovered that if they could merely override the disable feature on the hover aft switch and drive the aft rotor rearward in flight, they would in fact have a giant airbrake. They could then scream low level into an LZ, drive the aft rotor rearward, slow almost instantly, and settle quickly into an LZ before the bad guys knew they were there. How was this achieved? One of the pilots would simply reach out with his hand and cover the pitot tube, which senses forward airspeed, and fool the hover aft system into thinking the helicopter was just hovering and then drive the aft rotor rearward. Can't say I blame them. After all, I wouldn't be at all interested in hovering slowly into an LZ surrounded by bad guys with loaded rifles just itching to shoot me dead.

Unfortunately, the result of this activity eventually began to catch up with the CH-46 crews. The rear pylon that housed the transmission, rotor head, rotor blades, and other critical stuff wasn't built to handle the stresses being placed on it. Cracks developed that were not noticed during routine inspections and at some point, maybe many flight hours later and with a different crew, the mounts in the upper portion of the aft pylon failed, shedding the aft rotor system with catastrophic results.

Toward the end of 1967 all of the Marine CH-46s were grounded for inspection and, if necessary, repaired. The older, smaller H-34s were forced to pick up the slack. To their credit, the Marines somehow managed to get by until the CH-46s resumed flying.

11 | Fun and Games in the Que Son Valley

In the early months of 1966 the Marines began conducting large ground operations in the Que Son Valley, a basin roughly thirty-five miles south of Da Nang, astride the boundaries of Quang Nam and Quang Tin provinces. This area, comprising nearly six hundred square miles, contained a large population and, as a major producer of rice, a staple of the Vietnamese diet, was therefore a prime target for occupation by the Viet Cong and NVA.

The immediate area south of Da Nang and farther to the south and west into the Que Son Valley became the Marines' TAOR and by default, the Catkillers'. Pilots of the 3rd Platoon at Marble Mountain and their Marine AOs were scheduled daily flights to provide constant coverage of Marine ground units during daylight hours.

Tooling around one sunny August afternoon over the Que Son Valley, Rob Whitlow, my Marine AO, and I contacted a Marine company on a sweep. While we flew around we dialed up units to see if there was anything we could do for them. Rob gave them a call on the FM radio.

"Connive Mike; this is Blackcoat 3, over."

Our AOs had their own call signs and used them when talking on the radios, just as the Catkiller pilots used their personal call signs on the radio

"Blackcoat 3, this is Connive Mike. That you in the Birddog?"

"That's us, anything we can do for you today?"

"You sure can. We've been getting sniped at all morning by a couple of VC. We think they are a couple of hundred meters to the east of us, but we can't see them. Can you scout around in that direction and see if you can find them?"

"Sure thing, we'll head over that way now."

About that time a couple of big white birds suddenly flew up out of a clump of trees about three hundred meters east of the company's lead element. That grabbed our attention, and as we looked that way, we saw a leg disappear into the foliage. *GOTCHA!*

"Connive Mike, Blackcoat 3; I think we've got your problem spotted. They just ran into that clump of trees three hundred meters directly to your east where those two paddy dikes cross."

"Roger Blackcoat, we see the trees. We'll drop a few 60 mike-mike rounds on them."

"Roger Connive Mike, we'll stay out of your line of fire and keep an eye on the target to see if they try to get away."

Marine companies performing a sweep operation carried at least one 60-mm mortar with them. The 60-mm mortar wasn't quite as lethal as the 81-mm mortar, but it was lighter and the mortar rounds were not as heavy as those for the 81-mm, so companies could carry more of them. In combat, when it comes to bullets and other ordnance, more is good. Connive Mike lobbed a few mortar rounds into the clump of trees and suddenly two young males carrying rifles burst out of the foliage and began running along a paddy dike away from the Marines.

"Connive Mike, Blackcoat 3; we've got them running away from you, south along a paddy dike."

"Roger Blackcoat, we see them and we're taking them under fire."

"Connive Mike, it looks like you winged one of them. He's really slowed down. They've both ditched their rifles. Can you get some of your guys to drop their packs and go after them?"

"Sounds like a plan Blackcoat. Will you keep track of the other one for us?"

"We're on him now. He's hauling ass south on a paddy dike. We'll stay on him until you can get some folks over here."

With that, I descended and began making low passes at the VC who was in full stride running on the paddy dikes, trying to escape. For probably fifteen minutes, I'd dive for him and at the last instant he would throw himself prone in the dirt on the paddy dike. I would then pull up and do it again. Finally, the VC, shirt soaked with sweat, stopped in the middle of a dry rice paddy and "surrendered" to me. His chest heaving, he raised both of his arms as I flew around him in tight circles less than one hundred feet above the ground. He was rotating 360 degrees, facing me as I circled, with a look of resignation laced with fear written on his face. Several Marines soon arrived, and as we departed the scene, I could see the beginning of some intense interrogation. Connive Mike had resolved their sniper problem for today, but there would always be tomorrow.

On another day we just happened to be droning around in the Que Son Valley when my AO that day, Jim Sanders, and I got a call for help from a Marine company on a sweep toward one of the many villages that dotted the valley. As they approached the village, they began taking hostile fire from the edge of the village. Everybody hit the ground and they radioed for aerial support.

"Catkiller, Catkiller, this is Cottage Kilo, do you read?"

"Cottage Kilo, this is Catkiller 3-2. I've got Blackcoat 2 in the back seat. We have you Lima Charlie" [loud and clear].

Generally our AOs talked to the guys on the ground first for a couple of very good reasons. Our AOs were Marines, and they knew Marine tactics and Marine-think and probably even knew the CO of the unit we were talking to. Not only had all of our Marine AOs completed the Aerial Observer course, but many had done at least six months on the ground. They knew what the guy on the ground needed and how to give it to him. Catkiller pilots were well trained in how to fly the Birddog, but how to provide direct support to grunts on the ground we learned from our Marine AOs.

"Blackcoat 2, this is Cottage Kilo. We are taking fire from the ville to our west at Alpha Tango 923550. We are holding in our present position about three hundred meters to the east. Can you get some fixed wing or artillery in here for us?"

As we headed for Cottage Kilo's location, Jim transmitted, "Stand by Cottage Kilo, we'll get something cranked up for you ASAP."

Then to me on intercom: "Ray, see if the DASC has anything available, and I'll get more of a brief from Cottage Kilo as we head over there."

I checked in with the DASC on my UHF radio and was told I could have a flight of A-4s within just a few minutes. A short time later, true to his word, the DASC told me my flight was inbound and gave me a frequency and call sign to contact them. By then Jim had received a full brief from Cottage Kilo. We determined their exact location and told them we had fixed wing inbound and to stand by.

About that time I heard a flight of Marine A-4 Skyhawks checking in with the DASC, and then the DASC instructed us to switch to tactical frequency Orange. I changed the frequency in my UHF radio and in a moment heard the A-4s check in with each other and then call me.

"Catkiller 3-2, this is Love Bug 1–5-6 on Button Orange."

"Love Bug 1–5-6, this is Catkiller 3-2, read you Lima Charlie," I replied.

"Catkiller 3-2, Love Bug 1–5-6, flight of two Alpha Fours [A-4 Sky-hawks] inbound at flight level one-eight-zero, on the one-nine-zero at two-two off channel ninety-eight. We've each got six Delta One-Alphas, two Delta Sevens, and Pistols with three-zero minutes of fuel. What have you got for us?"

Perfect! Two United States Marine Corps A-4 jets, each carrying its standard close air support load of six 250-pound Snake-Eye high-drag bombs [Delta One-Alphas], two napalm canisters [Delta Sevens], and 20-mm cannons [Pistols] arrived on scene.

"Roger Love Bug, we're in an Army Birddog at one thousand feet circling off the two-zero-five at four-zero off Channel ninety-eight. Stand by for a target brief."

"Whenever you are ready Catkiller, go ahead with your brief."

"We've got a company on a sweep that has taken some small-arms fire from a ville about three hundred meters to their west. They are holding their position and will not be a factor for you. They have not received any automatic weapons fire. I want you to make your runs south to north on a three-six-zero heading. Your nearest friendlies will be three hundred meters at your three o'clock as you make your run. I want you to set up a right-hand orbit with a right-hand pull as you come off the target. I have received negative ground fire from the target. Plan on dropping your Delta Sevens in pairs on your first run, then we'll use the Snake-Eyes and your Pistols last if we need them. Target elevation is about four hundred feet. I'll be in a right-hand orbit at one thousand feet over the friendlies. Let me know when you see me and when you are set up for me to mark the target with a Willie Pete."

"Catkiller, Love Bug 1–5-6 flight has you. Go ahead and mark your target."

"Roger Love Bug, I'll be putting a Willie Pete in the center of the ville. We'll adjust you from that."

From my back seat Jim told me on intercom, "I've told Cottage Kilo that the jets are inbound and to keep their heads down. They said they're ready."

"Okay. I'm bringing it around for a rocket run."

As I completed my turn for the rocket run, I reached up and set the arming switches to fire one WP rocket and removed the safety pin on my control stick trigger. Rolling out of the turn I lined up on the center of the village, pulled on the carburetor heat to prevent the engine from quitting due to carburetor ice, and pulled the throttle back causing the nose to drop so the aircraft was pointing directly at the village. I squeezed the trigger and with a loud *BANG—WHOOSH!* away went a 2.75-inch rocket. It impacted near the center of the village in a large billowing cloud of white smoke. I immediately broke right so as not to overfly the target and any bad guys who might be waiting to hose us down with bullets. The billowing white smoke would continue for three or four minutes, providing ample time for the jets to identify the target and for me to make any adjustments for their ordnance drop. In this instance I wanted them to drop their napalm on the near end of the village to allow it to "splash" through the village in the direction of flight and cause the most damage.

"Smoke's away Love Bug, do you have it?"

"Roger Catkiller, Love Bug has the smoke in sight."

"Okay."

I then radioed the lead A-4, "From my smoke, six o'clock at one hundred meters with your Delta Sevens."

I quickly yanked my aircraft around to a heading of south so I could look for the lead A-4 as it was turning for its run on the target at about five thousand feet. I needed to locate it while it was still making its turn—usually by the flash of its wings in the sun—to ensure its run-in heading was correct; otherwise, I wouldn't be able to clear the pilot for the drop. Until the A-4 pilot heard me clear him "hot" he would not drop any ordnance. My job, and ultimate responsibility, was to ensure the jets were not going to drop anything on the friendlies on the ground.

"Turning final with two Delta Sevens, am I cleared hot?"

"Cleared hot," I transmitted.

I watched as the A-4 released its two large napalm canisters. They tumbled to earth, impacting on the south edge of the village one hundred meters short of the billowing white smoke from my rocket. The canisters exploded on contact with the ground, splashing liquid flame the length of a football field and incinerating everything in their path.

I then cleared the second A-4 and told the pilot to drop at three o'clock, fifty meters from the first drop. I wanted to take out the structures closest to the friendlies.

My AO, who had been talking with Cottage Kilo, thumbed his intercom button and said to me, "The guys on the ground say that's right where they think the gomers were shooting from and to keep pounding the ville."

We ran the jets for another fifteen minutes, walking 250-pound high-drag Snake-Eyes all over the village, leaving it nearly totally destroyed and devoid of any movement whatsoever. I controlled each drop by adjusting it from the previous one, using a simple clock system with the run-in heading as twelve o'clock. Left would be nine o'clock, right would be three o'clock, further would be twelve o'clock, and so forth. This system was simple, easy to understand, and very effective.

After the A-4s had expended all of their ordnance I circled the village once and then gave the departing jets their BDA.

"BDA follows," I radioed, "one hundred over eighty. Looks like three bunkers destroyed and a dozen structures. No bodies visible at this time, but the ground troops may find some when they sweep the ville. Great job. The guys on the ground say that they aren't getting any more fire from the ville and want me to thank you for them."

What I had just told the departing A-4s flight was that 100 percent of their ordnance had been on target and that the target was 80 percent destroyed. I would later call the DASC and give it the same information. This was how squadrons and the folks "higher up" kept score. Nobody wanted to return from a mission with a low BDA.

After the Marine jets departed, Jim and I got back with the folks on the ground to see if we could be of further help.

"How are things looking down there?" asked Jim.

"We're getting ready to move out. Would you take a look for any movement before we do?"

With that, I began to circle the village while Jim gave them an "Affirmative." As we circled the far side of the village, Cottage Kilo called and said that they were detecting movement on the edge of the village closest to them. We continued around and sure enough, there was movement, but not of a hostile nature.

"We have a woman with what looks like a baby in her arms crawling toward you along a paddy dike," Jim radioed the Marines on the ground. "She looks like she has been wounded in her leg. Can you send someone out to give her a hand?"

"That's a negative," they replied. "We still don't know if anyone is left in there to shoot at us."

"We don't see any threat at this time but we will continue to circle." And to me, "Ray, what do you want to do?"

"Let's go down and get slow and see if we can draw any fire," I replied.

I pulled the throttle back, lowered some flaps, and we began circling the village at about one hundred feet, daring somebody to take a shot at us. This may sound insane, but I was certain that anybody left alive in the village was cowering in the bottom of a hole. Besides, the woman and her baby needed attention now. Dragging the village low and slow was the quickest way I could think of to reassure Cottage Kilo that it was safe to come to her aid.

After circling the village twice and not receiving any fire, Jim keyed his mic and said, "Cottage Kilo, Blackcoat 2, we're not drawing any fire from the ville and we still don't see any movement. You should be good to send somebody out."

Cottage Kilo "Rogered," and as we circled the third time, we came upon a scene that will forever make me proud to have served in the military. On a paddy dike were three young Americans displaying compassion, coolness, and professionalism almost beyond description: They were between a village from which they had been receiving gunfire just thirty minutes prior and a company of United States Marines that were not in a particularly friendly frame of mind. A Navy Corpsman was kneeling beside the wounded woman applying a large bandage to her leg while two young Marines were calmly standing on the paddy dike. One held his rifle at the ready, facing the village, while the other had his rifle in his right hand, the butt resting on his right hip, and with his left hand held the baby, its bare butt (Vietnamese babies weren't diapered) resting on his other hip. This was a classic pose of Americans protecting those who cannot protect themselves. Something we have been doing for more than two hundred years. Sometimes going low and slow can ease a troubled mind and save a life in the process. Today that's called risk assessment, but back then it just seemed to be the right thing to do.

Not every flight into the Que Son Valley involved low flying and the risk of getting shot at. Taking unnecessary chances wasn't my job—

finding the enemy and supporting the Marines on the ground was. But sometimes just flying around looking for trouble wasn't good enough; I had to press my luck. I can't say that it was out of boredom, but rather just the absolute thrill of flying and the near euphoric feeling it sometimes generated in me. Anyone who has piloted an aircraft can recall a particularly beautiful sunset, or the sun's rays casting columns of light down through towering cumulus clouds, or something startling on the ground such as suddenly coming upon a waterfall deep in the jungle that could only be viewed from the air. The freedom of flight was still pretty new to me, and even in combat it frequently presented a new opportunity to experience that sense of well-being.

November 9, 1967, was one of those days. The Marines were being replaced in the Que Son Valley by units of the Army's American Division, but continued to maintain a presence in Antenna Valley just to the west. They had an outpost on top of a prominent ridge on the western end of Que Son Valley. From the air it appeared to be an observation post of some kind with just enough of a flat area on the top to land a helicopter. Marines in foxholes formed a perimeter but had no bunkers or anything of a permanent nature.

Earlier, my AO and I had made contact with a Marine company–sized force moving slowly through Antenna Valley and had checked out a few places for them that may have been hiding the enemy. We were headed back to Marble Mountain airfield via the Que Son Valley when I spotted a Huey sitting on the ridge top with its rotor blades slowly turning. Out of curiosity I decided to circle and have a look. Then I noticed one of the Marines wasn't wearing a steel helmet, just his cover (Marine-speak for baseball cap), and he appeared to have the attention of a small circle of steel-helmeted men that surrounded him.

The comedian Flip Wilson used to say, with an enormous grin on his face, "The devil made me do it." Well, it was something like that for me as well. I couldn't help myself. I just had to make a low pass over this little gaggle of Marines on the ridge top. I continued my circle until I was approaching the one with the soft cover from behind. I closed the throttle and swooped down, shoving full throttle back in just as I passed over them at about fifty feet. My AO had been talking with someone on the ground on the FM radio, and he now keyed his intercom button and told me, "Jesus, Ray! You just buzzed a two-star general and went so low you blew off his soft cover and he's pissed!"

Oops! I guess not everyone was as thrilled about my flying skills as I was.

Fortunately, my AO came up on the intercom again to tell me, "They said the general's men got a big kick out of it and they are all laughing and the general is smiling. Let's get the hell out of here before he changes his mind."

Whew! No risk assessment involved in that little stunt, but somehow it still seemed like the right thing to do.

12 | Catkillers and Special Forces

When the 220th arrived in I Corps, it was assigned a two-part mission. The first priority was combat observation support for all combat operations in I Corps Tactical Zone, which included the 1st and 3rd Marine Divisions, units of the 1st and 2nd Divisions of the ARVN, and the Army 5th Special Forces Group that had a total of ten camps with assigned A-Teams operating throughout I Corps.

The second priority was more difficult: continuous daylight visual reconnaissance of the entire I Corps Tactical Zone. Adequately fulfilling this intelligence-gathering requirement meant breaking I Corps into thirty-two sub areas, each with a letter and a number designation (C-3, B-4, etc.), then daily assigning the areas to individual pilots as primary and secondary areas for VR. The intent was that each individual aviator would become so familiar with his assigned area that he would immediately recognize any change from the norm. For each mission, the unit being supported would provide the observer in the back seat. Whether a Marine AO, a Navy ANGLICO, an ARVN officer, or a Special Forces NCO occupied the back seat of our aircraft depended on the type of mission and the area flown during that mission.

As soon as the 220th became operational, each sector and regiment of the different commands wanted an airplane for its own use stationed at small, remote airstrips located throughout I Corps. Although this arrangement was being used in other Corps Tactical Zones, Major Curry,

CO of the 220th, insisted on unit integrity and refused to allow this course of action. He felt it better to assign each individual platoon to the 3 major operational areas of I Corps and concluded if aircraft and pilots from each platoon returned to their home base each evening, a much higher level of mission accomplishment could be achieved. He reasoned that better maintenance and more latitude in aircraft and pilot scheduling would result. He was correct: The 220th aircraft availability rate remained at nearly 90 percent its first year, and the aircraft accumulated over 12,000 hours of flight time. During the 220th's six-and-a-half-year existence, the annual average availability never dropped below 85 percent. During this period, the 220th's aircraft accumulated 151,208 total flight hours with no more than 32 aircraft assigned at any given time.

Instead of scattering the 220th's Birddogs throughout I Corps, Major Curry sent the 1st Platoon to Quang Ngai on the coast near the southern edge of I Corps; there they supported the 1st Marine Division enclave at Chu Lai, a few miles north, as well as the 1st ARVN Division and the Special Forces (SF) camp at Kham Duc, near the Cambodian border. The 2nd Platoon went to Hue, a few miles northeast of company headquarters at Phu Bai. The dirt airstrip there was inside the city walls, next to the Citadel, the historical royal grounds of Vietnam's ancient rulers. These troops supported the 3rd Marine Division located in the Phu Bai enclave as well as the MACV headquarters and the 1st ARVN Ranger Battalion, both located at Hue. The 3rd Platoon was located at Da Nang Main Air Force Base along with Marine fixed-wing and rotor-wing aircraft until the Marines completed the MMAF in August 1965; at that time all Marine helicopter units were relocated there. The two-thousand-foot runway at MMAF was more than adequate to operate Birddogs, so the 3rd Platoon of the 220th went with them. The 3rd Platoon with its eight pilots and nine aircraft supported the 1st Marine Division activities around Da Nang and the Que Son Valley. It also supported the ARVN near the Hoi An sector headquarters and the Special Forces camps at A Shau and Thuong Duc. The 4th Platoon was initially detached to the 219th RAC operating to the south in II

Corps. The 220th was left with just three operational platoons (twenty-four aircraft) to cover all tasked missions in I Corps during its first twenty months in Vietnam. In April 1967 the 4th Platoon was brought back home and assigned to fly the DMZ out of Dong Ha, located some ten miles south of North Vietnam.

Although the support of the Army Special Forces in I Corps was not the primary mission of the 220th, our Special Forces brothers could always count on the Catkillers for support when needed. This was never more apparent than in March 1966 when the Special Forces camp at A Shau in the A Shau Valley fell under siege. On March 4 the Special Forces command requested a reconnaissance of the A Shau Valley. When the Catkillers of the 2nd Platoon flew over the Special Forces camp there, they found a massive force of Viet Cong surrounding the camp. Additional VR flights were conducted in deteriorating weather on March 5 and 6.

Early in the morning of March 8, 1966, the Viet Cong began a series of massive attacks that lasted for four days. During that period, pilots from the 220th flew visual reconnaissance, ran air strikes, and even evacuated a seriously wounded Special Forces sergeant. This was all accomplished under a solid cloud cover so low that Air Force Birddog pilots were restricted from flying beneath it. Not so the Catkillers. They flew a total of ninety-one sorties over the A Shau camp during a four-day siege and the eventual fall and abandonment of the camp. Because of their heroic actions under intense enemy ground fire, Catkiller pilots were recommended for a total of two Air Medals (with "V" device), eight Distinguished Flying Crosses, one Distinguished Service Cross, and a Valorous Unit Citation.

This action cemented the bond between the Catkillers and the U.S. Army Special Forces in I Corps. Because Special Forces were highly trained in unconventional warfare and counterinsurgency and their mission was the interdiction and border surveillance of enemy troop movements from Laos into South Vietnam, they always established their A-Team encampments in remote areas of I Corps astride enemy infiltration routes. They formed Civilian Irregular Defense Groups (CIDG) from minority ethnic and religious groups, commonly known as Montagnards. These were tribal people who lived in the remote mountainous areas of South Vietnam and did not like the lowland South Vietnamese or North Vietnamese. This made for a natural tendency for them to affiliate with U.S. Special Forces soldiers who lived with them and taught them military skills. The CIDG program was intended to provide an area secure from Viet Cong influence and terror, help the Montagnards develop their own self-defense program, and elicit their support for the South Vietnamese government. They seemed to be fairly successful at accomplishing the first two goals, but centuries of distrust between the Montagnards and the lowland Vietnamese precluded success with the third.

Air was the usual way of reinforcing and supplying these remote outposts, making it necessary to construct a primitive airstrip for cargo airplanes. The Army found its fleet of de Havilland Caribous met this requirement perfectly, and the Special Forces relied heavily on them for routine resupply of just about everything from medical supplies to bullets. They relied on the 220th pilots and their Cessna O-1 Birddogs for visual reconnaissance of their immediate areas of responsibility.

By the time I arrived at the 3rd Platoon in July 1967, the A Shau camp had fallen but, we still supported the reinforced Special Forces camp at Thuong Duc, which lay about twenty-five miles southwest of Da Nang and was located on a small hill overlooking the Song Vu Gia (River Vu Gia). Because the river ran east out of the mountains and the A Shau Valley and Laos were just thirty or so miles to the west, Song Vu Gia was a potential infiltration route into the area around Da Nang. That camp placement allowed Special Forces personnel and their indigent CIDG soldiers to monitor enemy activity. They patrolled and conducted ambushes and assorted small-unit actions in an attempt to discourage the NVA from infiltrating into the lowland built-up areas around Da Nang.

The thriving village of Thuong Duc was located just at the base of the hill below the Special Forces camp. The twelve-man Special Forces A-Team (A-109) that operated there maintained an active role in the community. Catkiller pilots of the 3rd Platoon flew frequent VR missions around Thuong Duc with the A-Team intelligence sergeant in the back seat. He always appreciated an aerial view of their area of operations. We would look for bridges, sampans, bad guys, and increased trail activity. The more frequently dirt trails were walked on, the shinier they became—a dead giveaway of increased infiltration by the Viet Cong and NVA. The Catkiller pilots themselves may have occasionally instigated the flights, but a working relationship had emerged out of the A Shau battle and we were always interested in keeping our Special Forces brothers under our wing, so to speak, through supporting them and their efforts.

Late in September I had flown a VR mission for them, and Captain (Duy Wi in Vietnamese, pronounced Di We) Edwards, the A-109 Team commander, subsequently invited me to come out some time and receive a guided tour of their camp and the village. I asked 1st Lt. Rick Vance, one of my fellow pilots, if he would be interested in the two of us flying out together, with Rick taking the Intel sergeant up while I took the tour. Rick said yes, and this set up a very interesting and enlightening day for me.

The Special Forces encampment was located on a small, elongated hill immediately west of the village of Thuong Duc. It had the trenches, bunkers, and firing positions of a typical A-Team facility, but instead of the usual triangle-shaped trench lines was oval in appearance and followed the contour line near the hilltop. The jungle-covered mountains of the Annamite Range rose abruptly behind the village all the way west to the A Shau Valley and Laos. The camp overlooked the village of Thuong Duc and the activity that went on there.

In the Thuong Duc small marketplace Vietnamese women, in black pajama-like pants and shirts and large straw conical hats, squatted behind baskets of everything from fish to vegetables while small children swarmed constantly around them. The level of activity could be compared to that of a small shopping mall back in the United States.

This activity began early in the day and generally continued until whatever they were selling or bartering was gone. The smaller Song Con

(River Con) flowed into the Song Vu Gia along the east side of Thuong Duc. A small concrete bridge spanning the Song Con was located on a dirt road that led past the two-thousand-foot grass landing strip and on toward Da Nang. The Song Con seemed to be the heart of activity in Thuong Duc: villagers washed their clothes and water buffalo, bathed, and fished there while the children played and swam there. It seemed likely the river was the disposal site for all of the village's waste and garbage; it looked pretty muddy to begin with, but that didn't seem to bother anyone.

A local industry seemed to be thriving there as well. I saw two men using a primitive bucksaw, cutting logs lengthwise to make lumber. They had placed the roughly ten-foot-long log in a "V" made from poles, with one end elevated. One man stood on the log, the other on the ground below. They were drawing the long saw blade back and forth in a steady motion. I asked Captain Edwards what they were doing, and he replied they were making lumber. My response was, "That sure seems to take a lot of time and effort for just a few boards." That was when I received my Sociology 101 lesson.

"The last thing they need is a labor-saving device. They all need to feel that they are a productive part of the community. It's a pretty basic human need and the glue that holds societies together," he said.

"Let me tell you a story, he began. "A few months ago, we *liberated* [Special Forces soldiers did a lot of that] a Mercedes Benz engine and large circular saw blade and built them a small sawmill. We presented this labor-saving device to the village chief, and there was a big celebration with lots of smiles all around. What we didn't realize was the last thing they needed was a labor-saving sawmill. Those two men you see down there sawing are considered craftsmen and hold very important positions in the community.

"About two weeks after we gave them the sawmill, the village chief came to me and told me that they couldn't use it because the blade was too thick and it wasted too much wood. He had probably spent the entire two weeks trying to think of a reason to not use the sawmill without offending me. Saving face is a very important concept in this culture, and to offend someone who has given you a gift is a dishonorable thing to do, so he had to come up with a reason that wouldn't offend me."

As the tour continued, I noticed other indications of everyone contributing. No one seemed to be just standing around. A man and a boy I assumed to be his son, probably around ten or twelve years old, came walking into the village from the jungle. Each was carrying bamboo poles. The father was carrying four or five poles that looked to be some fifteen feet long while his son was carrying the same number of poles, smaller in diameter and just five or six feet long. A simple task, but each in his own way according to his abilities, while contributing to the whole.

The next stop was the small, open school where a young Vietnamese Catholic priest was teaching what appeared to be first-grade children. I brought along several bags of candy I had purchased the day before at the Base Exchange at China Beach. I had asked Captain Edwards to inquire of the priest if he would allow us to pass out the candy, and he told Captain Edwards that it was okay. All of the children sat quietly, looking at the candy with very big eyes (how do children just know when something is going to taste good, even if they have never seen it before?) as it was passed out, not one of them touching any until the priest told them they could. There were lots of smiles as the sweets quickly disappeared. I noticed they had been writing in little tablets with double lines that were spaced farther apart, with a dashed line in between—exactly like tablets used by first- and second-grade kids in the United States. The only difference was that they were writing in Vietnamese. How similar most cultures are in wanting their children to be able to read and write. Maybe there is hope for humanity in spite of war.

I took some pictures of the market, of activity at the river, and of the children at the school. Then it was time to drive back down to the airfield, as I saw Vance was circling to land. For the first time I was seeing the Vietnamese people as they lived out their lives in their primarily agrarian society. These were the people who were affected by the war but were not part of the cultural interface between east and west I saw near Marble Mountain and anyplace where there were lots of American soldiers and Marines. These were the real people of Vietnam. They lived an uncluttered life. Granted, they were not at the pinnacle of Maslow's hierarchy of human needs, but they were finding ways to meet their basic needs of food, shelter, and social order under the protective umbrella of Special Forces soldiers who had extensive training in how to deal with, and integrate themselves into, the Vietnamese culture. My day at Thuong Duc had definitely been worth the trip.

I was becoming intrigued with Thuong Duc and what the Special Forces men appeared to be accomplishing there. I was seeing what I interpreted to be the positive side of the war. I began to think our being there would have a lasting effect, so I flew out there every chance I got. As I was soon to find out, Thuong Duc would also present another lesson or two.

A week or two later, I flew out there to take the Special Forces intelligence sergeant up for a visual recon of the surrounding hills and jungle. I had called Thong Duc Special Forces camp on the radio to tell them I was landing. By the time I had landed, taxied to the approach end of the grass runway, and shut down, I could see their three-quarter-ton truck leaving the camp and moving down the dirt road toward me. Just about then, a de Havilland Caribou (now belonging to and being flown by our Air Force boys in blue) whistled in and landed. It came to a halt some distance down the runway, turned back and taxied toward me and my Birddog, then did a 180-degree turn and pointed the nose back down the runway. As I stood there watching, the loading ramp at the rear of the Caribou lowered to about five feet above the ground, and one of the crew members pushed a wood pallet of supplies right to the edge of the ramp.

What I witnessed next will forever serve as a metaphor for the scorn the Air Force seemed to have toward any requirement to directly support the Army. Just as the three Special Forces NCOs drove their three-quarter-ton truck through the gate, no more than fifty feet from the rear of the Caribou and its semi-lowered ramp and in full view of the crew member standing there, the pilots applied full power to the engines and released the brakes. As the aircraft lurched forward, the crew member on the ramp literally kicked the pallet off the ramp and let it fall to the ground the remaining five feet. The Special Forces sergeants were livid! More than a few unkind words were shouted toward the Air Force Caribou and its crew as it departed.

At that moment I recalled a scene I had observed more than a year earlier in the casual bar of the Lawson Army Airfield Officers Club at Fort Benning. Air Force pilots were voicing their displeasure with being required to fly the Caribou. My suspicions that what I had just seen on the runway was an intentional act were confirmed by the three Special Forces sergeants: Air Force Caribou pilots frequently would not wait for them, and whatever fragile items were on the pallet, such as medical supplies, would probably be damaged and unusable. Had the pilots waited just a few more minutes, they would have backed the truck up to the ramp and off-loaded the pallet directly onto the back. The sergeants told me that when the Army flew the Caribous and resupplied them in their faraway little corners of Vietnam, their pilots always waited and the crew members always helped them load their supplies into their trucks.

Maybe the Air Force pilots were concerned about being shot at while they were on the ground, but nobody was shooting at me, and I had been standing there for several minutes beside my airplane with the engine shut down. Maybe they were behind schedule in their deliveries, but another three or four minutes on the ground couldn't have made that much difference. Or maybe, just maybe, they had a hot date waiting for them back at the Air Force Officers Club at Nha Trang or Saigon. We will never know, but we Army soldiers will always have our suspicions.

A more personal matter: on November 8, I landed at Thuong Duc with my Marine AO, 1st Lt. Rob Whitlow. We had been working in the Que Son Valley just across the mountain range to the south and were more or less heading home to Marble Mountain. There was just one problem: I really had to take a leak and knew I wasn't going to make it home in time. The little airstrip at Thuong Duc was just off to our left, and I knew I had to land there before my bladder burst.

I told Whitlow what I was going to do there and why, but he wasn't having any of it. His feeling was that I was putting him in jeopardy because it wasn't a "secure" airfield and I could damn well hold it until we got to a "safe" airfield, specifically Marble Mountain. Unfortunately, my discomfort was reaching epic proportions, and I let him know that we were landing there regardless of his feelings about a secure environment.

That was when my AO and friend, Rob Whitlow, threatened to shoot me with his .45-caliber pistol if I persisted. I quickly reminded him that if he shot me he would be losing his pilot and he just might have to walk the thirty or so miles through hostile territory to Marble Mountain.

Now my discomfort level was really spiking. I was either going to pee in my pants or get shot. Sweating bullets (almost literally), I pulled the throttle back, lowered flaps, and made a very short approach to one of my less remarkable landings. I didn't even taxi back to the approach end of the runway. I just braked hard to a stop, unbuckled my seat belt and shoulder harness, flung open my cockpit door, jumped out, and peed right beside the airplane not caring at that moment who might be watching . . . or shooting!

Rob didn't shoot me, and I was successful in relieving my discomfort. I did make a concession and left the engine running while I jumped out and peed, with Whitlow sitting in the aircraft and scanning the nearby tree line for hostile movement, M-16 rifle in hand. He grumbled at me during the entire flight to Marble Mountain and, to this day, periodically reminds me the only reason he didn't shoot me was because he didn't know how to fly the airplane himself. Marines do tend to have a strange sense of humor, and I still don't know for sure whether or not he was just kidding.

My last flight to Thuong Duc took place on Christmas Day 1967 and involved the 212th Aviation Battalion commander, a lieutenant colonel, and his favorite ice cream. Although the 220th RAC was operationally under the control of the Marines, administratively we were then under the command of the Army's newly formed 212th Aviation Battalion whose headquarters had been located at Marble Mountain in August. That meant the Marines told us where and when to fly. But our food, pay, records, and supplies were controlled by the Army's 212th Aviation Battalion.

We who flew low and slow in support of our brothers on the ground, exposing ourselves to the same hazards, tended to have disdain for those who didn't. They included very senior officers and their staff of administrative types, who spent their days in offices in buildings located within a secure perimeter of barbed wire and sentries armed with rifles and machine guns. We were willing to concede that those who fulfilled support roles such as logistics and administration did play a role in winning the war, but I think most of us who actually spent time in direct contact with the enemy felt our level of risk was substantially greater. Therefore, whenever we found an opportunity to "get one over" on those who we considered REMFs (rear echelon motherf**kers), we took it.

Two days earlier on a flight to Thuong Duc, I had asked the Special Forces guys if there was anything I could bring out on my next trip. I expected them to ask for adult beverages. Apparently they had all they needed in that department because they asked for milk and fresh vegetables—no particular kind as long as they were fresh. This simple request got me to thinking that maybe a little something extra was in order, so I enlisted fellow 3rd Platoon pilot 1st Lt. Jimmy Wall in a plot to take a carton of ice cream to the A-Team at Thuong Duc. After all it was Christmas.

All Army personnel at Marble Mountain Air Facility ate at the 282nd HC mess hall, which included the 212th Aviation Battalion headquarters personnel and its office-occupying senior officers. Every once in a while we were treated to ice cream for dessert, and I was determined to take some to our Special Forces pals at Thuong Duc. I knew better than to simply ask for it because mess sergeants tended to get quite possessive when it came to just giving away anything of value; they generally demanded something in trade. Since neither Wall nor I had anything to trade, we decided to simply liberate any ice cream we could get our hands on.

So there we were, Jimmy Wall and I, two young first lieutenants standing in the 282nd AHC mess hall, about to ask the mess sergeant if he could spare some fresh vegetables and a large container of milk for the Special Forces soldiers at their remote camp at Thuong Duc. How could he turn down a simple request like that? Wall and I introduced ourselves and presented our very short list of items.

"Hey sarge, the Special Forces guys out at Thuong Duc asked us if we could maybe bring them some fresh veggies and a container of milk the next time we flew out there. We're heading out there this morning and were wondering if you could spare anything," I asked.

"What've you got in mind, lieutenant?" the mess sergeant asked.

"Whatever you can spare. I don't think they really care, just so it's fresh," I replied.

"I think I might have an extra case of carrots and a two-gallon container of milk back in the cooler that I can let you have. C'mon, follow me back and I'll get them for you," our now magnanimous mess sergeant said, sort of getting into the whole Christmas Spirit thing.

After all it was just milk and carrots, and a lot of the troops he fed every day didn't appreciate fresh carrots anyway. He'd probably seen them end up in the garbage lots of times. So back we went to the mess hall storage area. There were shelves of canned goods and assorted non-perishable items like large cans of coffee and large jars of condiments.

To the Army's credit, it did try to feed its soldiers fresh food as often as it could, but when they were out in the boonies, about all they got were C-rations or Long Range Reconnaissance Patrol (LRRP) rations. Sometimes, they got nothing at all. LRRP rations were dehydrated or freeze-dried food. C-rations were small cans of food ranging from beans and weenies to scrambled eggs with ham chunks to—my least favorite—ham and lima beans. Each C-ration came in a small box that also contained such delicacies as peach slices (my personal favorite) or fruit cocktail. There was also either a small can of bread or crackers and jelly or peanut butter. Soldiers and Marines whose job was long-range patrolling for several days at a time preferred LRRP rations to C-rations because they were smaller and lighter. All they had to do was add water. When soldiers were humping the hills in the jungle of Vietnam with everything they needed to survive in a pack on their backs (including bullets), lighter was better.

In the back of the large storage area stood an enormous walk-in cooler and that's where we were headed. The mess sergeant opened the cooler door with a flourish and there inside was a cornucopia of culinary delights: several two-gallon containers of milk, boxes of fresh vegetables, meat, eggs, and other perishables—an enormous amount of fresh food, everything necessary to provide over 250 hungry men (flight crew, aircraft mechanics, and battalion weenies) 3 meals a day, every day.

He pointed to the milk containers and told me to go ahead and take one while he and Wall went deeper into the cooler to find a case of carrots. As I stepped out of the cooler I noticed a couple of large chest freezers against the wall. I quickly went over and lifted the lid of one of them. There, stacked one upon the other were several large cylindrical containers like the ones at Baskin-Robbins that just had to be ice cream. I quickly closed the lid and turned a moment before Wall and the mess sergeant exited the walk-in cooler, each of them lugging what looked to be about forty pounds of carrots in wooden crates.

Trying to look innocent, I inquired, "Hey sarge, are these freezers over here against the wall?"

"Yes, that's where I keep stuff that has to remain frozen, like ice cream and such," came the reply.

"Is that what's in this one?" I asked, pointing to the one I had opened.

"Well, that one has the colonel's ice cream in it. He really likes French vanilla, so when I get some of that flavor, I set it aside."

Jackpot! Wall caught my eye, and I could see from the expression on his face he was thinking, *No Ray, not that ice cream.* But it was too late. I had made up my mind and my thought process went something like this: *The colonel, the battalion commander, who sits here at Marble Mountain in his nice, cozy office all safe and secure while the Special Forces guys are out there hanging their asses out. Just how much ice cream does this guy need? There are four of those cartons in there and he won't miss one of them. A whole container of ice cream would be like manna from heaven to the Special Forces guys, and Wall and I are going to get it for them for Christmas.*

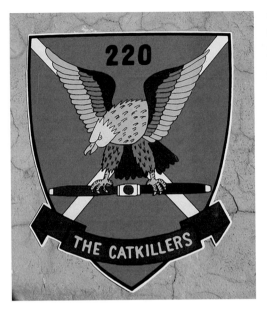

Catkiller Crest. Background is a shield with the white cross of St. Andrew in a field of red with a black border. It is based on the family crest of the first commanding officer of the 220th, Maj. Jerry Curry. A preying eagle clutching an aircraft propeller surmounts the shield in the center. The eagle exemplifies the ever-watchful and all-seeing eyes of aerial observation. On the shield in top center is the number 220, and across the bottom a streamer is unfurled bearing the legend THE CAT-KILLERS. *Author's collection*

Me and my Birdddog. Photo was taken at 3rd Platoon, MMAF. Note CAR-15 rifle and flak vest, our only personal protection. *Author's collection*

TPQ bombing of railroad bridge south of Da Nang. The bridge was already unusable. My role was to adjust the impact point of the bombs until they hit precisely on the eight-digit coordinates I had been given. The coordinates corresponded exactly with the north end of the bridge, thus calibrating the controlling ground site radar. *Author's collection*

Old French coastal fort. These forts were constructed when France occupied Vietnam and were placed periodically along the coast of Vietnam in I Corps. They were an interesting addition to the often beautiful Vietnam coastline. *Author's collection*

Wild Night in the Valley aftermath. The violence is well represented by the white napalm residue, the bomb craters, and the burned remnants of structures and tree lines. *Author's collection*

Birddog at Thuong Duc. Lt. Rick Vance with an SF NCO in the back seat after performing a visual reconnaissance flight around Thuong Duc while I was getting a tour. *Author's collection*

Cutting lumber at Thuong Duc village. The amount of activity along the river next to the village was amazing. People were fishing, washing clothes, and bathing while children were swimming, all under the protective umbrella of SF A Team A-109. *Author's collection*

Lieutenants Rick Johnson, Raymond Caryl, and David O'Hare at 220th company headquarters, Phu Bai, Christmas dinner 1967. *David O'Hare photo collection*

282nd AHC Black Cat Huey at Hoi An. The 282nd logo, a three-legged cat in a yellow circle, is clearly visible. Pilots CWO Dick Messer (on left), CWO Bart Colburn (on right, gloved hand sticking out of open door), and Sgt. Wade (crew chief). These young warrant officers and their crews were fearless professionals. *Author's collection*

Air America Pilatus Porter at Hoi An. This odd-looking aircraft could land and take off almost anywhere. This is the aircraft that a few minutes later startled the heck out of me at the other end of the runway. *Author's collection*

Dandy Dancer convoy traffic jam at bridge north of Hai Van Pass. The Marine convoy is moving from right to left and the lead element has already crossed the bridge. The ARVN convoy is attempting to cross from left to right and was second to arrive at the bridge. Result: Chaos. *Author's collection*

Missed me. Two AK-47 rounds came up from below while I was making a low pass, shooting my CAR-15 out the open side window at two NVA soldiers. Somehow the bullets came up through the open bottom of the engine compartment, missing both the engine and the firewall, exiting up through the left-side engine cowling. There are less than six inches separating the engine and its components from the firewall. My feet were just inches behind the firewall. It is good to be lucky. *Author's Collection*

The Ben Hai River looking west. This is the DMZ, and the Ben Hai River separates North and South Vietnam. North Vietnam is on the right. The entire DMZ was completely covered with artillery craters and bomb craters, giving it an eerie and threatening appearance. *Author's collection*

Bridge across the Ben Hai River. The North Vietnamese flag (red with a gold star) flies at the north end of the bridge. The bridge was named the Hien Luong and was also called the Peace Bridge. We Catkillers who flew the DMZ knew it as Freedom Bridge. We would occasionally try to blow down the flag using artillery and calling in a phony target south of the bridge, then adjusting the rounds north. *Author's collection*

Crash landing at Dong Ha. This "successful" landing on May 12, 1968, was caused by an exploding 1st Cav helicopter tearing the left main landing gear from my Birddog in flight, forcing me to return to Dong Ha and attempt a landing. The result was a perfectly good Birddog destroyed and an Army artillery observer and me wondering how we had survived. Note the smoke grenades attached to the fuselage beneath the observer's window. If the ground attack jets were having difficulty finding us, the observer would reach out and pull the pin in the smoke grenade, and we would fly in a tight circle trailing colored smoke. This modification was exclusive to the 220th RAC. *Author's collection*

Attempted R&R flight hijack at Da Nang. The alleged hijacker, second in line coming down the airstair in the dark jacket, had a .45-caliber pistol and wanted the Pan Am flight crew to take him to Communist China, not Hong Kong. *Author's collection*

Catkiller pilots Gene Frey and Gary O'Shields standing at the entrance to our company bunker at Phu Bai during Tet 1968. The "bunker" was constructed from fifty-five-gallon drums filled with dirt and set on end. Perforated steel planking (used to make temporary runways and parking ramps) was then laid on top with a layer of dirt-filled sandbags and dirt piled on top. It might have stopped a mortar round, but it would provide zero protection from an NVA 122-mm rocket. I did not like bunkers and would rather be in the sky getting shot at than hunkered down in one of these. *Author's collection*

Birddog over Hoi Ann. This is me attempting a Split-S, but our D-model Birddogs were so heavy that the nose fell through early. *Author's collection*

My partner in crime instantly picked up on what I was going to do and provided an excellent diversion by telling our friendly mess sergeant that we really didn't think the Special Forces guys needed two cartons of carrots and we could put one back. As soon as the sergeant disappeared back into the cooler, I grabbed the carton of ice cream in one hand and the two-gallon container of milk in the other and was out the back door like a shot. I heard Wall shouting "Thank you!" to the mess sergeant as I ran across the parking ramp toward my aircraft.

A few seconds later, as I was putting on my flight gear, Wall came puffing up carrying the crate of carrots. He didn't look too pleased that I had left him to carry the carrots while I had merely a couple of pounds of ice cream and milk. We both quickly loaded our swag into the back seats of our aircraft, securing it with the seat belts. A few minutes later we were airborne and heading for Thuong Duc, a flight of two bringing a little Christmas cheer to a lonely Special Forces outpost a long, long way from home.

Earlier, when I had done my preflight inspection of my aircraft, I'd asked one of the crew chiefs to secure a green and red smoke grenade under the wings and attach some safety wire to the pins so I could activate them in flight. Thuong Duc was approximately a fifteen-minute flight from Marble Mountain, and as we approached I dialed up their FM radio frequency and started singing "Jingle Bells." I cannot sing, so one verse was all they got, but it was enough to get the message across that we were inbound. I then pulled the safety wires on the smoke grenades and circled their compound at about two hundred feet, trailing red and green smoke. I told them that I had a "highly sensitive" item on board from Santa and requested that they immediately send someone down to the airfield to retrieve it.

Wall and I landed our Birddogs and taxied back to the approach end, then shut down. A couple of minutes later three Special Forces sergeants came rumbling up in their three-quarter-ton truck. Their faces lit up when Wall presented the carrots to them. They were still expressing their gratitude when I reached into the back seat of my Birddog and pulled out the two-gallon container of milk and the now slightly squishy carton of ice cream and announced, "Here's something special that we liberated for your Christmas enjoyment." The expressions on their faces were worth any repercussions I might suffer should the mess sergeant ever figure out what I had done while he was distracted.

We all immediately climbed into the truck and roared up the hill into their compound. By this time, the carton was beginning to really get soft as the ice cream rapidly reached the consistency of a milkshake. We rushed into the bunker that served as their Tactical Operations Center (TOC) and the celebration began. Each member of the A-Team got a canteen cup full, and seeing their sheer joy at downing the creamy liquid reaffirmed my feelings: it is the simple things in life that really count.

After telling them the story of how Wall and I had liberated some of the colonel's private stash, we were congratulated for being nearly as sneaky as they were at liberating things they needed that others weren't actually using. This being a long-practiced tradition of Special Forces, Wall and I felt honored to receive such a compliment from real pros. I had heard it said that a stolen watermelon was tastier than one that's been paid for, and now I was convinced the same holds true for ice cream.

13 | Kentucky Windage, Enemy Rockets, and a Near Catastrophe

Catkillers flew Birddogs armed with four WP rockets loaded into twin tubes mounted under each wing. We used WPs to mark targets for the fixed-wing jets; occasionally we popped one at the VC or NVA if we were too far out in the boonies to call up artillery or if the target simply didn't warrant scrambling a flight of jets to drop bombs and napalm.

One day in October, I was low bird on a two-ship visual recon flight in Indian Country west of Thuong Duc when I spotted two sampans making their way east on the Vu Gia River. Clearly visible in each sampan were two NVA soldiers clad in green uniforms with what looked like cargo hidden under tarps. As soon as the NVA soldiers in the sampans saw us they maneuvered to the riverbank and disappeared into the thick vegetation. Requesting a flight of jets to run on the sampans wasn't an option because we were short on fuel and could not wait for them to arrive. We were beyond the range of friendly artillery, so running an arty mission wasn't in the cards either. There was nothing left for us to do but try to hit the sampans with our rockets. I immediately radioed my high ship and pointed out the two sampans below. We quickly decided that the best course of action was to shoot our rockets at the sampans and see if we could at least destroy whatever cargo they had on board, because the NVA soldiers appeared to be long gone. As the low ship, I was first to shoot up the sampans.

This tactic came with a built-in caveat: the Birddog wasn't a gunship and didn't have a sighting system. Trying to hit a target without a gunsight was tricky. The phrase "Zen-State and Kentucky Windage" best describes the technique I used. Some of our Birddogs had a .25-inch-diameter rod vertically brazed to the front of the engine cowling that some of our pilots used as a front sight in conjunction with a grease pencil mark on the windscreen. To sight in on their target before firing rockets, they used the rod and the mark much as one would use the front and rear sights of a rifle. Each pilot would put his own grease pencil mark on the windshield so, over time, grease marks would accumulate and make it nearly impossible to figure out which one was yours.

This technique didn't work for me. Instead, I used another that didn't require a metal rod or a grease pencil mark yet proved to be very accurate when marking targets for the jet attack aircraft. In September I had discovered that "lagging" off a bit from the target but keeping it in sight worked well for me. Then, when I was just the right distance away (that was the Zen-State part), I'd turn back toward the target, pull on the carb heat so the engine wouldn't quit, close the throttle, and let the nose drop. This put me in a coordinated descent with the nose right on the target. During this maneuver, I'd arm a rocket by flipping an overhead switch and remove the safety pin from the control stick. Then, with my nose on the target with just the right amount of lead right or left (the Kentucky Windage part), I'd squeeze the trigger and . . . *BANG—WHOOSH!* the rocket was away straight and true to the target. Then I'd make a quick climbing turn away from the target and watch the impact over my shoulder. This way I never overflew the target and managed to stay out of range of enemy small-arms fire. This wasn't the way the Army had taught us to do it in flight school, but it worked very well for me and over time my accuracy improved significantly.

Unfortunately, this time my lagging off technique wasn't going to work because the river lay in a gorge and there were steep mountain ridges on three sides of the sampans' position. The best I could hope to do was climb a bit, chop the power, let the nose drop, and quickly fire a rocket before my airspeed could build up and cause the rocket to fly off target.

My wingman and I tried to make a game of it competing to see who could hit the sampans. We must have looked like a couple of demented buzzards the way we were maneuvering around in the restricted airspace of the steep-sided gorge. I did get the closest but still missed the sampans by a few feet, the muddy soil absorbing the impacts and mitigating the destructive ability of our rockets. All of that effort and still we caused no apparent damage to either sampan. Close only counts in horseshoes.

Damn!

Deciding that we had provided enough entertainment to our adversaries for one day, my wingman and I gave this one to Charlie and headed for home. I did call the Special Forces camp at Thuong Duc on their FM frequency and gave them the coordinates and description of what we had encountered. After we landed I wrote it up on the mission debrief form. The bad guys lived to fight another day, but we probably caused some soiled laundry with our antics. And they knew that we knew they were out there and would be constantly looking for them.

The NVA soldiers had some pretty interesting rockets themselves. Their 122-mm ground-launched rockets were not only lethal but psychologically terrifying because of the shrill screech they emitted as they flew through the air. They had a range of about ten thousand meters, and the NVA soldiers were masters at setting them up at a certain angle and pointed in the direction of whatever it was they wanted to hit. Pinpoint accuracy was not what they were looking for, but rather area targets such as an airfield or major encampment with lots of our troops in it. They would survey the point they intended to shoot from, mark it, and return at a later date under cover of darkness to unleash their screaming hell on unsuspecting troops or vulnerable equipment left outside such as aircraft or vehicles. As for a warning of incoming, forget it. By the time soldiers heard the screech it was too late; they were either going to be hit or not. Marble Mountain airfield and our company headquarters at Phu Bai were favorite targets for their 122-mm rockets. Once heard, their blood-chilling shriek was never forgotten.

One night at Phu Bai, after I had been transferred to the 4th Platoon, the NVA unleashed a volley of 122s, some of which seemed to impact in the 131st Aviation Company area right next to us. When dawn broke a few of the 220th Catkiller pilots emerged from their bunker and ambled next door to survey the damage. Word had spread that a couple of the 131st buildings had been hit, but fortunately no one had been injured or killed.

The 131st pilots flew the Grumman Mohawk, a powerful twin-turbine surveillance aircraft that located the enemy with side-looking airborne radar (SLAR) and infrared (IR) systems. When looking for enemy infiltration routes, they also had a platoon of Mohawks armed with 2.75-inch rockets, .50-caliber machine guns, and cameras that flew "out of country" missions over the Ho Chi Minh trail in Laos. They would conduct photo reconnaissance and were cleared to attack any targets of opportunity they should happen to find. These VR missions were flown only in the daytime whereas most IR and SLAR missions were flown at night. The SLAR and IR imagery as well as any photos were processed right at the 131st and then forwarded to higher headquarters for action. Because of all the developing and interpreting equipment they had and because the process was a 24/7 operation, the 131st had two large 150-kilowatt generators running continuously that were maintained by several young enlisted men. So critical were the generators that someone actually stood by them all night long.

On the night of the 122-mm rocket attack, the young enlisted guard was reclining on his cot in a sleeping bag to keep warm (it got cold in I Corps in the winter) when the barrage came screaming in. It was over as quickly as it had begun, and our young intrepid warrior had not even had time to budge much less scamper to a nearby bunker. We heard that one of the generators had been damaged, so we walked over to check it out. The young guard was still sitting on his cot, somewhat dazed and shaking his head as we approached.

"Rough night?" asked one of the guys in our group.

"Yes sir, it sure was," he replied in a voice that seemed to be a bit shaken about something that had already happened.

"You okay?" someone else asked.

Without saying a word, the young soldier simply pointed to a three-inch diameter hole in the clapboard wall about twelve inches above the head of his cot. He slowly shook his head and muttered, "I was lyin' down in my sleeping bag when that sucker went off and a piece of shrapnel flew right above me and through that wall. If I'd been sittin' up, it woulda gone right through me."

"Wow!" was the collective response from his small audience. For once, "lying down on the job" had paid a huge dividend: the guy was still alive.

Rockets were weapons that were dangerous not only to the enemy but also to those of us who had to handle them. The Army and Marine helicopter gunships used 2.75-inch HE rockets to blow stuff up. Birddogs used 2.75-inch WP rockets, commonly called Willie Petes, to mark targets so the jet attack aircraft could blow stuff up. There were some other types of 2.75-inch rockets the helicopter gunships used as well: two examples were flechette rockets containing little needles for shredding enemy soldiers and smoke rockets for masking activity from the enemy.

We Birddog pilots of the 220th stuck to Willie Petes to mark targets, which had to be loaded with care. Willie Petes were propelled by a solid fuel contained within each rocket but were ignited by an electrical charge delivered through a firing mechanism rotated over the rear of each rocket after it was loaded into the tube.

Part of our preflight check for each mission was to ensure the arming switches located overhead in the cockpit were off and the safety pin properly installed in the trigger switch located on the control stick. To arm the rockets we would start the engine, maneuver the aircraft so it pointed away from buildings and people, place our hands on the diagonal cross tubes above the instrument panel where our crew chief could see them, and give him a nod. This action assured him that we were not touching any switches and that he was clear to arm the rockets. He would then stand under each wing in turn and flip the metal contact arms so they touched the rear of each rocket. This was always a moment of concern because if for some reason the circuit to the contact arm was "hot," the rocket would fire and the crew chief could receive some pretty serious burns. Because of this danger the crew chiefs were provided with large, insulated gloves that extended up past the elbow to wear during the arming procedure. They rarely bothered to wear them, however.

The importance of using the gloves was driven home one morning when Sp4 José Munoz, one of our crew chiefs, was arming the rockets for one of our 3rd Platoon pilots. Fortunately, José was standing just to the side at the rear of the rocket tube as he flipped the contact arm or his burns would have been even worse than they were. They weren't serious enough to evacuate him back to the States or put him in the hospital, but he did spend several days with his arm and hand heavily bandaged. From that day onward, our crew chiefs wore the gloves when arming our rockets.

The Birddog electrical system was rudimentary and probably not designed for the rockets we carried, creating an occasional malfunction. Sometimes rockets wouldn't fire, or worse, they would fire when we did not want them to. The actual circuitry remains a mystery to me, but I'll never forget the day I nearly shot down a Marine H-53 with a Willie Pete.

My Marine AO and I had been working our tactical area of responsibility south of Hoi An where some NVA survivors of Operation Swift were still moving around. One of my rocket tubes had been written up as inoperative, so I was carrying only three Willie Pete rockets. We had run a flight of fixed wing on a target and had fired one of our rockets to mark the target. After that, the other two tubes wouldn't fire even though I had tried several times to get the remaining two rockets to fire. Murphy's Law was alive and well and residing somewhere inside the wiring of my Birddog.

To fire the rockets, I had to arm a rocket tube by reaching up to my upper left where a small panel containing four toggle switches, one for each rocket tube, was located. Each toggle switch had a cover and a corresponding light that illuminated when the switch was on and the circuit was "hot." I had to lift the cover of the toggle switch, pull the toggle switch back, look for the arming light to illuminate, reach down with my other hand and remove the safety pin from the trigger switch on the control stick, and then squeeze the trigger. It was a good process because a pilot had to make specific moves before he could fire a rocket—each step required a conscious effort and separate movement, nearly negating the possibility of accidentally firing a rocket and seriously wounding or killing someone other than the enemy.

The problem lay hidden somewhere in the wiring. I believe the arming system was an afterthought. Sometimes it simply didn't function as intended. I tried several times to fire the rockets, each time running through the complete sequence of lifting covers, pulling switches, checking the light, and removing the pin. Somewhere in that frustrating endeavor, I neglected to flip the cover back down on one of the arming switches. I had replaced the pin back in the trigger, so I couldn't squeeze it; but the system was still armed as I returned to Marble Mountain airfield.

As I approached the field for landing, I lowered flaps and turned on to final approach, lining up on the centerline of the PSP runway. At the other end of the 4,500-foot runway, two massive Marine H-53 helicopters were just lifting off heading south. I rounded out to touch down in the nose high, tail low, military three-point landing the Army recommended for its "tail-dragger" airplanes. This put me in a slightly nose high pitch attitude. The instant that I touched down, *BANG—WHOOSH!* one of the rockets that would not fire left its tube, rocketing straight toward the second departing H-53.

Oh my god, I thought. *I just destroyed a helicopter full of Marines!*

―――――

But the gods of aviation must have been smiling on me that day. Instead of climbing straight out, the two H-53s remained low and broke into a sharp left turn, so the rocket sailed right over the top of the second H-53, missing it by less than than fifty feet! All four crew members on that helicopter would have perished because of one small oversight by me and some infernal electrical gremlin inside my airplane.

As I taxied to our platoon ramp area feeling numb, I spotted Captain Stackhouse, my platoon leader, waiting with a none too pleased expression on his face. Thoughts of *Oh boy, here it comes!* flashed through my mind as I shut down the engine. Stack didn't even wait for me to get out of the aircraft.

"What the hell happened, lieutenant?" my platoon leader demanded.

"I don't know, sir." I then went on to explain the sequence of events ending with "The pin was in the trigger and I did not fire that thing. It fired itself."

"It went off when the grounding wire touched the runway, completing the circuit. Not your fault, the system is bad, but you'd better make damn sure that you have all of the switches off before you land from now on. I'm going to have to go over to battalion and explain what happened."

When he was finished, Stackhouse about-faced and stomped off toward the 212th Aviation Battalion headquarters building. I never heard another word about it.

One thing I did hear a week or so later was that the Army Special Forces compound just off the south end of the runway thought they were under attack when my Willie Pete rocket exploded in their midst. Fortunately, no one was injured. I learned years later that they were really pissed, and had they known whose rocket it was, they would have most likely hunted me down and done nasty things to me.

14 | The A Shau Valley from Fifty Feet

The A Shau Valley was a formidable place along the westernmost border of South Vietnam even before I ever flew there. It was an integral part of the Ho Chi Minh trail, a collection of NVA supply routes with traffic flowing south from North Vietnam through Laos, Cambodia, and the A Shau Valley. The trail's ominous reputation existed from March 1966 when the Special Forces camp at the south end of the valley was overrun during a four-day battle.

For the 3rd Platoon of the 220th RAC flying out of Marble Mountain airfield, the A Shau Valley was one of the areas we flew on a regular basis. It was always a two-ship mission; one low bird flying at eight hundred feet or so above the trees and a high bird tagging along behind five hundred feet or so higher. The low bird did the visual reconnaissance and the high bird was there to watch the low bird and call for help or mark where the low bird went should it run into trouble. I always thought this was a good idea when we flew over Indian Country up against the Laotian border; back there was nothing but dense jungle, mountains, and bad guys. We were well out of range of friendly artillery and a long time from any friendly assistance. Fortunately, as far as I know, we never lost a bird over the A Shau.

A number of separate aviation entities were constantly at work all over Vietnam at the time, but I didn't know it; we were rarely ever briefed on what the other guys were up to. We might be told to refrain from flying over a certain area because there was an "operation" being conducted there, but that's about as much information as we ever got. Because I had seen them, I did know the CIA's Air America pilots flew around in their white and blue striped Hueys and Pilatus Porters. They might turn up just about anywhere unannounced. I also knew some Air Force C-123 cargo planes flew in echelon formation lower than five hundred feet above the ground, spraying some type of chemical. I had seen them flying unannounced beneath me in the Que Son Valley.

Once a week we received a G-2 Air briefing that included grid coordinate locations of enemy radio transmissions, coordinates of where friendly aircraft had been shot at, and an estimate of the number of guns and their caliber. Yet I always had this nagging feeling that there were a lot of things they weren't telling us. And that bugged me because I felt since we worked directly with the troops on the ground and were their eyes in the sky, we should know everything going on in our area of responsibility.

These weekly briefings also failed to inform us about the Air Force F-100 "Fast FACs" that roamed the Ho Chi Minh trail and the A Shau Valley. We had no idea the Mistys (call sign for the F-100s) might be out there zooming around at four hundred knots while we were puttering along at less than one hundred knots. They were designated as Fast because they were jets. They were very difficult for the bad guys to shoot down.

Then there was the "secret" stuff, like what the Special Forces guys were up to; not to mention the Navy SEALs (back then, nobody even knew that's who they were), who had an island just off the coast at Da Nang for training so secret that the airspace around it was restricted. Even we weren't allowed to fly around or over it.

Last but not least was Project Delta initially run by Special Forces major Charlie Beckwith. "Chargin" Charlie's command was a mixed force of Special Forces soldiers and Vietnamese Special Forces who performed reconnaissance missions and "ran the trails" the NVA used in the jungle to glean information and wreak havoc on the enemy whenever possible. Project Delta had its own assigned helicopters and moved around the country, independent of any other U.S. or allied forces that might be in the area. During my tour the 281st AHC supported Project Delta. Everybody including helicopter crew members wore jungle camouflage "tiger suits" with no visible rank or unit insignia and often carried nonstandard weapons if operating in a "deniable" area like Laos. Even some of their aircraft were devoid of the usual "United States Army" on the tail boom of their Hueys, apparently for "deniability." Nobody we were fighting had Hueys, so it didn't take a college degree to know who these aircraft belonged to.

One sunny day in late October, Rick Vance and I—he was my high bird for the day—were flying a VR mission along the Laotian border. As was normally the case, I flew with one of our ARVN observers in the back. Vance was tooling along behind and above, keeping track of me while my observer and I were looking for signs of enemy activity. Prior to takeoff we had been briefed to remain clear of Charlie 6, a designated VR area just a bit south of the A Shau, because Project Delta was going to operate in there and they wanted no aircraft not specifically assigned to them flying around. That was fine with me. We still had to VR Charlie 3 and then move on north to the A Shau. A river with a prominent dog leg in it separated areas Charlie 3 and Charlie 6. I made the mistake of deciding to cut the corner at the dog leg, crossing just a couple of klicks of Charlie 6 on my way north to A Shau. Although I could see some Hueys working in the distance to the west and figured them to be part of Delta, I decided my shortcut was well away from where they were operating, so no harm, no foul.

It didn't work out that way.

My FM radio crackled with Vance's voice: "3-2 don't make any sudden turns."

"Why?"

"Just look out to your right and left," came the reply.

Oops, where the hell did those guys come from? I thought, looking out and seeing a Huey gunship on either side of me and slightly to my rear. I wagged my wings as a sign of recognition and in return noticed the door gunners in both helicopters had their machine guns trained on me. This was not good!

I switched to UHF Guard frequency and transmitted, "I'll be out of here in just a minute guys."

There was no response, just two heavily armed Hueys from Project Delta sticking to me like glue, their door gunners obviously just itching to shoot down a fellow Army aviator flying a fixed-wing Birddog. It all ended well, however. As soon as my flight path took me out of Charlie 6, the two Huey gunships disappeared as quickly as they had appeared without firing a shot, probably to the unending disappointment of their pilots and door gunners.

I was a little embarrassed at getting caught, thinking, *Damn Rotorheads, they wound up flying helicopters instead of airplanes and were wanting to get even—that's pure envy!*

As we approached the south end of A Shau Valley, lo and behold, right there on the trail below and in front of me were five guys carrying rifles. They were not part of Delta because Delta was back in Charlie 6. These had to be bad guys. A Shau Valley was way out in Indian Country, too far away to call up artillery or fixed wing, so I just armed a Willie Pete rocket, chopped the power, dropped the nose, and squeezed off a quick one. They saw the rocket coming and scattered into the nearby foliage. The rocket impacted right where they had been on the trail, but I didn't see any confirmed kill so for some strange reason kept the aircraft downhill and leveled out right over where they had been.

I could hear Vance on the FM radio, "3-2 what are you doing?"

"Just thought I'd go on down and see what I can see," I replied. "You just keep an eye on me."

"Roger," was his response, followed by a disgruntled, "You're nuts!"

It was several months into my one-year tour in Vietnam by that time, and I was feeling ten feet tall and bullet proof. I don't know if the guys on the ground experienced this, but it seemed to be pretty common among aviators. The feeling emerged after a couple of months in country and, unless something really bad happened, remained until a month or so before the end of the aviators' yearlong tour in country. That last month or so, they'd begin to worry about getting home in one piece and their flying tended to reflect a substantially more cautious approach to how they accomplished their mission. On this particular day I was feeling pretty cocky. Running the A Shau Valley low level seemed like a fun thing to do—I felt I just might see something I would miss from a higher altitude. Fortunately, my ARVN observer on this flight was Dui Wi Dan, a Vietnamese captain who was known among 3rd Platoon pilots for three things:

1. He probably had some sort of political connections, so he got to ride in an airplane and did not have to walk in the infantry.
2. He was a lousy aerial observer and basically never did anything once he got in the back seat.
3. He always went to sleep as soon as we took off and stayed that way until we landed no matter what we did with the airplane.

He didn't wake up this time either, and that was probably a good thing because I do not know what he would have done had he awakened, looked outside, and realized where we were and what I was doing.

So there I was, fifty feet above the ground, flat out at one hundred miles an hour, thinking that I was really something in my little two-seater, high-wing, single-engine Cessna. I flew past the now abandoned A Shau Special Forces camp and the wrecked Air Force A-1E that lay on the runway. Then, a bit further up the valley, I passed Ta Bat and still further, A Luoi. The only things I noticed were the bomb craters that permeated the road and the heavily used trail weaving unbroken through and around them. Some craters had been filled in with gravel to make them passable while others had standing water in them. It was very apparent that the valley floor was being heavily traveled because it was smooth and shiny despite the bomb craters.

Passing A Luoi, the road/trail turned west up and out of the valley and into Laos, immediately to the west. As I began my climb over the road, something happened that jerked me back to reality. I glanced to my left and there, neatly parked under the trees, were a yellow road grader and a yellow bulldozer.

I knew no friendly engineer outfits were out there, and if those two pieces of equipment were operational (and they appeared to be just that), then somebody was watching them—and me. Adding full power and initiating a climb, I knew one thing: I was going to get blown out of the sky. The maximum climb rate of my aircraft was maybe four hundred feet per minute, and I needed at least three minutes to get out of range of the AK-47 fire that was sure to commence. Those were the longest three minutes of my life.

For some strange reason, I did not hear anyone shooting at me nor did I take any bullet holes in my aircraft. The only explanation that I could think of was that either the bad guys were caught completely by surprise and I was past them before they could respond, or they didn't see me. Maybe they were too busy laughing at the "crazy Army Birddog pilot" to grab their rifles and shoot me down. Either way, I survived my risky escapade and was able to report accurate coordinates of the road grader and bulldozer. Then I was able to feel justified in flying low level out there, but I also realized that but for the grace of God or maybe just dumb luck, the outcome could have been much different.

15 | Pink Elephants, a Big Cat, and Funny-Looking Logs

Not everything in Vietnam was affected by the war. Every now and then I would happen upon something totally fascinating or border-line unbelievable. Once I got away from areas scarred by bomb craters and other evidence of violence, I came to realize Vietnam was a beautiful country. Some sections of the coastline in I Corps were quite rugged, breathtakingly beautiful, and pristine. The beaches were frequently littered with sampans used by the local fishermen but were beautiful nevertheless. Inland from the beaches the terrain varied from zero to several miles of sandy, slightly rolling terrain and rice paddies, then hills that suddenly rose to thickly vegetated mountains several thousand feet high. The flora beyond the foul-smelling rice paddies was incredible. Mother nature went to town in the warm, wet climate, producing a thick triple-canopy jungle in the mountains.

Vietnam was long considered the rice bowl of Southeast Asia; because of its agrarian culture, the country was conquered by other Asian countries. Every village was surrounded by rice paddies that the locals were constantly tending—depending on the season, they were either tilling with plows drawn by water buffalo, planting new rice shoots by hand, harvesting the rice, or burning dry rice stalks. They also seemed to have a fair quota of chickens, ducks, dogs, and water buffalo. The water buffalo didn't take kindly to any Americans but seemed perfectly tame around the Vietnamese. Small children could often be seen sitting astride these large, cranky beasts, and farmers used them extensively as tractors to pull primitive plows through the rice paddies. On the wilder side, there were tigers, very large snakes, creatures that lived in the water such as leeches, and things with lots of teeth. Even elephants could occasionally be spotted during VR missions deeper into the mountains.

The remains of several old French resorts near Da Nang were still visible, although the surrounding vegetation was taking them over. One of these old resorts located on a mountaintop just west of Da Nang was used by the Marines as an observation outpost.

For the grunts on the ground, Vietnam could be a very unfriendly place, not only because of the Viet Cong and NVA but also because Mother Nature herself didn't seem to be too happy with our presence. The advantage I had was that flying around at eight hundred to one thousand feet, I could see with total clarity yet be relatively safe from immediate threat. This bird's-eye view resulted in more than engaging the enemy and generated a few interesting tales.

In mid-October between some really rainy days, Lt. Rick Vance returned from a two-ship VR in Charlie 3, an area deep in Indian Country near the border with Laos. Several of us were standing around in the 3rd Platoon line shack getting ready to fly our missions. There we kept our flight gear, mission schedule board, mission debrief forms, and a large wall map made up of 1:50,000-scale maps taped together and covered with acetate. We had no-fly areas, shot-at report locations, free-fire zones, and other tactical information noted on the map in grease pencil. Vance seemed pretty excited when he came stomping inside.

Walking up to the wall map, he poked his finger at a prominent bend in the river that defined the border between Charlie 3 and Charlie 6 and proclaimed, "Right there! Right at the bend in the river, pink elephants!"

I wasn't sure that I had heard him correctly. "Pink elephants?" I asked. "Are you sure about that?"

Another voice in the small room wasn't quite so polite. "You're nuts. There isn't any such thing as pink elephants. Maybe you should go see the flight surgeon and have your eyes checked."

"No, I'm not kidding," Vance asserted. "There were five pink elephants hanging out on the riverbank at this bend in the river. I think Charlie [the VC] might be using them to carry equipment or supplies."

That elicited a couple of laughs from the small but now somewhat interested group. We were always eager to poke fun at each other, and this was beginning to sound like a great opportunity to pounce on Vance.

Lt. Bill Amberson, one of the Marine AOs, gave Vance just a sliver of credibility: "Ya' know, he could be right about the VC, or even the NVA using trained elephants to carry stuff. We don't know for sure that they aren't. But I'm not gonna buy into pink."

The conversation went on like that for a while until I noticed it was time for me to go fly, so I just sort of left it there. When I returned some two and a half hours later, Vance was still trying to convince those who would listen that he had actually seen five pink elephants. He dutifully wrote it up on his post mission brief, but I don't think anyone believed him. The next day, Vance requested the VR mission out to Charlie 3 just to look for those elephants. This time he didn't see them and had to admit the same because nearly everyone was asking about them. Now Vance was in a credibility conundrum, and it didn't help matters that nobody else who flew in that area for the next two days had seen them. Vance's reasoning was that because the VC were using the elephants to carry stuff, the animals were obviously working and couldn't be seen through the jungle canopy. The only reason he had seen them was because he must have caught them at some sort of rest stop by the river. And yes, they were pink!

Low clouds and rain prevented anyone from flying for the next few days, so no one could go back and check on the pink elephants. I think Vance was somewhat relieved because the pink elephant jokes began to taper off. Then five days later, Vance was vindicated. Capt. Lloyd Patterson flew a VR in Charlie 3 and discovered the elephants were again at the bend in the river. And they were pink!

Patterson was an easygoing but absolutely no bull kind of guy, so nobody was willing to dispute his claim. We never did discover if they were being used to transport supplies (that would have to be left up to a Recon team), but we did find out why they were pink. It seems that after the elephants would frolic in the river and get wet, they would roll around in the dirt on the riverbank, a red clay, and acquire a nice pink hue once the clay dried. Mystery partially solved. Vance's integrity was restored, although we would still jab him on occasion regarding his critical "pink elephant" sighting.

Vietnam was notorious for its big tigers. As a result, it was not surprising to hear stories circulating about tigers occasionally latching onto a grunt, usually after dark, and attempting to drag said grunt off somewhere to join him for dinner—dinner being the grunt.

My one encounter with a tiger, fortunately at no closer than one hundred feet, occurred on a nice sunny early November day. Not much was going on in the TAOR, so my Marine AO, Capt. Rod Chastant, and I decided to check out the area southwest of Da Nang called rocket city. The enemy liked to launch their 122-mm rockets from there to hit the Da Nang air base. Once in a while they'd switch targets and send them toward Marble Mountain. As soon as we got in the air we decided to fly over the top of Ba Na Mountain just west of Da Nang. There we would be able to see the remains of old stucco buildings that had probably been used as a resort or vacation spot for wealthy French aristocrats when Vietnam was a French colony. I was always interested in the old coastal forts and mountain villas the French had built during their occupation and exploitation of Vietnam. I was certainly in a position to get a unique bird's-eye view from above in my Birddog. Most folks could only see the wonders of Vietnam from ground level, while I got to see them from an exclusive vantage point. I just wish I had taken more pictures.

A bit west of Da Nang, I looked down and spotted an enormous tiger sunning himself along the edge of a very large bomb crater. This guy had to have been at least twelve feet long from the tip of his nose to the tip of his tail. What a serenely beautiful creature he was—completely in his element and, like any cat, just soaking up some afternoon sun without a care in the world. After all, who was going to bother a twelve-foot tiger?

Well, maybe me, but then I could afford to be brave from one hundred feet in the air. It would be entirely different had I been walking around on the ground in the jungle.

I pointed the tiger out to Chastant and suggested we take a closer look. Pulling on the carb heat and retarding the throttle, I began a circling descent down to a hundred feet or so above the terrain. The opposed 6-cylinder Continental engine tended to go *pop-pop-pop* when the throttle was retarded, so the ensuing noise disturbed the very large kitty. It was remarkable that Mr. Tiger didn't suddenly bolt off into the jungle in fear of the loud noise now invading his tranquility. He simply rose up and just like a common domestic house cat yawned and slowly stretched before looking up and ambling into the green vegetation. He was the king of that particular patch of jungle and he knew it. I had simply shortened his nap on this sunny afternoon. Had I not been soaring above him, we would probably have become an afternoon snack for disturbing his reverie. I may have disturbed him, but I'm pretty sure that I did not frighten him.

One of our VR routes that took us back into the mountains west of Da Nang was a valley we called Elephant Valley. The Cu De River ran through it and emptied into Da Nang Bay on its northwest side. To get there, I would fly low level around the north side of Da Nang airfield to stay below any aircraft in the traffic pattern. Buzzing the Vietnamese civilians on the beach was great fun as well.

Once clear of any airport traffic, I began climbing up to my VR altitude. Looking down, I noticed what looked like forty or fifty large logs, their ends moving back and forth like tails! There wasn't any current running and I couldn't figure out why they were moving. So I kept gaining altitude, but began circling the "logs," not sure what I was seeing. I was getting an increasingly creepy feeling up the back of my neck. Then it suddenly dawned on me. These things were bumpy and had eyes and long snouts. They were crocodiles—very, very large crocodiles and lots of them—some were swimming, some just lounging there in the water or along the banks of the river. And here I was in a single-engine airplane over the water, circling them. I immediately rolled out heading west and continued my climb. Better to be over the jungle and have an engine quit than over the bay and in the drink with those big fellas.

After the flight I made some inquiries and found they were Asian saltwater crocodiles, native to Vietnam. They are the largest species of crocodile in the world, reaching twenty feet in length and up to one ton in weight. Their natural habitat is the brackish water found at the mouth of freshwater rivers where they empty into salt water. Anything that size would have to have had a very big appetite and would not have excluded a human from its menu. I admit they had certainly been a complete surprise to me, and they were definitely one more reason I was glad to be flying the skies of Vietnam and not walking.

16 TPQ, MSQ, and Wild Navy Rockets

While flying in the 3rd Platoon out of Marble Mountain, I would occasionally be assigned a rather unusual mission with three (well, actually four if you counted the target) components. First was an AN/TPQ-10 radar system located somewhere in the Da Nang area; second was a bomb-laden Marine jet flying out of sight at 20,000 feet; and third was me tooling around about 1,000 feet above the ground in the general vicinity of the fourth component, the target.

We called such a process simply TPQ bombing, but to me it was PFM. The heart of it was the AN/TPQ-10 radar for ground directed bombing that used a combination of radar/computer/communications systems. The principle had been evolving since World War II but in Vietnam was refined to an almost unbelievable degree of accuracy. For any given mission the TPQ-10 people would provide bombing coordinates that were accurate to within 10 meters of the target. Using those grid coordinates, the radar control site would issue corrections of heading, altitude, and airspeed to the pilot of the bombing aircraft and tell precisely when to release the bombs. For the pilot, it was much like flying a ground-controlled radar approach to an airport landing. Very precise and surprisingly small corrections were issued to him as he actually flew a very narrow radar beam at 20,000 feet.

Maintaining that level of precision required occasional "calibration" of the system, and that's where I entered the picture—a set of eyeballs to verify the radar-directed ordnance was striking the ground exactly where it was supposed to. Such calibration was the difference between a TACA (me) controlling and adjusting close air support and someone else controlling and adjusting the impact points of bombs.

TPQ bombing required precision: the calibrated impact point of the bomb had to be within ten meters of the desired map coordinate. Thus I had to adjust the impact point to a precise eight-digit coordinate. The indispensable tool for all of the missions we flew was our 1:50,000-scale maps we carried with us in the aircraft. The scale of the maps made what we were seeing on the ground at eight hundred to one thousand feet easy to relate to the map information. The maps had been produced by the French when Vietnam was a French possession and were updated as recently as 1965. We trimmed the margins on individual map sheets, taped together those maps of whatever large area we were working in, and then folded them to fit in the cockpit. Everything we did was ground oriented: a Birddog pilot who had failed to take his maps with him on a mission might as well have never left the ground. That's how important those maps were to us.

Numbered vertical and horizontal lines on each map formed squares or grids. Each square (grid) on a 1:50,000 map represented 1,000 square meters or a klick (kilometer). A specific point within each square was expressed in numbers and called a grid coordinate. Normally, when giving the grid coordinate of a target to an artillery battery, we would use just six-digit coordinates, which narrowed the target down to a 100-square-meter area. From that point we adjusted their fire, using small increments expressed in meters: add, drop, left, or right. Calibration of the TPQ system required using an eight-digit coordinate that narrowed down the impact point to a 10-meter square. The PFM part of all this? None of the three players in this dance of precision could actually physically see each other. I was at 1,000 feet, the jet was at 20,000 feet, and the radar controller was hidden in a dark room looking at a radar screen.

My part of the mission started simply. G-2 Air at Da Nang issued a written request for me to be at a certain place at a certain time on a specific day for a TPQ mission and to contact the DASC on its UHF frequency. Someone in the 3rd Platoon participated in this process about once a week. The first time I was assigned the TPQ mission, I had no idea what it was all about. The explanation that I would be visually adjusting radar-controlled bombing didn't ring any bells. It couldn't be any more dangerous than what I had been doing for the past month anyway, so I decided to wing it. Captain Stackhouse did have a word of caution for me though.

"Lieutenant Caryl, I'd suggest that you fly a klick or two away from those coordinates until after you see where the first bomb impacts. After that, you can move in closer for your adjustments."

That simple statement did seem a bit ominous, so I decided to take my platoon leader's advice and err on the side of caution. I had been controlling jet attack aircraft for a couple of weeks by now and had no problem flying quite close to them when they were dropping bombs on their targets. After all, I was the one controlling them and adjusting their drops. It was the radar part of the TPQ bombing mission that had me a bit puzzled and apprehensive.

About an hour before my "on station" time, I took off from Marble Mountain and flew southwest toward the Que Son Valley. I had already checked in with the DASC staff when I departed Marble Mountain, so now I called them to let them know I was in position and ready to go.

"Land Shark, this is Catkiller 3-2. I'm on station for the TPQ, over."

"Roger, Catkiller 3-2," they answered, "contact Devastate Bravo on button Blue."

Devastate Bravo was the call sign of the TPQ-10 radar site that would be controlling the impending action. I assumed there was a radar controller sitting in front of a radarscope somewhere in Da Nang.

I reached up to my right overhead and switched my UHF radio to preset frequency Blue; then keying my mic button, I contacted Devastate Bravo and confirmed that the map coordinates I had been given were correct. When I had looked at my map I had discovered that the coordinates I had been given pointed to the exact location of the north end of a partially destroyed railroad bridge and wondered why they wanted me to blow up a bridge that was already destroyed. But mine was not to reason why, so I didn't bother to ask.

I found out why when I began adjusting the bomb impact points to hit exactly on the north end of the bridge: I wasn't there to blow up a bridge that had already been destroyed; my role in the process was to adjust each bomb that was dropped until one hit the north end of the bridge, verifying the coordinates and that the radar was accurately calibrated.

The TPQ-10 was used primarily at night or in bad weather to ensure positive control of all aircraft so ordnance delivered by air would be on target, not accidentally dropped on friendly troops. The radar system provided steering information to an attack aircraft, guiding it to the target by using the aircraft's speed and altitude to calculate the proper release point. This information was verbally relayed to the pilot or automatically programmed into an onboard electronic bombing system.

The TPQ system had its origins in 1949 when a small group of Marines formed an ad hoc group called the Marine Guided Missile Section, later known as the Marine Air Support Radar Team. They built a radar guidance system for the Loon, the U.S. version of the German V-1, with the assistance of German scientist Dr. Herbert A. Wagner, who had been brought to the United States as part of Operation Paperclip. While testing the Loon's guidance the Marines discovered they had actually developed an all-weather bombing system that could very accurately provide close air support. The system was put into service in 1951 and used in Korea. Out of this grew the AN/TPQ-10 bombing system or, as we referred to it, TPQ bombing. In 1967 it seemed like smoke and mirrors to me. With a properly calibrated TPQ-10 system, the Marines could bomb anyplace in I Corps in any weather—bad news for the bad guys and kind of nice for me, knowing I was playing an important role in technology.

The Air Force had a version of this same system, Combat Sky Spot, designation MSQ-77, with which it controlled the release point for their B-52 bombing strikes. Five Sky Spot locations were in South

Vietnam, and one was at the super-secret Lima Site 85 in the Plaines des Jarres, Laos, from which the Air Force controlled strikes over North Vietnam. The northernmost installation in South Vietnam was at Dong Ha, roughly ten miles south of the Ben Hai River and North Vietnam. The Air Force's B-52 strikes, called Arc Lights, were preplanned bombing missions over South Vietnam.

Navy inshore fire support ships fired rockets, in stark contrast to the ground-radar-controlled precision bombing and the close air support bombing that Air Force FACs and Marine and Catkiller TACAs controlled. Such Navy rockets were not the precision cruise missiles of today, but unguided 5-inch projectiles launched in a barrage. Of course, I had no idea that we were going to be involved in adjusting unguided rockets when my AO showed up for the mission one October afternoon in 1967. The way he briefed the mission, we would fly south of Hoi An, contact a Navy ship just off the coast, and adjust its fire on a large bunker complex at a certain set of grid coordinates. It sounded like a pretty normal mission to me. Turns out it wasn't.

I think my AO and I both expected to be adjusting gunfire from the heavy guns of a Navy cruiser, which would have been very similar to adjusting ground artillery by giving the firing battery crew a grid coordinate and adjusting their fire. We would observe the impact point of the first rounds and then instruct them to add, drop, move left, or move right so many meters to bring them on target. Once on target we would tell them to fire for effect. This sort of artillery/naval gunfire adjustment was usually quite accurate and could be safely used in the close proximity and direct support of friendly ground troops.

As we neared the target area, about a mile inland from the beach, we could see a large vessel that looked to be over a mile out to sea. Figuring that was our "shooter," my AO made radio contact with the ship and gave the appropriate target description, elevation, and six-digit grid coordinate. The fire direction center crew on board the ship rogered the coordinates and told us to stand by until they were ready to fire. When the ship signaled they were ready, my AO gave the command to fire and they did. What happened next was at first awesome and then downright scary. Instead of an individual burst of flame and smoke from a single, large gun as we expected, the entire deck of the vessel belched flame and a barrage of rockets launched themselves toward the shoreline.

Normally when I was directing artillery or naval gunfire, I'd hang a klick or two off to one side or the other of the gun-target line (an imaginary line between the gun shooting and the target coordinates) until I saw where the first round hit; then I'd creep in a bit closer to make finer adjustments. It was a little different when I was running close air support because I could see the jets and I knew they could see my smoke on the target. Artillery and naval gunfire are a complete mystery until you see the first round hit. In this particular instance I needn't have worried; the barrage of rockets impacted nearly two klicks south of the coordinates we had given them and I was two klicks north of the coordinates.

My AO gave them the adjustment "right 2,000," followed by what seemed to be more than a pregnant pause, before they transmitted back "Roger, right 2,000, over. Standby."

We circled for what seemed to be a long time, about fifteen minutes, and then they told us they were ready to fire again. Needless to say, I wasn't getting any closer to the target than I already was, and I may have actually flown a klick or two farther north just to be on the safe side. Their second barrage was on the correct gun-target line but this time impacted about a half klick short of the target coordinates. After that my AO and I began discussing the accuracy of whatever it was we were firing and whether or not he and I actually wanted to continue with the mission. We decided that we were just lucky that the area the rockets had impacted in was a free-fire zone and that there were no friendly troops anywhere close. One thing for sure, we agreed that we would never use this weapon system anywhere in direct support of friendly troops on the ground.

Realizing that we weren't doing anybody any good and that by continuing we risked the potential of a serious screwup, my AO cancelled the mission and thanked the crew for their work. We then flew back to Marble Mountain. My AO wrote up the mission report, and I just chalked it up to another weird occurrence in the petri dish that was the war in Vietnam. We never knew what bright idea we were going to encounter next.

Later I discovered that we had directed the fire of one of four converted World War II Landing Ships, Medium, Rocket LSM(R) the Navy had brought to Vietnam. The U.S. Navy had built a bunch of these ships during World War II to provide massive fire support during invasions. They would lay down barrages of rockets well in advance of the ground forces. Some were retained and used during the Korean War. After that, most had been decommissioned and sold to the highest bidder for scrap or transferred to allied naval services; but four were reclassified as Inshore Fire Support Ships (LFR) and sent to Vietnam. The rockets they launched were unguided, and the ship itself was positioned to determine where the rockets would impact the ground, some three miles away. Obviously these were "area fire" weapons—not something that could be used in direct support of friendly troops, as could artillery. They were used some in South Vietnam but probably had more success when assigned missions firing their rocket barrages into North Vietnam. No friendly troops were there; anywhere the rockets impacted was enemy turf, thus allowing the Navy to report, "All of the rockets hit their target."

17 | What the Hell Was That?

The world of aviation in the 1960s was full of surprises. For the fledgling civilian pilot, one was the likelihood of having a very difficult time finding a flying job. Nobody wanted to hire a new aviator with very little flying experience, and insurance companies weren't interested in insuring someone with less than five hundred hours flying time, even if he had a Commercial, Instrument, Multi-Engine pilot's license.

Not so for a military pilot fresh out of flight training with a mere two hundred flying hours under his belt and a war going on. Uncle Sam had just spent a half million or so training you and he wanted a return on his investment. So you're going to Vietnam! On the bright side, you weren't going to be flying junk and you were going to be well paid. Because you flew, an extra $110 was added to your base pay every month. You also got a $10,000 "free" life insurance policy and medical and dental coverage, and you didn't have to sleep in the back seat of your car. Life was good. You might get shot at, but what the hell, life was an adventure. And besides, you felt like you were ten feet tall and bullet proof, and you knew you'd wind up in Vietnam when you had volunteered for flight school anyway. But there were still some surprises in store.

A few phrases in military aviation have survived through the ages and will most likely continue until the end of time. The first responds to the question "Do you know the difference between a war story and a fairy tale?" Answer: "A fairy tale begins with 'Once upon a time,' and a war story begins with 'No shit, there I was.'" Another response is to this question: "What are the most commonly uttered last words of a pilot before a crash?" Answer: "Oh shit!" The third question is: "What the hell was that?"

I had heard and laughed at the first two in flight school and actually used the first one a couple of times at the bar with friends. I couldn't use the second when I was about to crash because I was too busy trying to land my wounded airplane. I wound up using the third one several times, because no matter how much you think you know, life is still full of surprises.

Nearly everything about flying in combat was unusual. The terrain was different, the rules were different, and people were trying to kill me. Believe it or not, uncertainty doesn't really apply to terrain, rules, and the fact that people were trying to kill me . . . because they were. Yet every now and again something would just jump out at me and leave me thinking, *What the hell was that?*

The first surprise happened deep in the Que Son Valley one December afternoon. The Que Son was our TAOR, and my AO and I had been working with a Marine company on a sweep for a couple of hours. The Marines hadn't run into any trouble, so we checked out and were heading east, more or less eyeballing the vegetation on our way back toward Marble Mountain. Suddenly three C-123 twin-engine cargo aircraft flew below me heading in the opposite direction. They were flying in an echelon formation well below five hundred feet above the terrain and appeared to be emitting some sort of spray beneath their wings. They looked just like giant crop dusters.

What the hell was that? I wondered as I keyed my intercom to ask my back seater if he had seen what I had. I did a 180 so I could take another look-see, and we watched as the three big airplanes continued their low-level trajectory, never wavering in their formation or heading. They disappeared into the distance toward Laos, looking to me like three very large lumbering, lucrative targets, ripe for shooting down by an enemy known to inhabit the Que Son Valley and the jungle-covered mountains to the west.

One thing was certain, flying straight and level like that was just asking for trouble. Whose aircraft were they? They looked like U.S. Air Force birds, but what were they doing? Why were they flying so low in formation? Were they really spraying something and, if so, what? This was my turf, so why wasn't I informed that they were going to be rumbling through here unannounced? Hell, had I been running an air strike or adjusting artillery, they could have been shot down or mid-aired another aircraft. All of these thoughts were the topic of conversation between my AO and me for the next few minutes.

It wasn't until years later that I found out about Operation Ranch Hand, which dispensed Agent Orange, the defoliant made to U.S. government specifications for the U.S. military by nine different chemical manufacturers. Agent Orange was actually a unique blend of two different herbicides that had been used separately in the United States since the 1940s. It got its name from the orange stripe painted on containers of the chemical. The stuff was pretty potent, and little thought was given to its potential long-term negative environmental and health effects. The military simply wanted to eliminate the enemy's use of jungle foliage for cover and concealment. Agent Orange has allegedly been linked to chronic disease in humans; today compensation has been granted to veterans exposed to it and suffering from not only certain cancer-related diseases but a fairly long list of other maladies.

This was turning out to be an eventful day after all. Just a few minutes after the C-123s flew under us, I spotted the next *What the hell was that?* incident. There below us, all by itself, was an H-13 helicopter hovering among the trees and bushes, its rotor wash pushing the foliage down as though it was looking for something. The Bell H-13, with it's distinctive Plexiglas bubble canopy and skeleton-like tail frame, presented a profile that was easy to identify. But the Marines didn't have any H-13s, only the Army did. What the hell was it doing out here all by itself?

It shouldn't have been such a surprise because we had been briefed that the Army was in the process of moving into the Que Son Valley to relieve the Marines. I knew there would be some overlap of coverage, but I thought the Army was operating a bit farther south in I Corps, so I certainly didn't expect to see this. What I was looking at didn't register as normal activity because I had never seen this tactic used before. A single slow, really low, literally unarmed helicopter hovering around by itself deep in the Que Son Valley seemed like a suicide mission to me. The Marine helicopter pilots didn't do anything like this, and I was certain the Army's 282nd Black Cats wouldn't either. Besides, this was the first H-13 I'd seen operating in I Corps since I had arrived in Vietnam in July.

I banked steeply and circled over the H-13 for a while as it went about its hovering routine, which was much like a honeybee in a field of flowers, sampling first one and then another. My AO and I discussed this new occurrence for a bit, then decided to break it off and head home, leaving the one lone H-13 to fate. As I rolled out of my steep turn on an easterly heading, the answer suddenly became very clear: two Huey gunships were heading right at me at my altitude. These two were so heavily laden with rockets, machine guns, and bullets that I could see the upward coning of their main rotor blades as they followed behind and above their little pal in the H-13. These two were fishing and using their little buddy as bait! Army helicopter pilots sure have a strange way of treating each other. This sight gave me one more reason to thank that lady at Infantry Branch for sending me to fixed-wing flight training.

Later I was to find out that what I had witnessed was a normal Army helicopter tactic, referred to as a Pink Team. The H-13 was flown by a scout pilot: a special breed of crazy helicopter pilot who knew his job was to be the bait. Those guys had balls of brass and probably clanked when they walked. The scout would slowly hover around suspected enemy locations until he found a bad guy. His observer (I've often wondered if he volunteered for the job) would then drop a smoke grenade, and they would quickly break away from the target. As soon as the gunships above saw this, they would roll in, firing their rockets and machine guns into the area the smoke was coming from. With luck, in all this wild and lethal madness, the scout pilot would safely escape to look for another target. What a way to garner flight time. It would be one massive adrenaline spike after another, day in and day out for a whole year.

Those two Huey gunships definitely looked like they meant business, lumbering along together, so I—being the more maneuverable and definitely more surprised—quickly turned to avoid them. The pilots were probably laughing their collective asses off at the dumb Birddog driver who got a bit too curious and almost ran into more than he bargained for.

My next *What the hell was that?* incident occurred at the short eight-hundred-foot airstrip at Hoi An. I had landed there to pick up a Vietnamese observer and saw a strange-looking Birddog parked on the dirt at the south end of the runway. It was painted a dull, flat black, and a large mouthful of sharklike teeth was painted on the nose, much like the P-40 Warhawks flown by General Chennault's famed Flying Tigers of World War II. There were no other visible markings on the plane to indicate who it belonged to, and I couldn't make out a tail number. Just as I was shutting down my aircraft, a lone American-looking Caucasian with dark hair and sideburns and wearing aviator sunglasses, cowboy boots, blue jeans, and a white T-shirt nodded to me and then climbed into the black Birddog and started the engine. My Vietnamese observer showed up right then, so I hustled him into the back seat, jumped in, and started my engine. The other Birddog took off a couple of minutes before I did, but as I climbed out from the airfield I could still see it off in the distance heading due west. I followed it for about five minutes at a distance, never able to catch up, but just wanting to see where it was going. Eventually it disappeared over the Annamite Range west of Thuong Duc. I was never to know exactly who the pilot was, who he belonged to, or where he was going. And I never saw a flat-black Birddog with shark's teeth again, but years later I found out about the Ravens. These guys were FACs who flew in the "secret war" in Laos. He must have been one of them.

The Ravens were volunteers who had previous experience as Air Force FACs in South Vietnam. Due to international treaties, the Ravens were "divorced" from the USAF. They wore only civilian clothes and usually operated out of small fields at different sites in the Kingdom of Laos. They had cover stories to explain their presence in Laos, but I don't think anyone believed the stories. Most Ravens knew little or nothing about what they were volunteering for, other than it was classified, exciting, and far removed from the bureaucratic battles and political rules of engagement in South Vietnam.

What this guy was doing at Hoi An that day is beyond me, but as I said, it was definitely one of those *What the hell was that?* moments.

I began to think these events came in pairs. A day or two later I found myself back at Hoi An after a two-and-a-half-hour VR mission. I had just shut down at the dirt ramp area so my observer could get out when a very strange-looking airplane suddenly appeared on short final and landed. It literally whispered as it went over me, so it had to have had a turbine engine. I was surprised to see it simply "squat" and come to a very rapid stop just a couple of hundred feet down the runway. This airplane had a very long nose, squared-off horizontal and vertical tails, a long wingspan with squared-off wing tips, and a very large exhaust pipe running back along the left side of its elongated snout. It was a dirty white and had a dark blue stripe running down its side with AIR AMERICA stenciled in small white letters. Brown stains around the edges of the passenger and cargo doors looked like corrosion. The plane had a U.S. civilian registration number starting with N, which was a bit unusual to me. *What,* I asked myself, *was a civilian aircraft doing operating in a foreign country, in a war zone?* Later I found out Air America was a CIA affiliate. Using a civilian aircraft was a clever way of supporting covert CIA operations (in plain sight to those in the know), while allowing the CIA to deny involvement.

The crew was still unloading baskets of something from the odd airplane when my observer departed, so I decided to go ahead and depart. Even without an observer on board, I would need just about the entire runway to take off and successfully clear the one-story buildings at the south end of the runway. There was a crosswind that favored a takeoff toward the south, which meant that I would have to taxi all the way to the other end of the runway. So I started my engine, checked to see if any other aircraft were coming in to land, and taxied to the far end of the airstrip. I performed my pre-takeoff checks and lined up on the centerline to take off. That was when I noticed the Air America pilot had his engine running and was taxiing out onto the runway. I grumbled a few naughty words to myself regarding his lack of propriety. Now I was going to have to wait for him to taxi all the way down to my end of the runway and wait for him to take off ahead of me even though I was first in line.

What happened next definitely fell into the *What the hell was that?* category: he poured the coals to his engine and started his takeoff run heading down the runway straight toward me. For just a brief moment pure shock ran through my body. *What in the hell is that guy thinking? This runway is only eight hundred feet long. He is trying to take off with a tail wind, which will make his takeoff run longer. I'm a sitting duck. He is going to run into me and we are both gonna die!*

Before I could react, the onrushing aircraft didn't use even half of the eight hundred feet separating us. The pilot yanked the nose up, and, at what seemed to me an impossibly slow airspeed, the airplane was flying. I could see the entire underside of the aircraft. It was literally hanging on the propeller with the nose pointing up at what must have been a 45-degree angle—an impossible feat for any airplane I had ever seen but well within the performance parameters of the legendary Pilatus PC-6 Porter STOL aircraft that had just left the ground in front of me. I'm sure I sat there with my mouth hanging open as "Mr. Air America" casually turned into the wind, continued to climb, and disappeared.

My most memorable *What the hell was that?* moment occurred one sunny afternoon near the DMZ in May 1968. I nearly got plastered by an Arc Light mission conducted by Air Force B-52 bombers.

The B-52, a big 8-engine jet bomber made by the Boeing Aircraft Company, was first introduced in early 1952 as a strategic bomber for conducting intercontinental nuclear strikes against the former Soviet Union. These monsters were 159 feet long, had a wingspan of 185 feet, and could carry up to 70,000 pounds of bombs. They were continually upgraded and modified for service in Vietnam so they would be capable of dropping 108 500-pound dumb bombs at one time—84 carried internally in the bomb bay and another 24 mounted on external wing pylons.

During an Arc Light mission the B-52s flew in groups of 3, or cells. A 3-plane cell could saturate a "box" on the ground with 324 500-pound bombs in under less than a minute, literally tearing asunder the earth and any vegetation upon it. The explosions of an Arc Light could be heard and felt on the ground miles away. The aircraft dropping the bombs flew well above 20,000 feet and could not be heard, so there was no time to run and hide. The earth would simply start erupting. In other words, if an enemy soldier out in the jungle encountered an Arc Light and it didn't kill or maim him, it would certainly scare the crap out of him and perhaps make him a little jumpy the rest of his life.

Arc Lights were preplanned, sometimes days in advance, and designed to interdict enemy troop and supply movement. There was, of course, a process for alerting friendly aircraft of an impending Arc Light so that they would avoid that airspace until after the Arc Light was over. Those of us flying in I Corps would hear a transmission on Guard frequency ten minutes or so before the strike was to commence. The controlling agency had the call sign "Panama." Panama was a radar facility on top of Monkey Mountain just northeast of Da Nang that was protected by a Hawk missile site and used the phrase "Heavy Artillery Warning" to announce Arc Light strikes conducted in I Corps.

It was incumbent upon all pilots to constantly monitor Guard channel on their UHF radios. There were occasions when I did not monitor Guard, and this just happened to be one of them. Once in a while my AO and I would get busy working with troops on the ground, running close air support and adjusting artillery supporting them. One of us in the aircraft would be talking to the jets on the UHF radio while the other was adjusting artillery on one of the two FM radios. At the same time, one of us would also be in contact with the ground troops on the other FM radio. This duplication of effort was necessary and included communicating directly with each other on the intercom as well. The last thing we needed to hear was some other entity such as the Air Force attempting to rescue a downed pilot in Laos, using Guard frequency.

At times like this the radio chatter simply became overwhelming, so I would reach up and turn off the Guard portion of the UHF radio. The UHF radio in our aircraft had several switches to control the frequencies we transmitted and received on; turning the switch from T/R/G (Transmit, Receive, Guard) to T/R eliminated Guard frequency and unwanted chatter. That was what got me into trouble that bright, sunny afternoon on the DMZ.

Earlier my AO and I had been busy working with some grunts in contact with a small enemy force. Some Snake Eye bombs and napalm along with a few artillery rounds had solved that problem. While we were engaged, a bunch of Air Force chatter suddenly popped up on the Guard channel, which I switched off in order to avoid being distracted; however, I forgot to turn it back on. Some thirty or so minutes later when my AO and I were trolling along above the hills along the western end of the DMZ, I suddenly noticed a series of explosions on the ground about a half mile ahead, moving rapidly toward us. *What the hell is that?* flashed through my mind before it suddenly dawned on me: *It's an Arc Light and if I don't do something FAST, it's going to be raining bombs on me. I gotta get out of here!*

I immediately made a 90-degree right turn toward the south, hoping to fly out of the path of the falling bombs. An instant later I saw a series of explosions parallel to the first ones, but a bit further south. I didn't know then that B-52s in an Arc Light mission flew in cells of three. What I was seeing ahead of me was the second aircraft in the cell unloading its bombs in front of me. I wasn't going to outrun them, so I yanked the stick to the left bringing the Birddog around in a 180-degree turn heading north trying to avoid disaster. That was when I saw the third series of explosions running parallel to the first series, but on the north side. By now my AO was furious. He had heard the explosions but hadn't seen them from the back seat and demanded to know what I was doing. When I told him what was going on and pointed out the explosions he calmed down a bit. "Okay," he said, "do the best you can, I'll sit back here and pray for both of us. But if we survive, I'm probably gonna kick your ass!"

There was nothing left for me to do but turn back to our original heading, start climbing to avoid flying debris from impacts on the ground, and pray we would thread the needle between the falling bombs. Somehow we managed to survive without a scratch and landed with another amazing tale to tell. My AO didn't kick my ass, but I never again forgot to switch the UHF receiver back to the Guard channel.

Not all of the strange things that I witnessed fell into the *What the hell was that?* category. A few were surprising, not startling or dangerous, but simply unusual. Let me be clear: combat causes a sort of paradigm shift in what is normal. In a combat zone the soldier experiences everything through an entirely different set of filters than the people back home would. It shouldn't be surprising that getting shot at is a new and therefore alarming experience, but a soldier must quickly learn to accept that new reality and react properly in order to survive. The new reality then eventually becomes the norm.

Oddly it can work the other way as well. I can recall how terrified I was when I returned home after my tour and rode upfront in a taxi cab on the freeway going sixty-five miles per hour. I hadn't gone that fast on the ground in a year and kept yelling at the cab driver to slow down even though he was just going the speed limit. Things were rushing by entirely too fast and I was not at the controls!

So it was that one afternoon in late spring of 1968, my AO, Lt. Denny Kendig, and I were flying over Leatherneck Square a few miles north of Dong Ha just trolling for trouble—another normal day on the DMZ. Off in the distance I noticed a lone Huey flying at about eight hundred feet altitude, parallel to the Ben Hai River, which divided North and South Vietnam. A couple of things about that Huey peaked my interest:

1. It was a slick, which was strange because Army Hueys usually didn't fly that close to the DMZ and never flew alone.
2. The Huey appeared to be flying at a constant altitude, heading, and airspeed. That was an open invitation for the North Vietnamese anti-aircraft batteries just north of the Ben Hai to shoot at him.

"Got any idea what that Huey is doing?" I asked Denny.

"Nope," came the reply from the back seat, "but I'll give the DASC controller a shout and see if he knows."

We got his call sign, Thirsty Red, from the DASC controller, who told us that he was working with Sundowner, the call sign for the 108th Artillery at Camp Carroll located just a couple of kilometers to the west of Dong Ha.

"Roger, copy, Southern Delta out." Then, "Ray," Denny asked over the intercom, "do you want to give him a call and see what he's up to?"

"Good idea Denny. I wonder if he knows that there is some pretty accurate Triple-A at Duc Duc and he's headed right for it?"

Anti-aircraft artillery, Triple-A, was lethal for slow-flying aircraft, particularly at altitudes below ten thousand feet. Pushing the transmit button located on the top of my throttle, I transmitted on UHF.

"Ah, Thirsty Red, Catkiller 4-2, what are you doing up there all by yourself?"

"We're working with Sundowner. We should be done here in about thirty minutes or so. Are we in your way?"

"Okay. No, you aren't in our way. I just wanted to let you know that there is some pretty serious Triple-A located at Duc Duc just a few miles ahead of you and on the north side of the river."

"Okay. Appreciate the heads-up," came Thirsty Red's reply. We watched the Huey pilot make a heading change to take himself further south and hopefully out of range of the guns at Duc Duc.

"Where are you flying out of?" I asked.

"Camp Carroll," came the reply, "but I'll refuel at Dong Ha."

"If you're gonna be working up here very long, I'd like to get together with you at Dong Ha so we can coordinate and I can bring you up to speed on our activities," I transmitted.

What I really wanted to know was what he was up to and give him some sort of briefing on known hazards and procedures because he was obviously a stranger to the DMZ. We Catkillers and the Marine AOs who flew there more or less felt "the Z" was our turf, and if anything was going on up there, we were either controlling it or were at least aware of it. It's good to know stuff when you are that close to North Vietnam and the NVA soldiers who were trying to kill you.

Two or so hours later I landed back at Dong Ha and taxied to the fuel pits. Parked near the JP-4 fuel bladders was Thirsty Red's Huey. Denny and I refueled our Birddog (pilots always take care of their trusty steed first) and then I taxied over to the Huey and shut down. The two pilots and their door gunner and crew chief were languishing in their bird, doors open, trying to stay out of the sun.

We crawled out of our aircraft as the two pilots ambled over. They were both warrant officers. One of them sported an enormous red handle-bar mustache that would have been the envy of any Wild West cowboy who ever lived.

Well, I thought, *that answers the Red part of the call sign; wonder where the Thirsty part came from.*

Introductions were brief. First on my list of questions was the call sign Thirsty Red. "Okay, I've got the Red part, but tell me about the Thirsty part," I asked.

They both chuckled as the copilot replied, "He really likes beer, and because we are on a special assignment, he just made up his own call sign."

They then went on to explain that the cargo hold of their Huey contained secret equipment that would provide extremely accurate coordinates for our friendly artillery to shoot at.

"I've got three civilian technicians from the States who ride back there," explained Thirsty Red. "They have a telescope that's hooked to a laser and run through an onboard computer so that whatever they are looking at through the telescope sends ten-digit coordinates to the arty Fire Direction Center [FDC] so they can shoot, hopefully, with first round hits. That way they don't have to bracket . . . they just shoot. It's still in the development stages and we are up here evaluating it. It's called VATLS. Right now, it's classified secret, so that's all I can tell you."

Wow! More secret squirrel stuff. Right here, right now, right under our noses.

That more or less ended our conversation. We did discuss call signs and some procedures, mentioning to always monitor Guard frequency for Heavy Artillery Warnings and what our role was as Birddogs. I added a request to be sure to let us know through the DASC if they were going to be up so they could avoid flying through any air strikes we were running or artillery that we may be firing.

Thirsty Red was only up there for a couple of weeks, and we did see him from time to time. Then as quietly as he had appeared, he was gone.

Years later, I learned that VATLS stood for Visual Airborne Target Locator System. Using a laser put it on the cutting edge of 1960s technology and made it the precursor to laser targeting systems so widely used by all of today's U.S. military. If nothing else, the conflict in Vietnam provided a tremendous amount of innovation.

I do not know if VATLS returned to Vietnam before the war ended. I do know it did not return in time to save the lives of 1st Lt. Donald Lee Harrison and his artillery observer, 1st Lt. Steven Neil Bezold. In the summer of 1968, the Catkillers were assigned the mission of flying several miles into North Vietnam, adjusting artillery out of Camp Carroll as well as the U.S. Navy battleship *New Jersey.* They were hunting NVA artillery batteries and attempting to destroy them. The mission, referred to as Tally Ho, was part of Operation Thor, which ran from July 3 to November 1, 1968. Lee and Steve were shot down over North Vietnam on October 30, 1968, just two days before the operation ceased. I've often wondered if using VATLS instead of flying single-engine slow-moving Birddogs directly over the targets would have saved their lives. I'm betting it would have.

18 | Tet and Technology

Tet, the Vietnamese lunar new year and arguably the most widely celebrated holiday in Vietnam, was supposed to begin at midnight on January 31, 1968. But it seems the NVA/VC in I-Corps misread their calendars and pulled the trigger a day early. In previous years, an unofficial truce was observed and the shooting diminished. Tet 1968 was different.

I had flown two missions during the day on January 30 and was spending the evening at the bar in the Black Cats' O-Club listening to Gary Puckett and The Union Gap sing "Woman, Woman" for the umpteenth time. The bartender had just placed my fourth double scotch and water in front of me when the sounds of explosions, automatic gunfire, and general mayhem outside suddenly inundated us. Naturally the club emptied in a matter of seconds, along with yours truly (after grabbing my double scotch and water, of course). Tracers were arcing across the sky as people were yelling that we were under attack and to head for the bunkers.

I don't mind saying I do not like confined spaces, especially a bunker where all one can do is hunker down and pray that a sapper doesn't toss a satchel charge into the one you're in. So I walked briskly to our line shack with scotch in hand, being careful not to spill any. I grabbed my flight gear, CAR-15, and a canvas bag of bullets and strode to one of the trusty Birddogs that one of our young intrepid crew chiefs was quickly getting ready for flight. Any military pilot will tell you that a good crew chief is worth his weight in gold. Ours were not only good, but were the unsung heroes of the 220th RAC.

As I was getting ready to climb into the cockpit, one of our Marine AOs suddenly appeared and calmly asked if we could go flying.

"Hell, yes!"

I couldn't wait to get off the ground and into the sky where it was safe. A quick preflight, a "thank you" to José Munoz, my crew chief, and we climbed in. Carefully placing my still nearly full glass of scotch and water between my legs, I strapped in, fired that Doggie up, and took off into the dark sky above.

We droned around south of Marble Mountain, watching the tracers fly back and forth—the red ones going down from the top of Marble Mountain as the Marines fired their weapons along with the intermittent flash of a recoilless rifle, and the green tracers of the enemy going back up, fired from VC/NVA automatic weapons down below. We tried to adjust some artillery and lobbed some rounds in the general direction of where the bad guys had fired several 122-mm rockets. I also fired my WP rockets in the general direction of the origin of green tracers. We couldn't see the ground well enough to accurately plot grid coordinates for the artillery, so we had the artillery battery fire at a preregistered point and then tried to walk the rounds into where we thought the enemy was. It wasn't a very precise method of directing artillery fire, and it certainly wasn't something we would have done if friendly troops were in the area; but it was the best we could do under the circumstances.

Somewhere near Hoi An, over a spot in the darkness that was spewing green tracers, I opened my side window and tossed out my empty scotch glass, hopefully nailing some VC on the head. Admittedly, I was in violation of regulations regarding drinking and flying and should not have been at the controls of anything, but I am convinced I was so pumped on adrenaline that any alcohol in my system (and there was a bunch of alcohol) was rendered null and void.

Two and a half hours later we landed back at Marble Mountain. We taxied in, refueled, re-armed, and went up again. When we landed two and a half hours later, day had replaced night and people were still shooting at each other; so we did the refuel/re-arm thing again. As we were getting ready to climb back into our aircraft, Captain Felton, my new platoon leader who had recently replaced Captain Stackhouse, strode up.

"Lieutenant Caryl," he loudly proclaimed, "I'll take your airplane. You go get some sleep."

Apparently he had not flown that night. A couple of things then occurred simultaneously: first, I took a half step back with my right foot and placed my right hand on the holster of my Colt .45, not realizing the openly hostile gesture that I was making; then, in a clear, unwavering voice I told the captain, "Go get your own airplane. This one is mine."

Felton didn't say a word. He just turned around and walked away. So off we went again in search of targets. We flew south toward the ARVN sector headquarters located at Hoi An, about five miles south of Marble Mountain. Throughout the night's earlier flights we had been listening to radio transmissions from the sector headquarters on our FM radio. We knew that the ARVN troops at Hoi An had been hit pretty hard by the VC/NVA and figured they could use some help from above. Sure enough, when I contacted the troops on the FM radio, they told me the enemy was shooting mortar rounds at them. They thought the rounds were coming from the large island in the middle of the Thu Bon River just to their south.

I rogered them and then dialed up the DASC, call sign Land Shark, to ask if it had any attack aircraft available. Land Shark replied that it had a Spooky looking for work and could we oblige him.

Timing is everything. Land Shark then gave me a radio frequency to work Spooky on and cleared me to switch.

Spooky (aka Puff the Magic Dragon, for the popular song by Peter, Paul, and Mary) was the call sign of U.S. Air Force AC-47 aircraft, the military's cargo version of the venerable Douglas DC-3. The C stood for cargo aircraft, but the A, which stood for attack, had given this aging icon of aviation a whole new mission in life.

Spooky was the long-term, often thwarted result of an idea presented in late 1927 by Army 1st Lt. Fred Nelson. He proposed engaging ground targets with automatic weapons mounted perpendicular to the long axis of an aircraft flown in a banked turn above the target. This technique required the pilot, while in the turn, to vary his bank, altitude, and airspeed in order to maintain a constant sight picture around a specific point. This maneuver, known as a pylon turn, had its origin in air racing in which the course was laid out using pylons. He argued that in using this technique, the pilot could keep the target in sight while delivering fire into it. Nelson successfully demonstrated this technique, but it was rejected as being too radical.

First Lt. Gilmore C. MacDonald submitted a proposal similar to Nelson's during World War II: an aircraft performing pylon turns and, firing .50-caliber machine guns, attacks German submarines with devastating results. Because the Air Corps had already begun modifying light and medium bombers with an increased number of heavy machine guns, MacDonald's suggestion was disregarded. MacDonald presented his idea again in 1945, this time using it against ground targets instead of submarines, but because the war was drawing to a close no one seemed interested.

Years later Lieutenant Colonel MacDonald did receive a spark of interest when, in 1961 he paired up with another lateral-firing enthusiast, Mr. Ralph Flexman, assistant chief engineer at the Bell Aerosystems Company. After discussing the merits of firing from pylon turns, Flexman proposed a side-firing gunship to the Behavioral Sciences Laboratory at Wright-Patterson Air Force Base in Ohio. He suggested that lateral fire from a slow-moving, low-flying aircraft could provide greater target coverage and the high angle of fire was more apt to pin down and destroy the enemy than the current straight-ahead strafing. His proposal was met with a litany of superfluous questions from a doubting audience of decision makers.

In April 1963 someone with final decision authority began to pay serious attention to this idea. For it was then that the MacDonald-Flexman consortium was joined by Air Force captain John C. Simons, a research psychologist at Wright-Patterson. Simons knew of a unique method of mail delivery used in the Amazon: light airplanes were flying tight pylon turns above small clearings and lowering mail bags on a long rope to the ground below. He sent a copy of Flexman's proposal to the Aerospace Medical Research Laboratory Office at Wright-Patterson for evaluation. The laboratory found the idea unsound, but before Simons was ordered to stop meddling outside his field, an unofficial copy of the proposal found its way to the Limited War/Special Air Warfare Division of the Aeronautical System at Wright Field, which had been set up to respond to the special requirements of the Vietnam War.

The folks within the Special Air Warfare Division took an immediate liking to the concept and initiated a project to test it named Tailchaser. The gunship idea had finally found its way to a segment of the military bureaucracy that took an active interest in it. Testing accelerated after Air Force test pilot Capt. Ron Terry, who had just completed a fact-finding mission in Vietnam, joined the project in the summer of 1964. Terry authored a proposal for hamlet and fort defense that was approved by senior leadership of the division.

In August 1964 live tests began at Eglin Air Force Base, Florida, using a General Electric 7.62-mm mini-gun mounted in the cargo door of a C-131. The GE mini-gun was capable of firing up to six thousand rounds per minute. The positive results obtained during the live fire tests impressed the Air Force 1st Combat Application Group. They wanted to find out if these planes could be used for ground support and asked if more than one of the guns could be mounted in a C-47 or C-123 cargo plane—a type already in use by Air Force Special Operations Command in Vietnam.

This was the opportunity Captain Terry was looking for. In September 1964, with three mini-guns mounted pointing out the left side of the aircraft, a C-47 was used to conduct live firing tests from various altitudes and slant ranges. The concept worked. To aim the guns an MK

20 Mod 4 gunsight was added to the left cockpit window and a selective trigger added to the cockpit so the pilot could fire either one or all three of the guns.

The first 2 C-47 gunships, designated as FC-47s, arrived in Vietnam and began operations in December 1964. They were armed with 3 mini-guns and carried a crew of 5, 24,000 rounds of 7.62-mm ammunition, and 45 flares that could be manually deployed in flight to illuminate targets on the ground. The initial designation quickly ran into trouble when the Air Force fighter community began to howl that a slow-moving cargo airplane could not be considered a fighter by any stretch of the imagination. The extended talons of the fighter pilot community were retracted when the designation was changed to AC-47 (Attack/Cargo).

As for the grunts on the ground, they couldn't have cared less about the official Air Force designation. Spooky, aka Puff the Magic Dragon or simply Puff, would prove to be a lifesaver when VC/NVA troops were attempting to overrun remote outposts in the middle of the night. Every fifth round was a tracer, and its red glow could easily be seen all the way to the ground. After dark, the volume of bullets spewing out of Spooky's mini-guns was so intense it looked like red water from a fire hose. A total of fifty-three AC-47s eventually saw combat in Vietnam.

Over the years, as the gunship concept evolved, larger, more sophisticated aircraft like the C-119 were brought into the picture creating the AC-119 Shadow and Stinger variants, the AC-130H Spectre, the AC-130U Spooky II, and the AC-130W Stinger II.

I saw my first Spooky working at night during Operation Swift in September 1967. I looked on from a distance and watched the red fire hose of tracers pouring out from the mini-guns as the AC-47 circled the Marines below. As I prepared to direct Spooky's fire, I had a pretty good idea of the devastation that was to follow. This was going to be fun.

I came up on the UHF frequency assigned to us by the DASC and checked in with Spooky. The Spooky pilot said that he had lots of bullets and a fair amount of loiter time left. Could we find him a target or two?

I put my last Willie Pete rocket in the middle of the island that seemed to be the source of the enemy mortar rounds, and Spooky went to work. I couldn't see the tracers from my vantage point because it was daylight, but what I witnessed was almost as impressive. The AC-47 rumbled over the island at about two thousand feet altitude, slowly circled once like a predatory bird eyeballing a field mouse, and then unleashed a torrent of bullets. It was like watching a Weed Eater at work. Trees, even palm trees, and brush—everything that had been sticking up on that island—was now lying down in every imaginable direction. It took a thirty-year-old aircraft armed with three 7.62-mm mini-guns less than twenty minutes to completely destroy every living thing on that island.

I released Spooky back to Land Shark with a 100 over 100 BDA and thanked him for Sector, who said they were no longer taking incoming mortar rounds. From my perspective, that was a solid understatement.

This wasn't the end of my morning's excitement, however. Land Shark notified me that I had a "Go-Go Niner inbound" and asked "Could you use it?" Go-Go Niner was a U.S. Army CH-47 Chinook helicopter; Chinooks were bigger than the Marines' CH-46. I knew what they were because I'd seen them at Fort Rucker, but although I had been in Vietnam since July, this was the first Chinook I'd seen anywhere in I Corps. I had no idea where it was from or what armament it was carrying. Land Shark switched us both to a UHF tactical frequency and then things went from different to dumbfounding.

"Catkiller, this is Go-Go Niner," a supremely confident voice boomed in my flight helmet.

"Go-Go Niner, this is Catkiller 3-2, do you have any ordnance?"

"You bet we do Catkiller, we have forty mike-mike, 50-caliber machine guns, and HE rockets."

Wow, I thought to myself, *this guy has some really bitchin' stuff. I'd best get him a really good target.* I'd heard about some CH-47s that had been converted to gunships and were being evaluated in Vietnam, but I had never expected to actually see one in action. Rumor had it that some kid had come up with the idea of hanging guns and rockets on Chinooks, putting armor plate over their fuel tanks, and loading them up with lots of bullets so they could remain on station a long time, protecting the grunts on the ground. Apparently the Army liked the idea and decided to try it out on a half dozen or so CH-47s. With a wink toward the current fad of go-go dancers, they were given the call sign "Guns A Go-Go."

Because rumors tend to abound in combat, I did not know the real story behind the inception and implementation of Guns A Go-Go until years later. It was an interesting story, much like that of the Spookys. It took a while for the idea of arming Chinooks to gain acceptance from above, but once put into action they were greatly appreciated by the grunts down below.

The CH-47 was a larger version of the Boeing-Vertol CH-46 that the Navy and Marines had in service. It was nearly 8 feet longer and 2 feet higher and could lift a heavier load. Boeing submitted a proposal to the Army to modify 11 Chinooks into heavy gunships. The first ACH-47A flew on November 6, 1965, and was delivered to the Army for operational training in March 1966. Three more ACH-47As were delivered in April 1966. Budget constraints limited the total number of ACH-47As to just 4, but the firepower they could produce was awesome. Under the nose was a belt-fed 40-mm grenade launcher. On each side of the aircraft, just forward of the sponsons were 2 stubby pylons that each held a 20-mm cannon fed by an 800-round container located inside the cargo hold. Each pylon also held a 19-round rocket pod that fired 2.75-inch HE rockets. Each ACH-47A also mounted 5 .50-caliber machine guns: two on each side and one mounted on the cargo ramp set to fire out the rear. Each of the .50-caliber machine guns had its own 1,000-round supply.

Anything this unique required a special logo and aircraft names. The logo was a skull with two three-bladed rotors on top and machine guns firing out of the empty eye sockets and the center of the mouth. Each of the four ACH-47As that entered service had its own name painted on the side. Their names, Co$t of Living, Easy Money, Stump Jumper, and Birth Control, were most likely known only to those who flew and maintained them. To the rest of us they were simply called Guns A

Go-Go—a very fitting moniker for these rotary-wing juggernauts. Their total operation time in Vietnam lasted only from May 1966 until February 1968, but during that nearly two-year period the grunts on the ground really came to appreciate their incredible firepower.

To select something for Go-Go Niner to blow up, I circled around Hoi An looking for a suitable target. On the east side of town my AO, with eyes still like a hawk after flying all night, keyed his mic and said, "Got us a target right down there. Some gomers crawling toward town in that trench line."

Sure enough, there they were. Ten little men dressed in pale green shorts and shirts carrying AK-47s, trying real hard not to be noticed.

"Go-Go Niner, Catkiller 3-2, I've got a target for you over here on the east side of town. Looks like about ten NVA soldiers in an east-west trench line. They have AK-47s, so you can expect some ground fire if you get too close. I don't have anything left to mark the target for you, but if you will fly over here I'll make a low pass and rock my wings when I'm right over them."

We maneuvered around until the Go-Go Niner pilot said he was in a position to watch my low pass, then down I went. After identifying the target, I climbed back up to one thousand feet and set up an orbit to watch the show. Sadly, what I witnessed was a comedy of errors.

Go-Go Niner trundled off to the south, climbing and bleeding off airspeed as it went. Then, at the apex of its climb, it rotated 180 degrees, pointed the nose downhill toward the target, and the pilot announced "Go-Go Niner's in hot."

"You're cleared in hot Go-Go," I transmitted and then waited, and waited. No rockets, no explosions, nothing but a big, lumbering helicopter descending toward our target at a blistering one hundred or so knots.

"Go-Go Niner is breaking off the run," came over the radio in a voice that was definitely less assertive than before. "We've got a minor problem. We'll make another run."

"Okay, Go-Go, you will still be cleared hot. Did you take any ground fire?" I asked, concerned that maybe the guys in the trench had somehow shot up Go-Go Niner's weapons system.

"This is Go-Go Niner. No, no ground fire. Just some switches that were not set correctly," came the response.

And that's how it went. Go-Go Niner made another climb and turn over the river and another thundering descent toward the target. I could almost feel the determination to obliterate the target emanating from the great, flapping beast. But obliteration was not to be. This time the rockets did leave the aircraft, but not screaming from their tubes belching flame and certain death. This time both rocket pods departed the aircraft with their unfired rockets still inside the tubes!

"Go-Go Niner off target, RTB" [returning to base], said the shattered-sounding voice over the UHF as Go-Go Niner turned south, departing the area.

I had to tell Land Shark that Go-Go Niner earned a zero over zero BDA due to some sort of system malfunction and that it was returning to its home base. I felt pretty bad for the intrepid crew of Go-Go Niner. They had made a gallant effort to help us out and I was sure that it would have been impressive to watch.

I was running low on fuel by now and was beginning to feel the fatigue of flying all night. I didn't have any more Willie Pete rockets and Land Shark was quiet, so I decided to head back to Marble Mountain. I flew over the guys in the trench line one more time. They appeared to be frozen in disbelief that they were still alive.

The irony in all of this of course was that although both Spooky and Guns A Go-Go were avenging angels for the grunts, one of them still had an Achilles heel. Spooky, an aging fixed-wing aircraft with state-of-the-art weaponry seemed to operate without a hitch; but Guns A Go-Go, a modern-day wonder in the world of complex helicopters, was still operating with glitches that had to be worked out. The mere fact that it was a helicopter immediately made it suspect to me when it came to reliability, and the ACH-47 was a very complex machine. This fact could have been a metaphor for the Vietnam War: We were fighting an enemy who often used primitive methods and resources and we were using modern-day technology. And modern technology wasn't always the answer.

19 | A Near Miss and a Missed Opportunity

Tet 1968 was two days old, South Vietnam was in chaos, and I was on my way to the 4th Platoon and the DMZ. I'd been hearing rumors since early January that the CO wanted to make some changes, so the transfer didn't come as a complete surprise. The 1st Platoon had already been sent north from Quang Ngai to augment the 4th Platoon on the DMZ. My name came up as having spent enough time in the 3rd Platoon "Country Club" at Marble Mountain, so I guessed it was time to trade places so some of the guys on the DMZ could have a break. I wasn't very enthused about giving up the amenities at Marble Mountain, but I realized that after six months in country a change of scenery might be good for me. Besides, I was starting to get a bit bored with the 3rd Platoon routine and I could see a potential problem with Captain Felton after our little dustup the morning after Tet started. Maybe it was time to move on.

As it turned out, change was just what I needed. I was given a new home at Phu Bai and a new call sign. I was now Catkiller 4-2. I had already been a Catkiller for six months, so the transition to flying the DMZ was merely getting used to the up-tempo of controlling close air support and adjusting artillery during every two-and-a-half-hour mission. Our missions were rarely devoted to exclusively visual reconnaissance. There was always something to blow up, blow down, or blow away. It made the job easier knowing anyone who moved on the ground that wasn't a Marine was the enemy and that my job was to kill him.

The 4th Platoon's area of responsibility was the DMZ between North and South Vietnam. Dong Ha was where the forward command post of the 3rd Marine Division headquarters was located and the northern-most airfield in South Vietnam, just ten miles south of the DMZ and North Vietnam.

The pilots in the 4th Platoon flew a three-day rotation in and out of Dong Ha from Phu Bai, got a day off at Phu Bai after the third day, and then started the cycle over again. Because Dong Ha was within artil-lery range of the NVA gunners on the other side of the DMZ, only two aircraft and pilots were left overnight at any one time. When the NVA artillery began to roll in, we could all head to the bunker. But our very valuable little Birddogs had to sit outside, unprotected, at the airfield. The accommodations at Dong Ha weren't all that bad, except for the sleeping bags. They had been there since early 1967 and were quite ripe by 1968. We used to joke that when artillery from North Vietnam would drop in during the night and we ran to the bunker, the sleeping bags, having a life of their own, would often beat us there. During the winter months it got cold enough that we needed good old military mummy bags. Once you crawled into a mummy bag, you never zipped it up all the way; that way you were sure to get out if you had to take cover in a hurry. We also slept in our flight suits with our boots close at hand.

One night one of our pilots, Capt. John Kovach, zipped his bag up. When the artillery rounds from North Vietnam came screaming in and everybody hauled ass to the bunker, his zipper jammed and he couldn't get out of his bag. He tried hopping across the floor toward the door but tripped. By that time he was like a giant inchworm making its way to the doorway and the bunker just outside, yelling for help. His buddies were too busy laughing at the scene to render assistance. After just a few rounds, the barrage stopped, but our hapless Catkiller was the brunt of some inchworm jokes for a while.

The 4th Platoon had a process in place for transitioning pilots and AOs new to the DMZ into this very intense flying environment. Both pilots and AOs flew their first couple of missions with a seasoned counterpart. This method allowed for the rapid assimilation of a very steep learning curve without jeopardizing the effectiveness of the mission. It worked very smoothly and was readily accepted by the old hands as well as the new pilots and AOs. For my first DMZ flight, I was paired with AO detachment commander Marine Maj. Jess Mulkey, call sign Southern Juliet. Major Mulkey was a soft-spoken, steady-as-a-rock professional who held the respect of every AO who worked for him as well as every Catkiller he flew with. I figured that I was in pretty good hands.

When I arrived at Phu Bai I was ready to go and excited about the new flying environment I was about to experience. Just one problem: Mother Nature had decided not to cooperate. It was raining with a cloud ceiling down to two hundred feet and visibility less than a mile, well below our standing operating procedure (SOP) weather minimums of a one-thousand-foot ceiling and three-mile visibility. An exemption to this rule allowed the pilot to fly if there were "troops in contact." At no time during my tour did I know of any Catkiller who refused to fly in poor weather if there were troops in contact. We always went, and our Marine AOs always went with us.

I had not received a troops in contact notification, but Tet had cast a very long shadow over I Corps, and if friendly troops weren't presently in contact, they might be at any moment, so Major Mulkey and I decided to go. I planned to fly low level north up Highway 1, past Hue Citadel and Quang Tri, and then turn left at the Cua Viet River to Dong Ha. This wasn't the best of plans under the circumstances, but I figured that whoever I was slated to relieve at Dong Ha would appreciate my effort. This would allow him to return to Phu Bai for a shower, clean sheets, and porcelain to sit upon. Phu Bai tower cleared me for a north departure, "special VFR," and off we went. The tower was telling me I was on my own, and if I really wanted to fly under visual flight rules in that nasty weather to go ahead. I departed the airfield boundary and was able to pick out Highway 1 heading north. The accepted protocol for following a highway is to stay to the right side of the roadway, just as you would back home in your automobile. This comes in especially handy when you can't really see any further ahead than a short city block, as was the case in this instance. Highway 1 led us past Hue and toward the Street Without Joy area, made famous by Bernard Fall's book of the same name.

We were on high alert for any NVA soldiers who might venture a shot or two at us, when suddenly something larger than a Greyhound bus with two rotor blades on top appeared out of the gloom, hurtling toward us at the same altitude on our side of the highway! It was an Army CH-47 Chinook, its nose tilted down at full speed, closing very rapidly. I had no idea what he did, but I broke right and after thrashing around low level in the gloom for a few minutes trying to regain some semblance of Catkiller "cool," I found my way back to Highway 1. One near miss a day was more than enough to convince me that flying up Highway 1 was no longer a viable option. Major Mulkey and I agreed to return to Phu Bai to wait and see if the weather improved.

About an hour after our return, a break in the cloud cover appeared above us. Civilians would describe it as a "sucker hole," Major Mulkey and I saw it as an opportunity to leap into the sky once again. I had planned on flying east to the coast to look for another break in the clouds to descend through, then follow the beach north to the mouth of the Cua Viet River, and turn west, following the river to Dong Ha. A simple plan, but still somewhat risky.

We took off and climbed through the break in the clouds, leveling out on top of the cloud layer at six hundred feet. In just a few minutes we were over the Royal Tombs outside and to the west of Hue. I could see 1st Cavalry helicopter gunships through sporadic holes in the overcast engaging the enemy. They had very limited room to maneuver beneath the clouds and were taking heavy volumes of ground fire from the entrenched NVA. A minute or two later we were over Hue, an enormous opening in the clouds revealing the Hue Citadel and the massive walls and moat surrounding it.

The Citadel had served as the royal capital of the Nguyen dynasty from 1802 to 1945 and had been the capital of Vietnam until it was divided into North and South Vietnam in 1954. Within the walled Citadel lay an inner sanctum known as the Purple Forbidden City surrounded by yet another wall, which had been the exclusive residence of the royal family. The people of Vietnam considered the Citadel and its inner sanctum a national treasure. It was targeted by the NVA and Viet Cong during the Tet campaign because of its psychological value. The battle for Hue between the NVA and U.S. forces was intense, with tremendous losses of both military and civilian lives and enormous destruction to the Citadel.

As we flew closer to the Forbidden City I noticed a large garrison-size flag flying from a flagpole high above the courtyard. Something about it bothered me, but for a moment I couldn't put my finger on it. Then it dawned on me: instead of the yellow flag with three horizontal red stripes that was the flag of South Vietnam, I was looking at a blue and red flag with a big yellow star, the Viet Cong flag. The NVA was claiming ownership of Hue Citadel and by extension, South Vietnam.

"Hey Maj, take a look down out the left side and tell me what you see," I calmly said over the intercom.

"Holy shit! Let's get something up and blow that damn thing down," he replied.

I dialed up the DASC and requested a flight of fixed wing.

"Stand by," replied the DASC, so we waited and waited.

"Uh, Catkiller, we don't have any flights available right now, but we'll get back to you as soon as we can."

Just then a voice that I recognized as belonging to Neil Ostgaard, a pal of mine who flew armed Mohawks, came up on the DASC frequency.

"Catkiller, this is Spud 3, can we be of any assistance?"

"Spud 3, this is Catkiller 4-2; yes, where are you?"

"Just look up Catkiller."

I did, and what I saw was a sight to behold: Right above me, no more than three hundred feet away, were two armed Mohawks from the 131st Aviation Company in a steep left-hand turn in close parade formation. These guys had a .50-caliber machine gun pod and a pod of 2.75-inch

HE rockets mounted under each wing, more than enough to make that Viet Cong flag go away.

The Grumman OV-1 Mohawk was a single-pilot, two-seat, midwing, twin turbine–engine surveillance aircraft. Every fixed-wing aviator in the Army wanted to fly it, including me. The OV-1 was created in 1959 to meet a joint U.S. Marine–U.S. Army request for a battlefield surveillance and utility aircraft. The Marines had backed out of the program before the OV-1s first flight, much to the relief of the Army because the intended mission requirements of the two services had diverged. Grumman had been building aircraft for the Navy since the early 1930s and understood the beating those aircraft had taken landing on aircraft carriers, so the OV-1 proved to be very stout and suitable for operating into and out of unimproved landing areas. The company wasn't called Grumman Iron Works for nothing. The Army loaded the OV-1A, B, and C models with cameras, SLAR, and IR sensors. It even hung pods with .50-caliber machine guns and 2.75-inch rockets on hard points under the wings.

Of the five Army Mohawk companies operating in Vietnam, only the 131st Aviation Company was authorized to fly armed Mohawks after the 1966 Johnson-McConnell Agreement. Its classified mission was to visually recon the Ho Chi Minh trail complex in Laos that wound south along the western border of South Vietnam. This mission was classified because the United States denied any action in "neutral" Laos. North Vietnam denied being there as well, even though it was moving tons of supplies and hundreds of soldiers daily through Laos on the Ho Chi Minh trail. The 131st flew two missions a day over Laos, with a flight of two armed Mohawks authorized to strike targets of opportunity, which they did often. I just happened to catch Neil and his wingman as they were departing Phu Bai and heading for Laos.

The sight of those two Mohawks ready to knock down that enormous Viet Cong flag got me to fantasizing. Visions of the headlines in the *Stars and Stripes* danced in my head: "Army Birddog Directs Mohawk Attack over Hue Citadel."

Sadly my fantasy was not to be. The DASC was not allowed to clear us to blow down the flag. Neil and his wingman departed, most likely to blow something away in Laos, and I was left with nothing but a shattered dream. The South Vietnamese considered the Citadel a shrine and were trying to limit the collateral damage. After nearly a month of intense fighting the flag was eventually blown or knocked down, and damage the Citadel sustained was extensive. Too bad, it was a beautiful walled city.

Major Mulkey and I did try to make it to Dong Ha, but once we reached the coast it was obvious that the low cloud cover was blanketing everything as far north as I could see. I decided I had pushed my luck far enough for one day and with Major Mulkey's concurrence, we returned to Phu Bai without further excitement. It had been a day of frustration, a near miss, and a missed opportunity.

I want to acknowledge that during the battle for Hue, Catkiller pilot Lt. Terry Bozarth was shot down and killed; his Marine AO, Lt. Bob Laramy, was severely burned while trying to extricate Terry's body from burning wreckage. On February 22, 1968, Terry and Bob had been dropping smoke grenades beneath a lowering cloud ceiling to mark enemy positions when Terry's Birddog was hit by rounds from an NVA 12.7-mm machine gun, killing Terry and causing the crash. Terry and Bob were doing what Catkillers and their Marine AOs always did: supporting Marines in contact with the enemy.

20 | One Hundred Ways to Die on the DMZ

Flying with the 4th Platoon out of Dong Ha, I covered an area on the DMZ that was actually small compared to the area I had been flying in before. It ran from east to west near the center of present-day Vietnam and was about one hundred kilometers (sixty miles) wide. The Demilitarized Zone, as it was formally known, ran along the Ben Hai River for much of its length. And although the DMZ was nominally described as being at the 17th parallel, almost all of it lay south of the parallel. It was established by the Geneva Conference of 1954 to separate the Democratic Republic of Vietnam (under the Communist leader Ho Chi Minh) and the Republic of Vietnam.

Because our operations involved a small area, all our activities were highly concentrated. It seemed that time itself was compressed because of the short distances between North Vietnam and us. When I flew from Marble Mountain with the 3rd Platoon our tactical area of responsibility in the Que Son Valley was a fifteen-minute flight away. At Dong Ha, we entered our tactical area of responsibility as soon as we took off. Obviously we didn't have a long commute to work. This closeness to North Vietnam meant we were well within range of NVA heavy artillery any time we were on the ground at Dong Ha. The enemy took advantage of that close proximity on a regular but unpredictable basis. These circumstances fell into the category of good news, bad news. The bad news was we never knew when an attack would come; sometimes in the middle of the night, sometimes in the morning when everyone was gathering at the mess halls for chow; the good news was it never lasted very long. The NVA soldiers never seemed to lob more than just a few rounds our way at any one time. I suspect it was because they were concerned about counter-battery fire from our huge artillery base at Camp Carroll, a couple of kilometers to the west. Yet they did manage to hit the ammo dump at Dong Ha twice during my tour, setting off massive explosions that went on for days and killed several Marines.

The Catkillers' area of immediate concern just south of the DMZ was called Leatherneck Square. It ran west from Gio Linh in the northeast corner, to Con Thien in the northwest corner, south to Cam Lo in the southwest corner, then back east to Dong Ha. Farther west of Leatherneck Square, the terrain became mountainous. In a broad valley just east of the Laotian border was the large Marine outpost and airfield at Khe Sanh. It was here that the infamous siege began on January 21, 1968, and lasted for seventy-seven days. The entire area that made up the DMZ encompassed roughly only three hundred square miles, yet it was arguably the most hostile flying airspace in all of South Vietnam.

The DMZ's proximity to North Vietnam and Laos meant the North Vietnamese could bring to bear against us just about any sort of anti-aircraft weaponry they had in their inventory. Everything from AK-47 automatic rifles and 12.7-mm machine guns to 57-mm anti-aircraft rounds was fired at me.

In the grand scheme of things, there are those who do get hit and those who don't. Those who do get hit fall into four categories: those who get hit a little, those who get hit a lot, those who take hits to their body and survive, and those who take hits to their body and don't survive.

Those who take serious hits to their body and survive generally get to go home; those with less serious wounds get bandaged up, take time off to recover, then return to flying, finish their tour, and go home. The unlucky ones wind up in a body bag. Some are very lucky and just take bullet holes in their aircraft. I was one of those guys.

So was my pal from the 1st Platoon, Capt. Tony Keltner. Normally Tony was pretty laid back, content to gnaw on the wood tip of his ever-present cheroot, professionally fly his missions, and, like the rest of us, quietly count down the days until he could go home. But during a two-week period in April he suddenly developed a talent for attracting a lot of hostile fire after relieving me "on station." On station means the pilot who is being relieved is involved in doing something, such as adjusting artillery for troops in contact, and cannot leave when his mission time is up. The pilot who is scheduled to fly next gets airborne at his scheduled departure time and is briefed in flight by the pilot he is relieving. He then takes over the mission in the air, or on station.

The first time Keltner relieved me on station, I was flying just north of the artillery base at Camp Carroll and had come upon two NVA 12.7-mm heavy machine gun positions located on a ridge line. Both positions were manned and had machine guns in them. My AO and I could see them tracking us, but for some reason they were not shooting at us. We had run two flights of Air Force F-4s on the machine guns' positions, destroying one but not the other. When Tony and his AO showed up, I gave him a thorough target brief, telling him the NVA soldiers seemed to be tracking us but were not shooting and that Dong Ha DASC had another flight of fixed wing on the way. Tony acknowledged the brief and took over, releasing me so I could return to Dong Ha.

I was taking a break before going back up for my afternoon mission when Tony landed, about forty-five minutes after I had left him. I went outside to see what was up and noticed that his airplane had a pretty good-sized hole in the tail. Tony got out of his airplane, looked at the hole, and said, "They opened up on me when the jets showed up. Look at the size of that hole! They scared the crap out of me when they opened up with that 12.7 machine gun." We never could figure out why they shot at Tony and not at me. Maybe they were just setting up when I found them and nobody had shown up yet with the bullets until Tony got there.

The second incident happened a few days later. I had been flying eastbound along the Ben Hai River at eight hundred feet, looking for evidence of recent river crossing activity by NVA soldiers. As we were tooling along, my AO and I began to hear the sounds of explosions. They were a bit different from the sound of something exploding on the ground; they had more of a sharp "crack" sound and they seemed to be going off in a regular rhythm. We looked down, but neither of us could see anything exploding. We were pondering the source of the noises as we reached the mouth of the Ben Hai and I rolled the aircraft into a turn back toward the west.

That was when I saw it: flak! Large, ugly black puffs of smoke hanging in the sky in a long chain that followed the flight path we had just flown, except the puffs were a few hundred feet higher. I immediately turned south, and the explosions stopped. We decided that it would be worth it to see if we could tell where the North Vietnamese guns were located by getting them to shoot at us again. I was convinced that because all of the rounds had been going off high and behind us, we had been too low for their guns to accurately track us. If I eased back toward the Ben Hai on a westerly heading maybe I could get them to shoot at us again, and we could spot where their guns were located and direct artillery fire from Camp Carroll. At the very least, we could let the other Catkillers know where the NVA guns were so they could be avoided. I flew north and then west, paralleling the Ben Hai. And sure enough, the flak started up again, and just as before, it was high and behind us; but we weren't able to locate the source of the enemy fire and after a short time it stopped. We continued with our mission and were shortly relieved by another Birddog flown by Tony Keltner, whom we had briefed as usual prior to departing back to Dong Ha. I then dropped off my observer and returned to Phu Bai for the night.

When I landed at Dong Ha the next morning, after flying up from Phu Bai for my first mission of the day, a pretty disgruntled Tony Keltner met me as I got out of my aircraft.

"Take a look at my airplane," he demanded, pointing to the shattered back plexiglass window. I asked him how he got it, and he told me that after he had relieved me the day before, he trolled back and forth along the Ben Hai for about an hour without getting shot at. Just as he was ready to give up and go do something else—they had begun to think my flak story was bogus—an anti-aircraft shell exploded close behind him, sending a large piece of shrapnel through the rear plexiglass window. Neither Tony nor his AO received a scratch, but it scared the crap out of them. Tony told me then that was when he was beginning to get a little wary about relieving me on station.

The third incident occurred three or four days later. My AO and I were working with a Marine company that had been in heavy contact with an enemy force at least the size of a company. The Marines had taken some casualties, and we flew overhead while the medevac helicopters came and went. The shooting had stopped, and it appeared that the NVA troops had departed the area to lick their wounds. Tony and his AO showed up, and my AO and I gave them a complete handoff briefing including that we had not been shot at for at least thirty minutes and that we thought the bad guys had pulled back. This information was not to be construed as a guarantee that the shooting wouldn't start up again, and Tony knew it. Heck, those of us who flew the DMZ expected to get shot at every time we flew. All I was telling him was that we had been getting shot at a while ago and that we were not getting shot at this moment. Well, you can guess what happened.

I don't know if Tony was buzzing something, flying straight and level too long, or if it just wasn't his lucky day, but about an hour after we left the scene somebody opened up on him with an AK-47 automatic rifle and stitched the tail of his Birddog. Tony flew back to Dong Ha and landed. He taxied to our little ramp area, shut down the engine, got out, and marched into our line shack mad as hell. He walked up to me chomping on the wood tip of his cheroot so hard I thought he was going to chew through it. He then proceeded to make it very clear he was NEVER going to relieve me on station again! And he didn't. That was when I started calling him "Magnet Ass."

Near the end of the seventy-seven-day siege of Khe Sanh in the spring of 1968, the 1st Cavalry moved into northern I Corps to begin

Operation Pegasus to relieve the Marines at Khe Sanh. At that time, the 1st and 4th Platoons were both flying out of Dong Ha, the 1st having been moved up from Quang Ngai in December. Still, there were days flying the DMZ when one of our Birddogs might be the only aircraft visible for miles, with an occasional flight of fixed wing that we were controlling or, off in the distance, a lone Marine H-46 or H-34. One can imagine how cluttered the sky became when the 1st Cavalry Division's seemingly hundreds of helicopters showed up at Dong Ha.

Immediately after Operation Pegasus wound down, two battalions of the NVA moved south over a span of two or three nights across the Ben Hai River into the area called Leatherneck Square. The trails became almost as wide as a country road, and the packed dirt was shiny. A few days later the ARVN Rangers were on a sweep south of Con Tien and ran into the NVA. One hell of a battle ensued. The 1st Squadron 9th Cavalry, 1st Cavalry Division (1/9 Cav), the wildest bunch of young killers one would ever encounter, pounced and began annihilating fleeing NVA soldiers.

In the span of two days things got very personal for me. On the first day my Marine AO and I were flying in support of a company of Marines advancing on a large group of NVA soldiers who had holed up in a bunker complex located just a couple of klicks south of the DMZ. I had dropped down to around four hundred feet above the ground looking at some bunker entrances when suddenly a lone NVA soldier appeared straight ahead in front of me. He aimed his AK-47 directly at me and began firing! I was heading right at him and could see the smoke coming from his rifle and his shoulder moving from the recoil; I was certain I could hear the bark of his AK-47 above the sound of the engine. I had been shot at before and had taken hits in my aircraft, but this seemed very personal. He unloaded an entire magazine at me and for some incomprehensible reason missed! I turned to my left to put some distance between us as I reached up and armed a rocket, intending to turn quickly back and smoke his aggressive ass with a Willie Pete, but he disappeared.

On the second day I was flying an artillery adjustment mission with an artillery observer with Headquarters, 12th Marines, Lt. Wayne Clevens.

We had just finished one fire mission and were watching the activity on the ground when I noticed two 1st Cav H-13 helicopters cross in front of me from right to left at my altitude. They then disappeared from my vision to my left rear. A minute or so later something impacted my Bird-dog with a loud bang and a bone-jarring force.

I immediately went straight and level, checked my instruments and controls, and goosed the throttle a couple of times. Everything seemed to be okay.

I then went through a mental checklist, examining my aircraft for damage. Looking out I saw the left tail, wing, and wing strut—all there. Then I looked back to my right and did another check: Observer with eyes as big as saucers. Okay. Right wing, wing strut, right landing gear. Okay.

Wait a minute—right landing gear okay, but no left landing gear!

Have you ever looked at something many, many times and not really noticed it? Then one day, something doesn't look right and you look again to be sure that it's there but it isn't. Keep in mind that I had just experienced a tremendous impact somewhere on my airplane. My heart rate was probably elevated. I did not know what had happened. It took me a few moments to actually see what was *not* there. The entire left landing gear strut and wheel were gone! Looking again to my left rear, I saw just one H-13 off in the distance and what looked like trails of white phosphorous forming a plume in the sky right about where the other H-13 should have been.

Thoughts of structural failure began creeping into my mind. *Let's see, the wing strut is connected to the bulkhead directly above where the landing gear strut is attached. Something impacting my aircraft with enough force to rip the landing gear strut from the bulkhead could jeopardize the integrity of the wing strut attachment, and if that fails, there is a good chance that my left wing will fold up and I will fall from the heavens.* This was not good. We had parachutes in the aircraft, but they had been in there since 1965 and never inspected or repacked. We never bothered to put them on, we just leaned against them.

Clevens closed out with the artillery battery, and I headed immediately for Dong Ha some nine miles away. I called Dong Ha tower, told them that I had an emergency and to alert crash rescue.

Because of heavy combat just north of Dong Ha, the single-runway airfield was extremely busy. Everything from Hueys to C-130s were landing and taking off in a nonstop procession. Landing with the missing undercarriage meant that a ground loop was unavoidable. I was also concerned about fire as my aircraft scraped along on the grit-impregnated Marsden Matting runway. So I elected to land in the dirt right beside the runway.

The aviation gods were smiling that day. Not only did whatever it was that flew from the exploding H-13 deliver a hit in just about the only place that wouldn't kill me and my observer outright or completely destroy my Birddog in flight, but also an old, abandoned foxhole just happened to be right beside the runway. I touched down in a three-point pitch attitude, and just as the lift in my left wing was departing and it started to drop, the right landing gear rumbled across and down into the foxhole and tore the right landing gear rearward. The plane was in a belly slide of a hundred feet or so with no ground loop! As I said, the gods were smiling. Crash rescue showed up and shot some foam on the ground where the fuel running out of the wing tanks was accumulating on the ground. Afterward we stood around for a bit, amazed we had survived.

An hour or so later I was summoned to the general purpose (GP) medium tent where a major from the 1/9 Cavalry sat behind a small wooden field desk. A young warrant officer standing outside the tent wearing a Cavalry hat and pistol told me "Wait here," went into the tent, said something, and came back out. All of this seemed quite stilted to me considering the circumstances and location, but the 1/9 Cav was a foreign entity to me, so I just tried to not look too impressed.

"The major will see you now," said the young warrant officer whose job apparently was to guard the tent opening. Stepping into the tent, I came to attention in front of the small wooden field desk, saluted smartly (I could play the Cav game too), and said, "Sir, Captain Caryl reports." The major returned a half-assed salute, seemingly showing his disdain for a lowly non–1st Cav aviator, and then proceeded to grill me on what had happened. I think he was trying to discern if I had collided with his helicopter in mid-air and if I was at fault. He was a cold, all business character, and when I said I was sorry he had lost one of his aircrews, he told me that the 1/9 Cav "expected losses" and to "get the hell out of my tent." I suppose he had to be hard core to command an aviation unit that was constantly losing pilots and aircraft, but he seemed like a certifiable jerk to me.

An hour or so later, my CO, Major Pederson, and now company operations officer, Captain Felton, arrived in the company Beaver to ascertain the particulars and return me to Phu Bai. As one might imagine, I was still extremely rattled by the experience, considering I had not only been nearly knocked out of the sky but had been thrown out of a GP medium tent to boot. The first thing out of Captain Felton's mouth upon arriving at the site of my almost new, now totaled Birddog was, "So, Captain Caryl, low-leveling again, huh?" This did not sit well with me, especially since it was within earshot of the CO, so I just glared at him and kept my mouth shut.

Yep, there are at least a hundred ways to die on the DMZ.

Years later, in 1992, I was a pilot in the Arizona Army National Guard, flying helicopters. I was in the 1/285 Attack Helicopter Battalion and at Fort Rucker, Alabama, for the Apache transition course. I was in the building at one of the stage fields waiting for my turn to fly when I noticed a full colonel with Master Aviator Wings who appeared to be waiting to fly as well. He had a 1st Cav patch on the right shoulder of his flight suit, indicating he had been with the 1st Cav in combat, so I struck up a conversation and asked when he had served with the 1st Cav. He told me 1968. Since my crash landing incident had occurred in May 1968, I inquired if he had flown for the 1/9 Cav on the DMZ in May and if he could remember an incident involving an Army Birddog and a 1/9 Cav H-13 helicopter.

To my amazement he told me that he did. I told him my story and that it had bothered me all these years that for no apparent reason that H-13 had exploded and those two crew members were gone in a heartbeat. He told me the Army never really found the exact cause but concluded that a WP grenade had gone off, instantly vaporizing the helicopter and its occupants. He related that the crews normally carried differently colored smoke grenades in a wooden box on the seat between them to use in marking targets. Although they were not supposed to carry WP grenades because of the intense heat they emitted, some flight crews did because the grenades put out very intense billowing smoke and burned hot enough to ignite just about anything they came in contact with. He said that because the flight crews straightened the pins in all of the grenades to make them easier to pull, investigators thought the pin may have vibrated out of the WP grenade, allowing it to go off.

That was a sad state of affairs. That mistake almost nailed me and my observer as well. In aviation if you fly long enough in environments that are hazardous enough, you will eventually accept the philosophy that when your time is up, your time is up. Yes, you can do stupid things to speed up the process or even acquire habits that may slow the process down, but the following from Anonymous is an absolute truth:

Should you seek the wondrous freedom of flight, one of two things will one day happen to you:

- One day you will go out to your aircraft knowing that it is going to be your last flight.
- One day you will go out to your aircraft *not* knowing that it is going to be your last flight.

Neither has ever caused those who seek the thrill of flight to avoid it.

Stranger from Another Planet

Life being at risk was common on the DMZ, but that had also become the norm for those of us who flew there on a daily basis. Even so, I discovered that we didn't need to be shot at, have bombs dropped over us, or miraculously dodge parts from an exploding helicopter to find ourselves in harm's way.

The chaos of Tet had diminished to a dull roar, and the once super-intense activity at Dong Ha had settled back to its normal level of insanity. The 1/9 Cav had left and taken its traveling circus somewhere else. Capt. Tony Keltner, our two Marine AOs, and I were languishing in our line shack at Dong Ha. There was an overcast sky with a low ceiling so we weren't flying. Our unit's SOP stated we had to have basic VFR weather before we flew; however, if there were "troops in contact" it was up to the pilot whether we flew or not. Catkillers always flew when there were troops in contact, but this seemed to be a slow day for the grunts too as nobody was calling for help.

There wasn't an on-site weather forecaster at Dong Ha, so when the weather was lousy we would conduct our own so-called weather check. We would go up to see how high the ceiling really was; but it was also an excuse to have a little fun. One of the guys and his AO would saddle up, take off, and head for the South China Sea low level following the Cua Viet River, which ran right past Dong Ha. Once feet wet, he would proceed north along the beach to the vicinity of the mouth of the Ben Hai River, arm all four WP rockets, point the nose toward North Vietnam just across the river, pull the nose of the aircraft up, and squeeze the trigger. With luck the rockets would hit something that belonged to the NVA, or at least piss NVA soldiers off. Such action was great fun when we were bored and needed a way of "verifying" the weather.

I had already done the morning weather check. The clouds were solid and down to about four hundred feet, and we were just hanging out in the line shack killing time waiting for someone to call. Suddenly we heard the distinct sound of a Birddog descending overhead. We weren't due to be relieved and besides, none of our Catkiller buddies down at Phu Bai would have been goofy enough to fly up to Dong Ha in that weather. Scrambling outside, we looked up to see a hole in the cloud cover right over the runway and a lone Birddog spiraling down through it. We stood around wondering out loud who it might be. Anyone flying up here from Phu Bai in this weather certainly couldn't be bringing good news.

As we watched, an unfamiliar Birddog landed, rolled out, turned around, and taxied back to our small parking ramp in front of the line shack. We knew right away that it wasn't one of our Birddogs. Instead of two rockets under the left wing, it had an M-60 machine gun. The strange Birddog rumbled up and shut down, and a tall, lanky, rather confused looking lieutenant climbed out.

"Hi," he said, looking around as if to get his bearings.

"Hi," we replied, wondering who this stranger was and what he was doing this far north.

The lieutenant paused, no doubt a bit embarrassed, knowing that he was about to commit the cardinal sin of all aviators: conceding that he had no idea where he was.

"Uh, just where is this?"

You cannot imagine the glee with which the four of us said, "Dong Ha!" In response, his puzzled look told us that he had no idea where in the hell he was.

"You're less than 20 klicks south of North Vietnam. Dong Ha is the northernmost friendly airfield in South Vietnam," Tony told him with that million-dollar grin, his wood-tipped cheroot clamped firmly between his teeth.

"C'mon inside and we'll show you on the map."

It was with great satisfaction that we showed our visitor how close we were, indeed, to North Vietnam. His reaction was to quickly slump down on one of the wooden benches attached to a table and quietly shake his head. We offered him a can of semicold soda from our little refrigerator, and gradually he told us his story.

His Birddog company, the 21st RAC, the Black Aces, had recently moved into the southern part of I Corps, and he was on a solo, single-ship visual reconnaissance mission. Somewhere west of Chu Lai in the vicinity of the A Shau Valley, he had encountered low clouds and climbed above them hoping to find a break in the cloud cover and descend through it to continue his mission.

This guy, I thought, *must have been a rookie.* Nobody in his platoon must have bothered to take him under their wing, because what he was attempting to do solo was something the Catkillers would have never done. He had no idea what could have easily happened to him had something gone wrong back there. He would have simply disappeared. That area was Indian Country and a two-ship mission for the Catkillers. He had not been able to find a break in the clouds, did not know exactly where he was, and had consumed over half of his fuel when he decided to head to Da Nang using his ADF navigation radio. Apparently his ADF wasn't functioning correctly so he flew past Da Nang on a northerly heading. With his fuel getting critically low he just happened to look down and see the runway at Dong Ha through a break in the overcast. That's when we heard the *pop-pop-pop* of his spiraling descent. Had he not landed at Dong Ha, we calculated that on his last heading and with the fuel he had remaining he would have run out of gas over Vinh, an airfield in North Vietnam.

After a bit of conversation, we helped him refuel his Birddog and spent a little time oohing and aahing over the cool M-60 machine gun mounted under his left wing. I was secretly thinking that trying to use that thing would just get you killed. Our job was to find the target and then get somebody else to blow it up.

We said our goodbyes, pointed him toward the beach, and gave him instructions to "turn right when you get to the big lake and follow the beach back south." Just another lost soul flying around in Vietnam who might as well have been a strange visitor from another planet.

21 | Sharkey, Poz, and the Miracle of the Six-Holer

Combat tends to cast a slightly different light on events that one might otherwise describe as normal (back in the USA). The things we laughed at and found humor in might well be considered nearly insane by folks back home. It was as if I was living in Joseph Heller's book, *Catch-22*.

Like the characters in *Catch-22*, many of my fellow warriors had survived near-fatal incidents that, in terms of both reason and probability, seemed to defy the odds. A near-fatal incident didn't have to involve direct combat; it could encompass run-ins with extremely irate senior officers, seemingly innocent endeavors such as a visit to one of our primitive "powder rooms" (in this case a four-holer), or simply an encounter with a 122-mm enemy rocket. A near-fatal incident didn't even need to leave a visible mark on the victim or cause a severe case of post-traumatic stress disorder; it could merely leave the individual involved in—or witness to—the event wondering *How in the hell did I [or he] manage to survive?* Such was the case with a warrant officer Catkiller pilot I will refer to simply as Poz.

Field sanitation is an important element in the health (and success) of any military unit engaged in combat. Victory over an enemy occurs only when troops are standing on the contested ground and the enemy is no longer able to mount a counterattack or has retreated from the field of battle. If combat troops become sick or infected with disease because of contaminated food or water or improper disposal of waste, they experience a self-inflicted wound every bit as lethal as an enemy bullet.

One thing I always felt comfortable with was knowing that wherever I went in the Army, I could count on uncontaminated food and water. The water may have come from a Lister bag and tasted like iodine and old canvas, and the food may have been cold C-rations, which I happened to like anyway (except for ham and lima beans); but I knew that what I ate and drank wasn't going to make me sick. Human waste was another area of concern, but the military had an answer for that too.

In Vietnam many of the permanent bases actually had complete sewage systems attached to porcelain commodes. Some of the less improved sites, like Dong Ha, had aboveground wood-constructed latrines with wooden benches placed above fifty-five-gallon drums cut in half and strategically fixed below. The drums were partly filled with diesel fuel used to incinerate the waste. These latrines (or heads, in Marine-speak) were commonly referred to by their number of seats; one with just two seats was a two-holer, one with three seats was a three-holer, and so forth.

At Dong Ha, adjacent to our dirt Birddog parking area next to the runway, we were blessed with a four-holer. It was an impressive structure— about nine feet high, five feet wide, and eight feet long with a door at one end. Privacy was never an issue; there wasn't any. If you needed to use it and someone else was already occupying a seat, you would simply drop-trou, sit down on an empty seat, and do your business, all the while trying not to notice the guy sitting right next to you trying not to notice you.

Periodically some hapless junior enlisted Marine would show up to "burn the shitters." This chore involved lifting a hinged wooden door on the back of the four-holer, dragging a nearly full half drum out from under each seat, and placing it a few feet away from the wooden structure. If he was careful he might be able to accomplish this without slopping any of the contents on himself. Once all four containers were a safe distance from the structure, he would light some rolled paper and toss it into each drum to ignite the diesel fuel and burn the contents. Billowing black smoke and a rather disgusting odor indicated that field sanitation was in progress. Thirty minutes later, after the drums had cooled, the empty waste receptacles would be restocked with diesel fuel and slid back under the seats. A less than desirable but necessary task accomplished until the next required iteration. Had I been a young enlisted Marine, I certainly would not have wanted to get on the wrong side of my company first sergeant because this task was ready-made for resolving disciplinary problems.

The four-holer at Dong Ha was to become the center of one of the most extraordinary near-fatal incidents I witnessed during my tour in Vietnam or for that matter ever since. It happened one morning just after I landed to relieve one of the pilots who had been staying overnight. Tony Keltner and Poz were in the line shack when I landed and wandered over as I shut down the engine on my Birddog. Poz was a chain-smoking, 5-foot 10-inch skinny as hell pilot whose flight suit fit so loosely it would flap in the breeze like a flag; if he turned sideways and stuck out his tongue, you could easily mistake him for a zipper.

As we got caught up on the latest scuttlebutt, Poz ambled over toward the four-holer and disappeared inside. A minute or so later, probably just enough time for Poz to get comfortable, what should suddenly appear but a Marine H-53 helicopter. Those things are monsters, and the rotor wash is strong enough to knock you off your feet should one hover over you at a hundred feet. This one had a very large net hanging beneath it full of some sort of cargo. It was heading toward the ramp across the runway from our parked Birddogs and decelerating as it descended. It slowly passed above us, peppering us with dirt and small rocks kicked up by the downwash from its rotors. I'm told that a heavily laden H-53 pulling maximum power in a hover can create winds nearing one hundred miles per hour. I believe it. Our Birddogs were rocking violently as the downwash caught their wings, but fortunately the helicopter was moving rapidly enough that it didn't create any damage to our aircraft. But as it slowly moved over the four-holer occupied by Poz, disaster struck.

The entire structure rose about five feet from the ground, then almost in slow motion it rolled, inverted as the rotor wash moved with the passing H-53, and then crashed back to earth.

"Hey, Poz is in there!" Keltner yelled.

"Damn!" muttered one of the AOs, and we all ran toward the now completely shattered four-holer. Boards were broken and laying askew. The diesel and excrement-filled drums were scattered about, their contents now coating everything.

"He's moving," someone said as our little band of would-be rescuers came to a screeching halt just short of the nastiness running in rivulets on the ground.

"Poz, you okay?" someone asked, as Poz, covered with diesel fuel, pieces of used bathroom tissue, and excrement, slowly crawled from beneath the broken pieces of wood that had once been a magnificent four-holer. As concerned as we were, nobody offered to help him to his feet. We all just sort of backed away with worried looks on our faces. I guess that helping a friend in need does have its limits.

Poz didn't answer other than to mutter something derogatory regarding helicopters and to state he didn't think that any of his body parts were broken. Thank goodness for that. I doubt that Poz weighed more than a 110 pounds—that's probably why the four-holer went airborne so easily. He didn't weigh enough to keep it on the ground, and the structure itself had so much lightweight surface area that it simply went flying in the rotor wash as the H-53 hovered above.

We escorted our soiled friend to a nearby water trailer, a water buffalo in Marine-speak, which was really nothing more than a large tank mounted on a trailer with spigots and NON POTABLE stenciled in large letters on the sides of the tank. Water buffalos were strategically placed near latrines that didn't have running water. The water within was not for drinking but was clean enough for washing your hands. Field sanitation at work.

Poz shed his flight suit, boots, and underwear and then literally lay down under the spigots while someone handed him a bar of soap. Two of us held the spigots open as he scrubbed his scrawny body. One of the AOs offered to let Poz use an extra flight suit that he had, so he wouldn't be forced to fly back to Phu Bai naked. It was four sizes too big, but that didn't seem to bother Poz one bit. He managed to salvage his boots, but the rest he tossed back into the debris that had once been our four-holer.

Once again a Catkiller had survived contact with the "enemy," this time cleverly disguised as a Marine helicopter and a germ-laden four-holer.

Poz's fateful encounter was in stark contrast to an unbelievable incident—later to become known as The Miracle—that occurred the night of August 27, 1967, at the Marble Mountain Air Facility during an NVA rocket attack. This was the stuff of legends. An old Marine master sergeant, stumbling back to his hooch after a long evening at the NCO Club, decided to stop at a nearby six-holer for a sit-down. As he was seated, the structure took a direct hit from a 122-mm rocket, which blew the entire structure to smithereens, leaving him sitting there on one small remaining section of seat, entirely unscathed! Rumor had it that he got up, pulled up his trousers, stumbled to his hooch, then passed out on his bunk. The only damage seemed to be to his hearing; the sharp crack of the exploding rocket rendered him all but completely deaf for a couple of days.

The next day Whitlow and Sanders walked down there to see the place of The Miracle. Except for the spot where the old sergeant had been sitting, nothing was left but splinters and roofing tin. They said that the master sergeant didn't have to buy a drink at the NCO Club for the rest of his tour. The Mox said it was just another example of the good Lord looking after fools and drunks. Young Marines stopped by to marvel at the wreckage for days, as though going to visit some kind of religious shrine. Always the deep thinker, Sanders said that it should have been a front-page story with photographs in *Stars and Stripes*. It never made the *Stars and Stripes,* and the structure was never rebuilt. It simply sat there as a tribute to the fickleness of the Grim Reaper and to whatever angels in the heavens above protect senior Marine Corps non-commissioned officers.

To us Catkillers and our AOs, "a non-fatal incident" could also describe an occurrence or event with the potential to end one's military career unexpectedly under adverse circumstances—that involving Capt. Mike Sharkey being a case in point.

Mike was an exceptional pilot, but then he was a Catkiller, so none of us were particularly surprised at that. What set Captain Sharkey apart was his resourcefulness and gift of gab. Mike was cut from the same cloth as *Catch-22*'s Milo Minderbinder; he just didn't have the same sense of self-aggrandizement as did the movie version of Milo, portrayed by Jon Voight. Mike definitely had the ability to quickly and decisively solve problems. Sometimes, as in the case of our volleyball court, this got him into trouble.

The volleyball court in question was located next to the Officers Club belonging to the 220th. Everyone in the company was welcome to join in the spirited games frequently played there. Volleyball was a great way to let off steam and certainly added to unit cohesiveness among our pilots, enlisted crew chiefs, and maintenance guys as well as our Marine AOs.

Then came monsoon season. Our volleyball court quickly became a muddy quagmire. Morale plummeted as frustrated would-be volleyball participants could do nothing but stand and look at the nasty, slippery mess—until Capt. Mike Sharkey came to the rescue.

Sharkey just happened to be standing outside the Catkiller O-Club one afternoon when he spotted a Navy Seabee driving a large forklift along the dirt road that cut through our company area. The forklift was laden with some sort of metal panels roughly three feet by ten feet. Instantly recognizing a possible solution to our volleyball dilemma, he ran back into the O-Club, grabbed a bottle of booze from behind the bar, ran back outside, and stood by the roadside waving the bottle and motioning for the Seabee to stop.

Enlisted Marines and Seabees were restricted in their consumption of alcohol. Monthly they were issued a card that was punched every time they procured a beer, usually warm. They never even got a chance to imbibe in the hard stuff. And there stood Captain Sharkey waving a bottle of hard liquor before a young enlisted Seabee. The Seabee stopped the forklift.

"What are those panels that you have on your forklift?" shouted the good captain.

"It's Marsden Matting, sir," the young Seabee yelled back above the noise of his forklift.

"What are you going to do with it?"

"It's for the runway extension, sir."

"Shut that thing off and let's talk."

The negotiations were brief and quickly agreed to. Captain Sharkey would trade several bottles of bourbon for enough Marsden Matting to construct a volleyball court and the Seabees would install it.

The very next day a contingent of Seabees did in fact lay out enough Marsden Matting to complete a regulation size volleyball court next to the Catkiller O-Club. Morale at the 220th soared! Captain Sharkey was a hero! The troops were again engaged in one of their favorite pastimes, monsoon season be damned!

There was a downside though. Marsden Matting was created to replace perforated steel panels (interlocking steel panels with holes in them that worked well as temporary runways for aircraft until it rained and they would get wet—then they became slicker than snot). Marsden Matting was light metal alloy panels with no holes that were interlocking and had a sandpaper-like gritty surface that prevented aircraft tires from slipping when wet. The matting was great for runways, although not so great for volleyball courts. The nonskid surface produced at least one sprained ankle on a Catkiller pilot and was cause for his being grounded from flying for a week as he hobbled around using crutches. Such are the vagaries of war. Sprained ankles or no, the Catkillers were able to resume their outdoor pastime and not get muddy.

About two weeks after Captain Sharkey's momentous achievement, a dark cloud hovered over our O-Club in the form of a Marine major, the airfield commander at Phu Bai. Simply put, he was in charge of and responsible for just about everything associated with the airfield, from the refueling facility, to all support vehicles, to structures, to the runway itself. His job was not an easy one, nor was it devoid of responsibility. If something went wrong anywhere on his airfield, his superiors would look to him for immediate answers. It is not difficult to see why the major was a man under constant pressure, a man who saw little humor in anything that ran contrary to good order and discipline.

It was early evening and the major had stopped by the Catkiller O-Club for some libations and friendly conversation. Eventually nature called and the major inquired as to the location of the head. Someone piped up, "It's right out that side door, sir. Just go straight and you can't miss it."

Out the door went the major, who happened to glance to his right as he was walking and see the beautiful Marsden Matting volleyball court. Forgetting all about his head call he performed a 180-degree turn without breaking stride and stormed back into the O-Club.

"Who authorized that volleyball court?" he demanded in a very loud and authoritative voice. A hush fell over the O-Club, which by now was full of Catkiller pilots and Marine AOs.

"That's about twenty feet of MY runway out there, and I want to know how in the hell it got there, and who in the hell is responsible for it!"

From somewhere in the room a voice said, "Captain Sharkey."

"Captain who?"

"That's me, sir," said Sharkey, sliding down off his stool at the bar where he and fellow platoon leader Capt. John Kovach had been drinking and playing their nightly game of Flinch. With a big grin on his face, Sharkey calmly walked up to the nearly apoplectic major. The rest of us sat frozen, knowing we were about to witness Sharkey receive at least an Article 15 or worse, a court-martial at the hands of one seriously pissed-off Marine major. From the look on the major's face, a beheading might not be completely out of the question either.

Sharkey calmly suggested the two of them go outside and check out the problem. We watched through the open doorway as Sharkey and the major engaged in earnest conversation for several minutes. At first, there was quite a bit of arm waving by the major, then, amazingly, laughter, a firm handshake, and smiles as the major departed. Sharkey ambled back into the club, refusing to answer a hundred questions—"What happened?" "Is he gonna hang your ass?" "Are we gonna lose the volley-ball court?"—and simply remounted his stool at the bar with an "It's all taken care of, no sweat." He then returned to his game of Flinch with

Kovach, which usually seemed to end in Sharkey getting slugged on the shoulder and knocked off his barstool. Why he persisted in playing that game with Kovach, a former college linebacker, remains a mystery to this day.

The next day a group of Seabees showed up and to our dismay removed the Marsden Matting. And then, to our astonishment, they laid out the forms and poured a regulation-size concrete volleyball court exactly where the major's "twenty feet of runway" had been. In just a few days we were back in the volleyball game, this time with no twisted ankles.

Captain Sharkey once again modestly assumed the mantle of local hero. He never would tell us exactly what had been said as he and the irate major stood outside the O-Club, but we all knew Sharkey's quick wit and sense of humor had somehow kept him undamaged, alive, and out of jail and had made us all the beneficiaries of an expensive volleyball court.

22

Low-Level Flight
The Good, the Bad, and the Ugly

The Catkiller standard operating procedures were pretty specific about flying low level: "Thou shall not do it!" There were times, however, when flying close to the dirt simply could not be avoided. Admittedly, almost all Catkiller pilots were in their early to mid-twenties and tended to be type A or at least A- personalities; it wasn't surprising to find us occasionally expressing our exuberance while in flight. Most of the time we were all business, and if we broke a rule or two, we had a damn good reason. Yet, we were young, ten feet tall and bullet proof, being paid to fly a single-pilot, fun-to-fly airplane Uncle Sam had given to us for a whole year. Temptation was never far away singing her siren song.

In truth, the minimum altitude rule—eight hundred to one thousand feet—was a pretty good one. Flying at this height would put you just out of range of accurate AK-47 fire; and if you frequently threw in some turns and a bit of uncoordinated flight, the rule would generally keep you from getting hit by machine-gun fire as well. Of course, once the bad guys knew you had them spotted and you began shooting artillery or running fixed wing on them, all bets were off.

Supporting "troops in contact" put everything in a special context if you were a Catkiller. I'm not saying pilots in other Army Birddog units wouldn't fly low to help their brothers on the ground when the situation warranted, but merely that I never knew or heard of a Catkiller who wouldn't fly his Birddog right up an NVA soldier's ass if that's what it took to get the job done.

This was exactly the situation my AO and I found ourselves in during late afternoon on May 10, 1968. We were flying near the dirt road running south from Con Thien on the west side of Leatherneck Square right near the foothills. The shadows from the hills to the west of the road were getting long, and we were heading back to Dong Ha for the night. Suddenly we heard a voice whispering to us on our FM radio.

"Catkiller, Catkiller, this is Sand Box, over."

I figured that it was a Marine recon team because they always whispered. Usually they just wanted to check in to have us help them verify their location. They would have one of the team members lying on his back in the brush popping a red panel. We would fly over and then fly off a short distance (they tended to get nervous if we circled them) while we located their position on our 1:50,000 maps.

We would then use the sophisticated code "First and third on the side of the bird" to tell them where they were. By using the first and third words painted on the side of our aircraft, *UNITED STATES ARMY*— which contained exactly ten letters, none of them repeating—we could give them the digits of the coordinates. For example, the grid coordinates YD 990543 would become Mike, Mike, Yankee, Echo, Tango, India. They would already know they were in grid YD; all they needed were the numbers. Primitive? Yes. Could the bad guys figure it out? Maybe. But because we did not have current communication security codes, it was the best we had and it did seem to work. We didn't use it very often, only when the recon guys needed to know exactly where they were. This time, however, the recon team knew where they were, they just needed help fast!

"We are at your three o'clock in a bomb crater and need an immediate extraction," came the call over the radio.

"Roger Sand Box, we think we see where you are. What is your situation?"

"We are completely surrounded by at least a platoon of the NVA, and if we can't get out of here pretty soon, we're not going to make it through the night."

That got my attention. I dialed up the DASC on UHF and asked it to scramble a couple of flights of fixed wing and some helicopters for an emergency extraction. In the meantime my AO was getting the specifics from Sand Box on where all of his people were, exactly where the NVA soldiers were, what kind of weapons the NVA had, and how much longer Sand Box felt they could hold on.

Under these circumstances, it was definitely okay to circle the recon team. We could see they were all lying in a very large bomb crater facing outward in a 360-degree circle. We could also see that lots of men in pale green shorts and shirts had the Marines nearly surrounded and were closing in fast. Knowing that it was going to be a while before the jets coming off the hot pad at Chu Lai could come to the rescue, it was decision time.

"They are in some real deep shit Ray," my AO said over the intercom. "How long before the fixed wing are going to show up?"

"About twenty minutes, maybe thirty," I replied.

"That's too long; we need to do something to get the gomers off their backs."

I thought for a few seconds about our options and said, "Well, we can always go down and try to distract them by shooting out of our windows. You up for that?"

"It's all we've got, let's do it."

So down we went. Both of us were firing our rifles out the open side windows, buzzing over the NVA soldiers as close as I dared to go. Every time we made a low pass, the bad guys would start scrambling around, and that was taking the heat off the recon team. This tactic went on for a while, just how long I'm not sure, but it seemed like an eternity. All the while I kept thinking, *Come on jets we need you NOW!*

I must have fired nearly all of the bullets in the spare magazines I carried in a canvas bag by my right foot, and my AO shot nearly all the ammunition he had. By this time we were shooting our .45-caliber pistols. I'm not sure we hit anything, but we were making lots of noise and annoying the hell out of the NVA soldiers. They must have thought we were nuts! Good. We were. Fortunately, before we ran completely out of bullets the DASC called to tell us our extraction helicopters were en route and that two flights of A-4s were inbound, call signs Hellborne 2-0-3 and 2-0-5, and to work them on button Yellow.

I reached up to my right and switched my UHF radio to tactical frequency Yellow and listened to the two Hellborne flights check in with each other, their voices strangely muffled by the oxygen masks they were wearing. I advised Hellborne 2-0-3 to proceed inbound and 2-0-5 to hold over Dong Ha. In a few minutes the 2-0-3 flight of two A-4s showed up.

"Catkiller 4-2, Hellborne 2-0-3," came the call of the radio. "We each have six Delta One-Alphas, two Delta Sevens, and Pistols." Hellborne had just told me he and his wingman were each carrying six 250-pound Snake-Eyes, two 500-pound canisters of Nape, and 20-mm cannons. Exactly what we needed in this close air support situation.

"Okay Hellborne 2-0-3," I responded, "here's what we've got. A recon team is hunkered down in a bomb crater just to the west of the dirt road that runs due south out of Con Thien. They are completely surrounded by NVA soldiers that are within 50 meters of them. Your drops will be danger close. Target elevation is 800 feet with rising terrain to the west. I want you to make your runs from south to north on a 360-heading parallel to the dirt road with a right-hand pull. I'll be over the friendlies in a right-hand orbit at 800 feet. Nearest friendlies are in the bomb crater. So far, they are reporting only small-arms fire. We have been making low passes on the NVA soldiers to keep them busy, and we have not taken any hits that we know of. Let's start with your Delta Sevens, just one at a time so we don't get any on the friendlies. I say again, we are danger close [emphasizing that we were going to be extremely close to the Marines]. All of the friendlies are in the bomb crater, and they are keeping their heads down. We'll use the Delta One-Alphas next and then the Pistols if we need them."

"Dash One has you in sight," came the reply. "Go ahead and mark the target."

As I was communicating with the flight of A-4s, my AO was briefing Sand Box on what we were going to do and ensuring the recon team was okay with what was about to happen. Dropping any ordnance that close, especially napalm, fell into the category of danger close and required the full concurrence of the folks on the ground. They understood the danger, but they also understood that was the only way we could get them out alive. "They said that they will keep their heads down and hope we don't screw up."

I brought the Birddog quickly around, activated the arming switches, and carefully set up to put a Willie Pete exactly where I wanted Hell-borne 2-0-3 to put the first Nape. *Please God,* I thought to myself, *let this be the most accurate rocket I've ever fired.*

Under normal circumstances, putting a rocket within twenty meters of where we wanted the fixed wing to drop their ordnance was called good. We would then tell the jet pilots to adjust their distance and direction using the clock system, for example, from my smoke, twenty meters at nine o'clock. In this instance, close wasn't good enough—my WP marking rocket had to be perfect. I was pretty low so I simply pulled the throttle closed, let the nose drop, and squeezed the trigger on the control stick. I then banked sharply away as the rocket impacted about fifty meters to the right of the bomb crater, right where I wanted it.

"Put your first Delta Seven right on my smoke. I have you in sight and you are cleared hot."

"Roger Catkiller, I have your smoke. One's in hot," came the reply.

Now it was all up to the accuracy of the A-4 jock. His napalm canister impacted just to the right of the billowing white smoke of my Willie Pete rocket, exploding in a cascade of intense flame and certain death to anything in its path.

"Perfect, Catkiller. That really nailed them. Keep it coming," I heard Sand Box shout on the FM radio, no longer bothering to whisper.

Marine A-4s were incredibly accurate with their ordnance drops under normal conditions, but this time they outdid themselves. The A-4s could not carry the amount of ordnance that the F-4s could. Unlike the F-4s they were not supersonic; but when Marines on the ground were in dire straits and we needed absolute perfection, a Marine pilot in a Marine A-4 was always just what the doctor ordered.

Hellborne 2-0-3 flight made repeated passes, dropping ordnance dangerously close to the Marines in the bomb crater. After the napalm came the Snake Eyes. These bombs were specifically designed for close air support of ground troops. Once they are released from the aircraft, a set of high-drag fins pop out, retarding the bomb's forward motion so that it explodes well behind the releasing aircraft; this means bombs can be dropped as low as two hundred feet, which improves accuracy and ensures the aircraft dropping the bomb is out of shrapnel range when the bomb explodes.

Then I heard a radio transmission that no TACA ever wants to hear.

"Catkiller, Catkiller, you're too close! We're taking shrapnel!"

"Hellborne flight," I nearly shouted into my mic, "go high and dry, we're hitting the friendlies."

My AO immediately started talking to the Marines on the ground to determine what had happened and the extent of injuries to members of the recon team. After a few very tense moments, Sand Box responded in a rather contrite tone. "The drops were perfect," he said, "but one of my people was standing up taking pictures and got nicked by some flying shrapnel. Sorry about that, they'll keep their heads down. Go ahead with your drops."

Sometimes you just can't predict what a young Marine is going to do. Here they were almost completely surrounded, fighting for their lives, and they felt confident enough in what we were doing to expose themselves so they could take pictures! Foolish, probably; confident, absolutely; brave, beyond measure. But I bet that the recon team leader chewed some serious butt down there in that bomb crater.

"Hellborne 2-0-3 flight, Catkiller 4-2, we got the problem straightened out. Your drops were fine, just somebody standing up taking pictures."

By now the sun had set behind the mountains to the west and the only illumination around the Marines was the burning brush from the napalm. Just as I was releasing Hellborne 2-0-3, the two extraction helos, call sign Chatterbox 1-3, showed up.

"We have you in sight Catkiller. We're ready to make the extraction when you clear us in," came over the radio.

My AO, who had stayed in contact with the Marines on the ground, advised that they had identified a landing zone two hundred meters south of their location. They weren't taking as much fire as they had been, so we must have been doing some good. They were going to make a break for it, he told me, as soon as the helos were on final approach. "They have a strobe light," he said, "and will turn it on as they move to the landing zone. They'll stay in the bomb crater until we give them the go-ahead."

"Sounds good," I said over the intercom, "tell them to get ready to saddle up."

Next, I went back to the helicopters. "Roger Chatterbox," I radioed, "I'm going to have the fixed wing make two more drops and then we'll get you right in. The LZ is two hundred meters due south of the bomb crater the recon team is in. I want you to fly north about two klicks and then turn back south for your final approach."

As Hellborne 2-0-5 flight was making the last drops of their Snake Eyes, the helicopters radioed they were turning south and inbound to the LZ.

Looking down, all I could see of the two H-46s were their top red rotating beacons as they passed beneath me and, then, total darkness as the Chatterbox pilots extinguished even those lights to avoid drawing enemy fire. I watched the blinking strobe light moving toward the LZ and then it went out. Suddenly, the total blackness was lit up with dozens of intense bright flashes of light, right about where the LZ was.

Oh my god, I thought, *they've been ambushed!* I was nearly overwhelmed with anguish. *So close and we aren't going to get them out*, was all that I could think. Total darkness enveloped everything again as the bright flashes ceased; and then, silence. My heart was in my throat. A feeling of absolute failure went like a spear straight through my chest. *How can this be? We all worked so hard.*

Then, out of the darkness, a radio transmission: "Catkiller, Chatterbox 1-3, we've got all of them. We're heading for Dong Ha. Lights are coming back on. Thanks for the good work."

A feeling of relief washed over me as I watched the red rotating beacons of the two Chatterbox H-46s climb up to altitude and turn toward Dong Ha in the distance. We had flown low and lives had been saved.

"Ah roger Chatterbox, Catkiller 4-2, I thought you were ambushed back there when the LZ lit up," I managed to say over the UHF radio.

"Oh, that was just them shooting out of the portholes as we lifted," was Chatterbox's calm response. Later I was to discover that it was standard procedure for recon teams to stick their rifles out of the portholes on the sides of the helicopters and fire on full automatic as the helicopter lifted from a "hot" LZ. This gunfire was meant to encourage any nearby enemy soldiers to keep their heads down while the helicopter was most vulnerable. The bright flashes I had seen were the muzzle flashes of the recon team shooting, not the enemy. The sudden disappearance of the strobe light was the recon team running up the rear ramp and disappearing into the helicopter. I also learned that all of the Plexiglas in portholes on helicopters that supported recon teams was removed; when a team boarded the helicopter, they expected to be able to fire as the helicopter lifted so they would smash out any portholes they found with Plexiglas in them.

Not all low-level flights were this successful. A month earlier we had been flying in Leatherneck Square when we got a call from a Marine platoon on a sweep just north of Cam Lo.

"Catkiller, Catkiller, this is Mad Minute 2-6 X-Ray, do you read, over? Can you get us a medevac bird in here? We have two routine medevacs at this location."

Looking down, my AO and I could see several Marines walking around in the brush near two shelter halves erected together with two pairs of bare feet sticking out of one end. The way they were milling around gave the impression they were not in contact with the enemy and gave us cause to wonder why the two men were lying under the shelter halves, so my AO keyed his mic button and asked about the nature of their injuries.

"We have two heat exhaustion cases, and we need to get them medevaced so we can continue our mission, over."

"Roger," replied my AO, "I'll see what we can do for you." Then to me on intercom he stated, "It looks pretty calm down there, so we probably won't have a hot LZ. Let's give the DASC a call and see if we can get something up for them."

"Roger that," I told him on the intercom and then went ahead and requested a routine medevac from the DASC.

It was a slow afternoon, so we decided to hang around for a while to direct any inbound helicopters, to the Marines' location. A few minutes later, Mad Minute called again to ask if we had any word on the medevac, requesting that it now be upgraded to a priority medevac.

Marines in the bush in Vietnam not only ran the risk of getting shot, they struggled with the loads they had to carry in the heat and humidity. It typically took a couple of weeks before new replacements became acclimated, and in the process many of them had to suffer through bouts of heat exhaustion. The only way to snap someone out of it was to get them out of the sun, cool them down, and have them drink lots of water. I called the DASC and passed on the upgrade request. More time went by and still no helicopter.

"We are now requesting an emergency medevac," radioed Mad Minute. "They [the casualties] are going into thermal runaway. We need that medevac now!"

Hearing that transmission from the ground, I began thinking maybe there was something I could do to get those two young Marines to safety. Back at Dong Ha, there was a medical station with two large stainless-steel tanks, each full of ice-cold water with ice cubes actually floating in them. Normal procedure for a heat injury was to strip the patient and submerse him in the ice-cold water. This would drive all of the blood, which had gone to the body's extremities in an attempt to mitigate the increased body temperature, back to the vital organs. After that the patient could then be stabilized, and he would recover in a matter of hours. The key was to get him to the tanks before he went beyond his body's ability to recover. Heat exhaustion can kill!

As I looked around, I decided I could land on the dirt road just to the west and take them to Dong Ha myself. I lowered flaps and tried an approach to the road as I told my AO what I was thinking. "Tell them that if they will just get their people to the road a half klick to their west, I'll get them to Dong Ha."

"Negative," came the reply from the ground. "We can't risk an ambush taking them to the road."

That was when I broke into the conversation. "I'll come down and troll for bad guys. You let me know if you hear anyone shooting at me, okay?"

And that's what I did. I slowly flew around between Mad Minute and the dirt road at about fifty feet above the ground. I was a nice, ripe, and very desirable target for any NVA soldier in the area. I started another landing approach that would have brought me down right next to the Marines' location, but quickly realized that even if I could have landed without flipping over on my back, I would not have been be able to take off again—the earth was too soft to land on, having been so torn up by previous artillery strikes. By now frustration was beginning to get to me. I couldn't land at the Marines' location, they refused to get their two heat casualties to the dirt road, and I couldn't get the DASC to spring just one damn helicopter loose from whatever it was doing.

Two young Marines died that day. Not from bullet wounds or enemy activity, but heat exhaustion. They died because nobody tried hard enough to save them. I should have come up on Guard frequency and made a blanket transmission for any helicopter that could hear me to come to their rescue. The DASC could possibly have redirected a helicopter on another mission to take a fifteen-minute detour and pick them up. The Marine commander could have trusted me when I told him it was safe to take them to the road and then done so. None of that happened. Instead two mothers' sons died in the span of about an hour, lying barefoot beneath two shelter halves in the hot sun, less than five miles from two stainless steel tanks filled with ice water and salvation. That sad memory haunts me to this day. Sometimes you fly low and it still ends in tragedy.

Other times you fly low and it gets ugly. That's what happened to me one day in February. I'd just had two pretty good days of flying on the DMZ. I'd blown some stuff up, run a few flights of fixed wing on three or four excellent targets, helped out some Marines in trouble, and adjusted artillery on a bunker complex. Life was good and I was heading back to Phu Bai for a day off. The sun was shining, there was hardly a cloud in the I-Corps sky, and the ribbon of Highway 1 beneath my wings was leading me home to a shower, cold beer, and clean sheets.

In the distance ahead of me I noticed a lone Huey flying low level, parallel to the highway. There he was, a Slick, all by himself in the Street Without Joy area, flying down the wrong side of the road. He even had the side cargo doors closed, with no evidence of a door gunner sitting behind an M-60 machine gun on either side of the aircraft. Nobody except Dustoffs—Army medevac helicopters—flew unarmed Hueys in Vietnam, and they had big red crosses painted on them. But this Huey didn't have red crosses. I was in a D-Model Birddog, faster than a Huey, and the temptation was just too great for someone in as good a mood as I was: I had to pass him. Besides, only a complete idiot would fly a lone Huey low level in that neck of the woods. So, down I went gradually overtaking the unsuspecting Rotorhead in my spiffy, superfast D-Model Dog, jumping the wireless telephone poles along the right side of the highway. It wasn't long before I had passed the Huey, a good two hundred yards to its right, and then climbed back up to one thousand feet and proceeded to Phu Bai. It all seemed like harmless fun to me.

But not to the commanding general of the United States Army's 1st Cavalry Division, Maj. Gen. John J. Tolson; it was his UH-1 Huey helicopter flying low-level "solo" I had passed near the Street Without Joy. The next day I was awakened and told to report to my CO, Maj. Gary Clark, for an undisclosed reason. Puzzled, I did as I was told, and the outcome wasn't pretty. It seems that General Tolson had been on board that lone Huey flying low level near the Street Without Joy. He had taken umbrage at my "telephone pole hopping" antics and was demanding that I be severely punished.

"Sir, Captain Caryl reports," I said, coming to attention exactly three steps in front of Major Clark's desk and popping a most excellent hand salute.

Major Clark just looked at me with scorn written all over his face and asked, "Captain Caryl, did you pass a Huey yesterday coming back from Dong Ha, jumping telephone poles as you went by him?"

"Yes sir, I did," I answered, a sort of numb feeling creeping up my body.

"Well, that Huey belongs to General Tolson, and he was in it and he got your tail number. He wants you charged with reckless and dangerous operation of an Army aircraft. I have to do it and I'm not very happy about it."

The numb feeling crept higher.

"Here's what I'm going to do. While I figure out whether to court-martial you or just give you an Article 15, you are going to put on your steel pot and your flak jacket, take your rifle, and ride shotgun on a truck in the resupply convoy between here and Hue Citadel. You are grounded! Understand? Now get out of my office!"

I managed to squeak out a "Yes sir," saluted, about-faced, and, I'm certain, stumbled to the door. *Oh man, how quickly a seemingly harmless act conducted in a moment of high spirits can turn sour, especially when a general wants a piece of your ass.*

For the next three days I remained in a state of depression. I had really screwed up. A perfect example of how a whole bunch of "attaboys" can be wiped out by just one "aw-shit." According to an old Army aviation saying, there is a very fine line between an Air Medal and an Article 15; the latter is nonjudicial punishment, and I had crossed that line. On the bright side, riding shotgun in a five-ton truck pulling a flatbed trailer wasn't all that bad. I got to see Vietnam low level without worrying about pissing off some general. Of course, there was always the chance of hitting a mine or getting shot at, but that concern was overshadowed by the joy of looking at the little kids who lined the road. They were always smiling; the resilience of children in the worst of conditions never ceased to amaze, and for a brief time I felt real compassion for the Vietnamese people and their plight.

One little girl who I saw each day stood out from the rest of the children. She was probably six or seven years old, appeared to have some French in her ancestry, and wasn't as aggressive as the rest of the children in the group. She wore a tattered dress and was barefoot, had long black hair, big dark eyes, high cheekbones, and a pretty smile. All this tugged at my heartstrings; I wished that somehow I could scoop her up and send her home so my folks could clean her up, put nice dresses on her, send her to school, and give her an opportunity to live a full life free from danger and want. Children should not have to experience war. I couldn't do it, though, so I tossed her candy and some C-rations as we rumbled by, silently praying that somehow she would survive this hell she was forced to live in.

While I was grounded, Major Clark apparently wasn't too excited about having to really nail me to the wall as the good general had demanded. Capt. John Mulvany, one of the good guys and a pal, had become the company operations officer; he was close to Major Clark and, I guess, sort of a confidant. Years later I learned learn that over drinks at the Catkiller O-Club bar, John had convinced Major Clark I was really a darn good pilot, knew my job, and did it well when not irritating generals. I think my having taken the assigned task of riding shotgun without complaint may have been factored in as well. Anyway, after three days on the ground, my name showed up on the mission board and I was back in the sky flying the DMZ.

23 | Homeward Bound

When I arrived in country in July 1967, pilots in the 220th RAC were granted two leaves for rest and recuperation (R&R) during their tour of duty in Vietnam. I would like to believe the two R&R gift was granted because somebody somewhere felt Catkillers hung their asses out just a bit more than Army Birddog pilots in other companies. Those pilots slated for R&R could choose to fly to one of six possible destinations courtesy of Uncle Sam: Bangkok, Kuala Lumpur, Australia, Tokyo, Hong Kong, or Hawaii. We only had to pay for our own lodging and entertainment while we were there. Most of the guys who were married went to Hawaii where they were able to spend a week with their wives. For the rest of us, the world awaited.

Initially I planned to take my first R&R in February of the coming year. I'd go to Australia because it was summer Down Under and rumor had it the ladies of Australia loved the young men fighting in Vietnam, just as their mothers had loved World War II Yanks who had served in the Pacific. Then, I'd take my second R&R in June in Hong Kong, just before completing my tour and rotating home, so I could do some shopping.

And then at the end of January Tet happened. It was starting to look like the NVA was getting serious about the war and our two R&R tradition would soon become a distant memory. Consequently, buying stuff in Hong Kong became more important than any hedonistic pursuits in Australia. Ah, the difficult choices we are forced to make in the quest for happiness. Reluctantly, I decided to forget about Australia and head for the mall.

My R&R adventure got off to a spine-tingling start even before I left Vietnam. By this time I had gotten used to total strangers trying to kill me and figured there weren't any more surprises that would snatch my attention. So there I was on February 9, 1968, comfortably seated about twenty rows back in a Pan American DC-6 parked on the ramp at Da Nang preparing for departure to Hong Kong. I was wiping accumulated sweat from my face with a warm, damp cloth the stewardess had just handed to me and excitedly anticipating my week of rest and recuperation in Hong Kong.

Suddenly the sergeant who had herded us all on board was now moving rapidly down the aisle, telling us all, "Get off the airplane NOW! Do not take anything with you, just get up and get off the airplane." He wasn't kidding. We all quickly got up and rapidly descended the boarding stairs and then were led away from the aircraft to an area inside a low fence just outside the terminal building, about one hundred feet away from the aircraft. Naturally, there was quite a buzz among all of us as to why we were standing outside in the bright Vietnam sun and not on our way to Hong Kong. We were soon to find out.

As we watched, numerous pieces of ground-handling equipment were moved in close proximity to the aircraft, completely surrounding it. The aircraft was now blocked and could not move. Several jeeps and assorted military vehicles filled with Air Force Security Police carrying M-16s arrived quickly, and the police positioned themselves with their weapons pointed at the aircraft. This was not normal procedure.

One of the Air Force sergeants ambled over and told a few of us the aircraft was not going anywhere; there was an AWOL Marine, charged with shooting a fellow Marine, in the cockpit waving a .45 around, demanding to be flown to Communist China. The word had come back down the chain of command, all the way from General Westmoreland himself: the aircraft was not to move, regardless of any threats to the

Pan Am crew. Right about then I was thinking that being a Pan Am airline pilot could be almost as dangerous as being an Army Birddog pilot in I Corps.

Suddenly there was a flurry of movement inside the cockpit and the starboard forward galley door was flung open revealing several uniformed men with rifles pulling the young handcuffed Marine through the doorway and down the airstairs that had been hastily rolled up to the side of the aircraft. He was not looking all too happy. At the bottom of the stairs, more military personnel surrounded him immediately and he was quickly swept out of sight. I had my camera out and was taking a few pictures of the hapless would-be hijacker when the thought crossed my mind he would probably never be seen nor heard from again.

The next day a replacement Pan Am aircraft took us to Hong Kong, and I began my week of rest and recuperation, which quickly became a week of restlessness and reflection. Once I had gotten over the excitement of the attempted hijacking at Da Nang, the magnificent city of Hong Kong was like being in another universe. Just a couple of hours before I had been in a combat zone and now I was safe and secure in the luxurious Hong Kong Hilton.

My first night in Hong Kong was a memorable one. I had turned in early after an excellent steak dinner and a couple of drinks at the hotel bar. Deep in a sound sleep, I was awakened by what I thought was the terrifying scream of a 122-mm rocket! I launched myself from the bed still mostly asleep and, acting out of pure reflex, tried to slide under the bed. I came fully awake wondering why I couldn't get under it, then realized the bed was elevated on a platform, not legs; there was no open space. That was when I realized that the screech I had heard wasn't an incoming rocket but rather a jet passing over the hotel to land at the Hong Kong airport. I may have been physically safe here in Hong Kong, but that damned war wasn't going to let go of my subconscious.

The next morning I was up and quickly adjusting to my new surroundings. I decided to do some shopping and explore this beautiful, cosmopolitan metropolis full of so much familiar Western culture. Capitalism was in full bloom, with shops and stores everywhere selling everything from stereos and cameras to custom-tailored suits. Yet just across the bay lay a country with an enormous population wrapped in Marxism. Even though Hong Kong was a British colony, I began to wonder about the hypocrisy of a Communist government that seemed very eager to leave this door of capitalistic endeavor open to the rest of the world. And that thought wasn't the only cloud that began to creep into my consciousness.

Oddly, by the end of the second day I began to feel a sort of unease at being here safe and sound while my brother Catkillers, just a few hours away by air, were at war. I just couldn't shake the thought that, since the onset of Tet, the level of combat intensity had increased and with it the level of risk and potential for getting shot down. Then came the guilt: What if one of my fellow Catkillers got shot down and I wasn't there to help him? We argued and gave each other a hard time, but we loved each other exactly like brothers. I was here on R&R safe and they were not. It is difficult to explain, and only those who have faced danger over a protracted period of time and grown very close to those who have faced it with them will know, but the feeling of guilt for not being "there" with them is almost overwhelming. And I had a huge dose of it.

By day three of my long-anticipated R&R, I was ready to go back to Vietnam. I felt the same stream of emotions I would feel later, when I returned home at the end of my year in Vietnam. It was survivor's guilt. I was lucky. I figured it out. But a lot of guys didn't and they, along with their families, fell victim to that awful residue of war that is so damned difficult for them to verbalize and work through.

The week finally ended, and I returned to Vietnam looking forward to getting back to work. Because of bad weather, I had to spend three nights at Marble Mountain waiting to catch a flight to Phu Bai. On February 20, I was back flying the DMZ, getting shot at, and feeling normal. The week away had allowed me to clear my head and gain a new perspective. The war had changed. Some of it subtle, like the fading support from the folks back home. The massive assault of the major cities throughout South Vietnam by the NVA and Viet Cong had come as a complete surprise and seemed counter to previous claims that we were winning. Now the press was reporting that we were losing, and although U.S. troops had never lost a major battle, the die was cast. In the eyes of our loved ones at home we were losing, and we were losers.

Needless to say, what Cronkite and the boys back home were saying wasn't sitting well with the Catkillers. We were flying more hours and getting shot at more than ever and the NVA just kept coming. Now our bitch sessions not only included how we were being told to fight the war with one hand tied behind our backs, they also included our new enemy, the press. We were definitely feeling increased pressure from the NVA throughout I Corps and it was taking its toll on the 220th RAC.

At Dong Ha we were taking incoming artillery from North Vietnam nearly every night and during the day as well. The weather wasn't co-operating much either. Normally I would spend just one night up there out of every three, but because of bad weather I wound up spending five of the last eight nights of February stuck at Dong Ha—nobody could get up to Dong Ha from Phu Bai to relieve. The NVA soldiers took full advantage of the low clouds to shoot artillery at us, probably realizing we weren't flying so we couldn't spot them. The constant pounding was aggravating. I just wanted to get into the sky and adjust some of our artillery on them for a change.

On February 28, 1968, my AO and I were refueling our airplane when artillery from North Vietnam came screeching in. I threw down the nozzle, closed the fuel cap, and we both jumped into the aircraft. Neither of us bothered to buckle his seat belt or shoulder harness until after we were safely in the sky. We agreed it was better to be airborne unbuckled than sitting on the ground waiting for the next explosion, especially when parked at the refueling point.

I was at Phu Bai in a deep sleep on the night of March 8 when a low-flying jet went over. I had the same reaction as my first night at the Hong Kong Hilton and launched myself out of my bed while still somewhat asleep. This time I landed on my steel helmet I had placed on the floor next to my bed, open side up. The sharp edges caught me in the small of my back. *Ouch!* I must have been getting "short-timer's disease" and become jumpy. It was easy to control when I was busy flying and taking it to the bad guys, but it seemed to creep up on me when I was sleeping with my guard down or on the ground feeling vulnerable. The only place I felt safe anymore was in the sky.

Capt. Rick Vance, whose room in the hooch at Phu Bai was just across from mine, had slept through the frequent mortar attacks we had been experiencing. He begged me to wake him up the next time one occurred so he could join the rest of us in the bunker. I agreed and attempted to wake him up the very next night. He simply would not wake up! I'd never seen anybody sleep that soundly, especially with explosions going off nearby, so I left him and ran to the bunker. Vance was pretty pissed at me the next morning. I pointed out that if I had stood there and been blown away too, then the company would have been short two pilots, one of them very good (me) and the other sort of mediocre (him), so it was better to lose just one (him). For some reason Vance failed to see the humor in my comment. "Funny" takes on a whole new meaning in combat.

On March 9, 1968, I got a close-up glimpse of what the Marines were experiencing during the siege of Khe Sanh. I had walked into my hooch and saw a dirty, disheveled, bearded, mud-covered Marine lieutenant standing in the middle of the hooch as though he was looking for something. His eyes were sunken and had the strange glint of a trapped animal, like a cornered rat. I had never experienced seeing a human being that looked like that guy did. He introduced himself and asked if I knew where Lt. Bob Happe was. I answered that Bob was up at Dong Ha but would return the next day. The lieutenant told me he was Happe's pal and that he was at Phu Bai from his unit at Khe Sanh to pick up the pay for his troops. He said he would have to leave the next morning and wondered if he could sleep in Happe's room that night. I told him yes, Happe probably wouldn't mind if he racked out on his bunk. He said, "No, that's okay," and with that, the strange lieutenant lay down on the concrete floor right in front of me and fell instantly asleep. Just what kind of hell those Marines were going through at Khe Sanh, I could not imagine. One thing I did know was that I had witnessed the most serious case of chronic fatigue I had ever seen.

By the middle of April we were directed to fly at least five hours a day with no days off. My suspicions were confirmed: even the higher-ups were beginning to get the message that the North Vietnamese were not anywhere close to giving up the fight.

Then came what I considered the final insult. Periodically officers were required to fill out what we called our Dream Sheet. On it we would list, among other things, any schools we wanted to attend and aviators indicated any aircraft transitions we wanted. I had always put the Grumman OV-1 Mohawk as my first priority for aircraft transition; when I received orders to attend the helicopter qualification course at Fort Rucker after completing my tour in Vietnam, I was not at all pleased. I was a fixed-wing pilot and wanted to stay that way. Helicopters were dangerous, and I had been witness to enough helicopter mishaps during the past few months to probably feel that way forever. The only thing that I could do was wait until I got back to the United States, contact Infantry Branch, and see if I could weasel my way out of helicopters and into Mohawks.

During the first week of May there was a three-day bombing halt. We continued to fly but were relegated to visual reconnaissance only. We weren't allowed to shoot anything at anybody. All this did was give the NVA three days of uninterrupted movement of soldiers and supplies south across the DMZ into South Vietnam. On one of my flights I circled several NVA soldiers sitting on the edge of a large bomb crater full of water, soaking their feet and smoking cigarettes with their AK-47s close at hand. We waved to each other. That was the same day my engine tried to quit twice on me during my second flight. I wonder if they would have been as nice to me had I been forced to land next to them because of a dead engine. I nursed my airplane back to Dong Ha, thinking that I was getting down to less than two months left on my tour and that maybe the engine wanting to quit was some sort of omen. Circumstances were beginning to pile up, and they were not in my favor. Of course, as soon as the bombing halt was over and some politician somewhere was happy again, the shooting on the DMZ picked right back up.

June 2, 1968, I requested and was granted my second R&R. I decided to return to Hong Kong primarily because I was familiar with the city and knew I could hunker down and relax rather than because I harbored any desire to visit some new and exotic surroundings. Nobody tried to hijack my airplane, the week went by quickly, and I only encountered a slight touch of survivor's guilt. In hindsight, I guess I was emotionally extracting myself from the war in Vietnam and all of the what-ifs that had plagued me during my first R&R. I had come to grips with the knowledge that the war wasn't going to end soon and that it would probably end badly.

By June 8 I was back at Phu Bai and the daily grind of flying on the DMZ. The excitement of it all had disappeared and, after my R&R, so did some of my aggressiveness. I still had a job to do, but I may have been just a bit more cautious in the way I did it. The thought that I may get out of there alive and in one piece shaded the exuberance of my actions. Basically I just wanted to go home. I was winding down.

June 17, 1968, I was introduced to my replacement, 1st Lt. Jerry Bonning. An eager young kid, he was all eyes and ears wanting to pick up any scrap of information that would help him survive his year in hell. Can't say as I blamed him. I tried to help him get his maps organized and give him a few tips, but I just told him that what he was about to do was learned by on-the-job training and to just soak up as much as he could as fast as he could. Unlike helicopters—in which the Army put the newbie pilots with experienced pilots in the same aircraft—we flew single-pilot aircraft. There wasn't another pilot to give the new guy advice once he climbed into the cockpit; so we always put experienced AOs in with the newbies. The practice went a long way toward mitigating the new-guy problems.

As they say, timing is everything, and that proved to be true for me when I turned in my beloved CAR-15. That little rifle Capt. Kenny Trent had issued to me nearly a year ago had never failed to fire when I wanted it to. And most of the time I had fired full tracer ammo at bad guys out the open window of my Birddog. Other pilots who were issued the standard M-16 rifle complained that occasionally they would experience a problem, generally attributed to the gas port getting fouled by the tracer bullets' coating that made the bullets glow when fired. I never experienced that problem with my CAR-15.

Elements of the 101st Airborne Division had moved into northern I Corps early in the spring of 1968. All of a sudden we were being told to turn in all of our CAR-15 rifles because the 101st Airborne wanted them. Maybe I'm just the suspicious sort, but I think some 101st Airborne colonel saw one or two of our pilots with their CAR-15s and decided that the staff weenies at the 101st headquarters would look really cool if they could parade around with CAR-15s on their shoulders. I was determined to not give up mine until I was no longer flying. For almost three weeks I managed to be somewhere else when my platoon leader came looking for me to turn my weapon in. The day after I flew my last combat mission, I turned in my CAR-15. I was the last Catkiller to do so, a statistic I am quite proud of. Screw a bunch of 101st Airborne brass. If they had wanted CAR-15s so badly, they should have brought 'em with them. The CAR-15s fit perfectly in the cramped cockpits of our little Birddogs and never malfunctioned when we needed them.

Four days after flying my last combat mission on June 26, I received new orders sending me home. I departed Phu Bai on a Marine CH-53 heading for Da Nang and then caught a C-130 flight to Cam Ranh Bay where I encountered one last oddity. I bumped into an Army master sergeant I had known at Fort Ord, California. His job was overseeing the scheduling in and out of Vietnam for the 101st Airborne personnel who were going on R&R. He told me he could put me on an airplane to any of the six R&R locations that I wanted to visit. He said Uncle Sam had already paid for every seat on the airplanes, that many times they left with empty seats, and that I could go to several before I rotated home as long as I had the money to spend once I got there. When I naively suggested my orders didn't allow that, he laughed and told me that orders got "lost" all of the time and not to worry about it. I really should have taken him up on his offer.

July 3, 1968, 25 days after returning from my last R&R, I boarded a Pan Am 707 with more than 150 other happy, lucky souls heading east to the good old United States. The anxiety was almost palpable; would the VC lob one last mortar round our way or would we get out of here in one piece? Every one of us was anxious to get on board and get the hell out of Vietnam!

The big Boeing 707 lifted off the runway at Tan Son Nhut. As the landing gear was coming up an enormous cheer erupted. We had made it! We were heading home. We landed in Japan to refuel but were not allowed to get off the aircraft, probably because the flight crew didn't want to have to waste time rounding up all of us and getting us back on the airplane. I don't think anybody really minded. Every minute we spent here would be a minute's delay in getting home. I spent most of the flight playing Hearts on the floor of the galley with a couple of the flight attendants, so the time seemed to pass pretty quickly.

We landed at McChord Air Force Base near Tacoma, Washington, at about 4 a.m. The sun wasn't up yet and we had to sit on the airplane for an hour waiting for the U.S. Customs folks to show up to clear us back into the United States. Finally an airstair was rolled up to the airplane and we began deplaning. I was one of the last ones off. As I stepped through the open doorway I paused at the top of the stairs. The sun was just coming up on a beautiful, warm July morning, and the fresh smell of evergreen trees filled my senses. I was a Pacific Northwest boy, and this was the sweet smell of home.

AFTERWORD

I served on active duty for a total of six and a half years, remaining in until September 1970. Upon discharge I immediately joined the Georgia Army National Guard, and there I achieved my dream of flying Grumman Mohawks. In 1973 I was hired by the U.S. Forest Service as a pilot in the Southeastern Region. After finally earning my college degree from Embry Riddle Aeronautical University in 1979, I was transferred to California where I flew as a Forest Service lead plane pilot until 1986. I then transferred to the U.S. Customs Service and flew drug interdiction missions in South America, Central America, Mexico, and along the southern U.S. border, before retiring from federal service in 1998.

Not ready to give up flying, for more than two years I flew a helicopter for a local television station in Tucson, Arizona. Eventually that contract ran out, so I returned to flying on forest fires for four years, as a contract helicopter pilot. I hung up my spurs in July 2004 after nearly thirty-eight years of flying as a professional fixed-wing and rotary-wing aviator. Throughout all of those employment changes and transfers, I remained in the Army National Guard and Reserves flying military aircraft until 1997.

Looking back, it has been one heck of a ride. I have two observations I feel are worth sharing:

1. Do not reject serving in the U.S. military as a stepping-stone to lifelong success and satisfaction.
2. The best thing that I can say about my 3,200-plus hours of helicopter flight time is that *I survived!*

APPENDIX

The lyrics of the Catkiller theme song, "CATKILLER 8-0-1," have been attributed to Capt. Kenneth Trent as the sole author. Ken will be the first to admit it was a corroborative effort, spanning several evenings and quite a few adult beverages in the newly constructed 220th Officers Club at Phu Bai in 1967. The song lives on long after the 220th stood down in December 1970. Here is the result of that effort.

"CATKILLER 8-0-1"
(set to the music of "Wabash Cannonball" [trad.])

I was called to operations, one cold and rainy day.
Said they had a mission and they wanted no delay.
I donned on all my armor, my rifle, pistol too,
and headed for the briefing to see what I had to do.

The S-2 was awaiting, he said "I'll give it to you straight,
Ole Charlie's out in the A Shau, I hope we're not too late."
The weather it should be okay, fixed wing is on the way
So let's go get ole Charlie before he gets away.

"Hello Phu Bai Tower, this is Catkiller 8-0-1
Sitting on the Birddog ramp request to taxi one."
"Well, taxi to 2-7, that's the active for today
Hurry with your run-up, you're in a C-130's way."

I lined up on the active, I winged into the blue
Tower cleared me to change freq's, good day, good flight to you.
I headed out to A Shau, the ceiling was pretty low
Told my Marine observer, we'll try to make a go.

When we arrived on station, just like the S-2 said
Ole Charlie was in the valley and most were still in bed.

(The next two lines are spoken to the music.)
"Well hello Catkiller 8-0-1, this is Condol 8-5-2
Two Fox Fours on a 1-8-5, thirty miles from you.

Lock on channel 69, come out the 2-5-4
I'm in an Army O-1, skimming the valley floor."

(The next two lines are spoken to the music.)
"Tally Ho 8-0-1, now this is 8-5-2,
I've got you at my three o'clock, now what're we gonna do?"

"I'll run you in on a 1-8-5, drop your Delta 9s"
Then we'll use the pistols, I think that'll work out fine."

(The next two lines are spoken to the music.)
"Number One is on the base leg,"
"Now you're cleared in hot!
From my target marking round, 20 meters at one o'clock."

Those F-4s were great today, as they roared in out of the blue
Ran six flights on Charlie, Charlie only shot down two.
We've given everyone their BDA, now they're headed home.
The jets, they have all left us, now we're out here all alone.

"Hello Phu Bai Tower, this is Catkiller 8-0-1
Turning on the downwind, my prop is overrun.
My engine's overheated and my chip detector's bright
So, light up that old runway, 'cause I'm landing here tonight."

(The next two lines are spoken to the music.)
"Well, hello Catkiller 8-0-1, now this is Phu Bai Tower
I'd like to wake the crash crew up, but it is their coffee hour.

The runway lights are broken and the generator's down
So Catkiller 8-0-1, take that bird around."

Website

To learn more about the 220th Reconnaissance Airplane Company, visit
the Catkiller website, www.catkillers.org.

SELECTED BIBLIOGRAPHY

Bechett, W. H., K. P. Price, and M. E. King. "OV-10 Story: Innovation vs. the System," http://www.blackpony.org/ov10story.pdf

Buckingham, William A. *Operation Ranch Hand: The Air Force and Herbicides in Southeast Asia, 1961–1971.* Washington, D.C.: Office of Air Force History, 1982.

Callahan, Shawn P. *Close Air Support and the Battle of Khe Sanh.* Quantico, VA: History Division, U. S. Marine Corps, 2009.

Davies, Peter. *U. S. Marine Corps F-4 II Units of the Vietnam War.* Oxford: Osprey, 2012

Edgar Allan Poe Literary Society, Inc. "Who Are the Ravens." www.ravens.org

Gilbert, Ed. *The U.S. Marine Corps in the Vietnam War: III Marine Amphibious Force 1965–75.* Oxford: Osprey, 2006.

Greenberg, Lawrence M. "'Spooky' Gunship Operations in the Vietnam War." *Vietnam Magazine,* April 1990. http://www.historynet.com/spooky-gunship-operations-in-the-vietnam-war.htm

Hays, Phillip R. "Details of the First Talos RGM-8H Anti Radiation Missile Combat Firing." www.okieboat.com/Talos antiradiation shot.html

Lester, Robert E. *Records of the U.S. Marine Corps in the Vietnam War* [microfilm]. Bethesda, MD: University Publications of America, 1990.

Monsanto Company. "Agent Orange: Background on Monsanto's Involvement." http://www.monsanto.com/newsviews/pages/agent-orange-background-monsanto-involvement.aspx

"One Powerful Helicopter Gunship—the ACH-47A 'Guns A-Go-Go.'" Tails through Time website. http://www.tailsthroughtime.com/2011/02/one-powerful-helicopter-gun-ship-ach-47a.html

Shulimson, Jack. "The Marine War: III MAF in Vietnam, 1965–1971." http://www.vietnam.ttu.edu/events/1996_Symposium/96papers/marwar.php

Shulimson, Jack, with Leonard A. Blasiol, Charles R. Smith, and David A. Dawson. *U.S. Marines in Vietnam: The Defining Year, 1968.* Washington, D.C.: History and Museum Headquarters, U.S. Marine Corps, 1997.

Stanton, Shelby L. *Vietnam Order of Battle.* Washington, D.C.: U.S. News Books, 1971.

Telfer, Gary L., Lane Rogers, and V. Keith Fleming. *U. S. Marines in Vietnam: Fighting the North Vietnamese 1967.* Washington, D.C.: History and Museums Division, Headquarters, U.S. Marine Corps, 1984.

United States Army Aviation Museum. *Vietnam Memorial Exhibit,* www.armyaviationmuseum.org.

Weinhert, Richard P., Jr., and Susan Canedy. *History of Army Aviation.* Fort Monroe, VA: Office of the Command Historian, U.S. Army Training and Doctrine Command, 1991.

Wilson, Gene, and Dennis Currie. "Battle and Fall of A Shau March 1966," 220th Aviation Company website. http://www.catkillers.org/history-1966-Battle-of-A-Shau.pdf

Woolley, Bobby Jack. *The Bird Dog Tale: The Combat Service of the Cessna O-1 Aircraft within Southeast Asia, 1962–1972.* Seattle, WA: Peanut Butter Publishing, 2010.

INDEX

ABOUT THE AUTHOR

Raymond G. Caryl's aviation career began in 1966 in the Army and extended until 2004. After leaving active duty, he continued to fly in the Army Reserves and National Guard until 1997. He has flown as a pilot for the U.S. Forest Service and U.S. Customs Service and as a contract helicopter pilot.